Airside by

Airside

Distributed by

gesta1ten

Die Gestalten Verlag GmbH & Co. KG
Mariannenstr. 9-10
D-10999 Berlin
Germany
Tel: +49 (0)30 726 13 2000
Fax: +49 (0)30 726 13 2222
Email: sales@gestalten.com
www.gestalten.com

Published by
Airside
339 Upper Street
Islington
London N1 0PB
UK
Tel: +44 (0)20 7354 9912
Email: studio@airside.co.uk
www.airside.co.uk

Bibliographic information published by
the Deutsche Nationalbibliothek.
The Deutsche Nationalbibliothek lists this
publication in the Deutsche Nationalbibliografie;
detailed bibliographic data is available on
the internet at
http://dnb.d-nb.de

ISBN 978-3-89955-244-7

Typeset in Bodoni, Akkurat, DFPLeiGaSo and
Hiragino Kaku Gothic Pro

Printed in the UK by
Cambrian Printers Ltd
ISO-14001 accredited with award winning
Environmental Management Systems
For more details see
www.cambrian-printers.co.uk

Printed on
FSC Mixed Sources paper
from certificated forests and controlled sources.
Chain of custody number TT-COC-2200
www.fsc-uk.org

FSC

Mixed Sources
Product group from well-managed
forests and other controlled sources
www.fsc.org Cert no. TT-COC-2200
© 1996 Forest Stewardship Council

Interviews and commentary by
Fiona Sibley
Japanese translation by
Rumi Takahashi, Anna Takimoto, Andrew Thomas
Japanese edit by
Yoshinobu Ku, Hiromi Tsuchiya

インタビュー&作品解説：
フィオナ・シブリー
日本語翻訳：
ハイブリッド（高橋流美、滝本杏奈、アンドリュー・トーマス）
日本語編集：
區祥信、土屋弘美

CONTENTS

目次

FOREWORD

序文

Adrian Shaughnessy I first became aware of Airside when I saw their name mentioned in the design mags. At the time, they were lumped in with all the other fledgling web design companies. But they seemed more interesting than just another band of Flash jockeys. I also noticed their famous calendars on sale in the Virgin Megastore – alongside Justin Timberlake and Kylie calendars – and I sensed that they were part of a new entrepreneurial development in graphic design that was beginning to take root.

For the first time in its history, graphic design had emerged from under its cloak of professional anonymity and was now being enjoyed for its own sake, often by people who weren't necessarily working designers. This small but growing development felt like a challenge to the design hegemony which decreed that designers were anonymous servants waiting patiently to do their clients' bidding. Here was a trend (if not quite a movement) amongst designers to use their skills to produce artefacts to be sold direct to the public. Designers were becoming their own clients.

In 2004, I wrote an article for Creative Review about this phenomenon. In my essay I mentioned Airside's calendars. Shortly after the piece appeared, their director Nat Hunter contacted me. She said Airside were going through a tough patch and had been cheered up by what I'd written. She added that they were worried about going out of business. I was surprised to hear this. I'd assumed they were overwhelmed with work. We agreed to meet.

I went to the Airside studio in Islington. Fred, Nat and Alex all struck me as smart and thoughtful. Fred reminded me that he had shown me his portfolio shortly after he graduated from Central Saint Martins. Back then I was creative director of Intro, the design company I co-founded.

エイドリアン・ショーネシー 僕がエアサイドのことを知ったのは、デザイン雑誌でその名前を目にしたのが最初だった。当時、彼らは他の新進ウェブデザイン会社とひとくくりに紹介されていたけれど、月並みなFlashの使い手たちよりも面白そうに見えた。それに彼らの噂のカレンダーが、ジャスティン・ティンバーレイクやカイリーのカレンダーと一緒にヴァージンメガストアで販売されていて、彼らこそ、当時ちょうど根づき始めていたグラフィックデザインをビジネスにしていける会社のひとつなんだと認識したね。

あの頃、グラフィックデザインは、歴史上初めて「匿名のプロフェッショナル」の殻を破り、デザインに携わっていない人々も含め、デザインそのものが楽しまれる時代になりつつあった。この小さいながらも確実な進化は、「デザイナーはクライアントに選ばれるのを待つ、名も無きしもべ」という、当時のデザイン界の常識に対する挑戦にも思えた。これにより、デザイナーの間では、自分たちが作った作品を、直に顧客に売ることが(ムーブメントとまで言わずとも)流行になった。デザイナーは、自らクライアントへと変身を遂げたのだ。

2004年、僕はこの現象について「クリエイティブ・レビュー」誌に記事を書き、その中でエアサイドのカレンダーに言及した。雑誌が店頭に並んで間もなく、ディレクターのナット・ハンターから「エアサイドは厳しい現状に直面しているけれど、あなたが書いてくれた記事に励まされた」と連絡をもらった。倒産を心配していると聞いて、僕は驚いた。てっきり彼らは引っ張りだこで仕事に追われているに違いないと思っていたから。こうして僕らは会って話をすることにした。

イズリントンにあるエアサイドのスタジオを訪れた僕は、フレッド、ナット、アレックスが、いずれも知的で深い思想を持っていることに感銘を受けた。フレッドは、セント・マーチンを卒業後間もなく、僕にポートフォリオを見せに来た話をしてくれた。当時僕は、共同設立者の1人として、イントロというデザイン会社でクリエイティブ・ディレクターを務めていて、面接して欲しいと言う人を断ることはほとんどなかった。自分が

I very rarely said no to anyone who asked for an interview. I'd been snubbed a few times when I was job-hunting and I always remembered how dispiriting it had been. I also fancied myself as a bit of a talent spotter. But I had no recollection of seeing Fred. Some talent spotter I was.

—————————— I liked them immediately, and over lunch they listed their problems. It was the stuff that the non-design world knows how to deal with, but which we designers usually struggle with. No one tells you how to manage growth. No one tells you how to organise your studio. No one tells you how much to charge, or what to do when someone

tells you they are not paying a bill. Designers have to find out the solutions to these problems the hard way – usually by making lots of mistakes.

—————————— Later I spent a day trying to help them introduce some structure to Airside. It was clear that they'd reached a critical point in their growth. They'd grown rapidly and were faced with the dilemma of deciding whether to muddle along by retaining the freewheeling attitude that had served them well in their early years, or to look at introducing a more systematic approach that would help them avoid the snake pit of business failure, but which would also enable them to continue to

do good work, and carry on looking after the staff that they had accumulated.

—————————— It's a familiar conundrum that all idealistic designers have to confront. We imagine that if we adopt business practices we will lose our creative soul and personal integrity. The great American illustrator Brad Holland has noted that: "A lot of artists seem to think they'll be better artists if they're bad businessmen." But of course, the opposite is true: it's only by adopting rational (and ethical) business practices that we can hope to preserve the creative integrity that many designers crave.

—————————— Nat, Fred and Alex have since told

職を探していた頃、冷たくあしらわれて、滅入るような経験をしたからね。それに、タレント発掘には、ちょっとした自信もあった。ところがフレッドと会ったことは、記憶からすっかり抜け落ちていた。「タレント発掘」が聞いて呆れるな。

—————————— 僕はすぐに彼らのことが好きになった。一緒に昼食をとりながら、彼らはエアサイドが直面している問題を列挙した。いずれも、他の職種に就いていれば、どう対処すべきかわかりそうだが、大概のデザイナーたちが苦労する類いの問題ばかりだった。どうやって会社の成長をマネージメントしていけばよいのか、どうやってスタジオを組織していけばよいのか、クライアントにいくら請求したらよいのか、支払いをしないと言わ

れたらどうしたらよいのか。こういったことは、誰も教えてはくれない。デザイナーたちは皆、試行錯誤しながら、こうした問題の解決法を見つけていくのだ。

—————————— 後日、ある種のビジネス構造をエアサイドへ導入する方法を、丸一日かけて彼らに説明した。エアサイドが成長の限界点に到達しているのは明らかで、あまりに急成長を遂げた彼らの前には、2つの選択肢が立ちだかっていた。初期の発展を支えてきた自由奔放な態度を保持しながら、なんとか難所をやり過ごしていくか、あるいはビジネスで苦境に陥らないよう、もう少し体系だった方法を導入してみるか。そして、どちらを選べば、今まで通り、いい作品を作り続けられ、かつエアサイドが

培ってきたメンバーたちの面倒を見ることが可能なのか。

—————————— 理想を抱くデザイナーなら、誰もが直面する難問だ。みんな、ビジネス運営術を取り入れたら最後、創造的な魂や個性を失ってしまうのでは、と思い込んでいる。アメリカの偉大なイラストレーター、ブラッド・ホランドは、かつてこう言った。「アーティストたちの多くは、ビジネスに疎ければ疎いほど、良いアーティストになると思い込んでいる」でも事実は、逆なのだ。つまり、合理的で、倫理にかなったビジネス運営術を取り入れさえすれば、多くのデザイナーたちが望むところの、クリエイティブ精神を保つことができる。

—————————— 以来、ナット、フレッド、アレックスは、僕と

Foreword
序文

me that the day I spent with them (for which they paid me) was useful. Yet I can only remember doing a lot of listening, and my instinct from the outset was that they were smart enough to prosper without my advice. At the time I felt like a Northern mill owner in a black and white British movie telling his wild son that the party was over and that he had to give up the bright lights and come home to run the family firm. I felt a bit of a killjoy.

My first instinct was right, though. Not only have they prospered, but what was good about them then, is still what's good about them now. There's a sense of playfulness about Airside

that distinguishes them from lots of other studios. Play is a dirty word in our post-Thatcherite world. You can't imagine Sir Alan Sugar or Donald Trump telling any of their wannabe 'apprentices' that they would like to see more playfulness from them. But playfulness in the world of communication, branding and advertising, is a rare and valuable commodity, and in the way Airside integrate it into their work I'm reminded of Push Pin, the brilliant design and illustration collective that boomed in late-sixties, early-seventies New York.

Push Pin was founded in the 1950s when Seymour Chwast, Milton Glaser and others

banded together to produce a monthly magazine that became known as the *Push Pin Graphic*. They were pioneers of self-publishing. They combined design and illustration in a seemingly effortless way, and they produced work that appealed to other designers rather than to the moguls of big business. When you think about it, this could be a description of Airside, too.

Yet perhaps the most important aspect of Airside's rise is the fact that none of the three founders comes from a conventional design background. Fred did an English degree and then an MA in Graphic Design. Nat did an MA

過ごしたあの日は、ものすごく有益だったと言ってくれている (謝礼まで払ってくれた)。でも僕は、ただ話を聞く以外、大したことはしなかったと思う。僕のアドバイスなんかなくても成功できる手腕の持ち主たちだと、直感的にわかっていたから。なんだか、イギリスの白黒映画にでてくる北部の工場主が、放蕩息子に「パーティーは終わりだ。いつまでも華やかな気分に浸っていないで、故郷に戻って家業を継ぐように」と諭しているような気分だった。我ながら白けたことを言ってるなぁと思ったよ。

だけど、僕の直感は正しかった。彼らは見事に繁栄しただけでなく、当初からの持ち味を今も失っていないからね。彼らが他のスタジオと一線を画しているのは、そ

こに遊びのセンスがあるからだと思う。「遊ぶ」という言葉は、サッチャー以降の時代では禁句で、アラン・シュガー卿やドナルド・トランプが、彼らに憧れる見習いたちに「君たちの遊び心をもう少し見せてくれないか」なんて注文することは、まず想像できない。けれど、コミュニケーションやブランディング、広告の世界において、「遊び心」というのは大変な希少価値で、エアサイドがそれを巧みに織り交ぜていく様は、60年代後半から70年代前半にかけて、ニューヨークで一大ブームを巻き起こした、デザイン・イラストレーション集団プッシュ・ピンを彷彿とさせる。

プッシュ・ピンは、1950年代に、シーモア・クワスト、ミルトン・グレイサーらによって結成された。その後何

人かが加わって、後に「プッシュ・ピン・グラフィック」として知られるようになる月刊誌を作った、いわゆる自費出版の先駆的存在で、デザインとイラストを難なく自在に融合させた彼らのスタイルは、ビジネス界の大物たちよりも、他のデザイナーたちに刺激を与えた。こういった現象は、エアサイドにも当てはまると思う。

けれども、エアサイド台頭の一番重要な点は、3人の創始者が皆、いわゆるデザイン畑出身ではないという事実にあると思う。フレッドは英文学の学位を得てから、グラフィックデザインの修士を取得、ナットはRCA (ロイヤル・カレッジ・オブ・アート) でインタラクティブ・マルチメディアの修士を取得。そしてアレックスは同じくRCAでインテリア建築の

in interactive multimedia at the Royal College of Art. Alex – also at the RCA – did an MA in interior architecture. These are hardly standard routes to running a graphic design company, but I think their chosen start-points have equipped them intellectually and practically for working life in the modern, media landscape. In fact, a conventional graphic design background is increasingly anachronistic in a screen-based interactive world. The Airside mix of illustration, animation, interactive, technical and communication skills is a potent combination in the 21st century mediascape.

But time and again you come back to the playfulness. Today they work for advertising agencies, record labels and direct clients, but the work is never po-faced or humourless. It always has wit and vim, and it always has the Airside signature embedded in it somewhere. They've moved on from the vector-based imagery with which they made their reputation. They make commercials, movie title sequences, and have even created an entire DVD of motion graphics for Lemon Jelly. Nor have their self-initiated projects dried up. Despite an increasing workload, the Airside shop still does a brisk trade in cyberspace, and this book is evidence that the urge to take control of their own destiny hasn't evaporated.

The instinct that told me that Nat, Fred and Alex were going to thrive in their first decade tells me that they will do the same in the next one. The next ten years will see them grow in importance within the design and communications world. There's a new studio to be occupied. There's talk of movie deals. Nat wants to save the world through her work with Three Trees Don't Make a Forest. Whatever happens, you can bet that the trademark playfulness and intelligence will be visible in everything they do.

修士を取っている。いずれも普通ならグラフィックデザイン会社の設立に到底繋がらないところだが、スタート地点がデザインではなかったことが、知的にも実用的にも、彼らが現代のメディア業界で上手く仕事をする土壌を作ったのだと思う。事実、グラフィックデザインのみ学んできたという経歴は、画面上でデザインをすることが当たり前のインタラクティブな世界では、もはや時代遅れになってきた。イラストレーション、アニメーション、インタラクティブ、テクニカル、コミュニケーション能力を兼ね備えたエアサイドこそ、21世紀のメディアの領域において、有力な集団なのだと思う。

そして、何よりもやはり「遊び心」というポイントに辿り着く。現在彼らは広告代理店やレコードレーベル、あるいは直接クライアントと仕事をしているが、作風は決して堅苦しくなりすぎず、ユーモアも健在だ。常にウィットと活力を感じさせ、どこかに必ずエアサイドらしさを光らせている。ベクターベースの作品で評判を得て以来、CM、映画のオープニング映像、またレモン・ジェリーのDVDでは全曲のモーショングラフィックスを手がけるなど、快進撃を続けてきた彼ら。多忙な日々を送る現在も、自主プロジェクトの勢いは衰えることなく、相変わらずエアサイドのウェブショップを賑わせている。そしてこの本こそまさに、運命の手綱を自ら握っていこうとする、彼らの意欲の証であろう。

ナット、フレッド、アレックスと出会ったあの日、これから10年のうちに、エアサイドは成功を収めるだろうと告げた僕の直感が、これからの10年も、彼らは上手くやっていくだろうと告げている。今後10年のデザイン・コミュニケーションの分野で、エアサイドは必ずや大きな役割を果たすことになるであろう。新しいスタジオも手に入れ、映画のオファーの噂もある。ナットは「Three Trees Don't Make a Forest（3本の木じゃ、森にはならない）」という活動を通じて世界を救いたいと願っている。何が起ころうとも、彼らの手がけるものには、今後も必ず、エアサイドらしい遊び心と知性が光輝くことは間違いないだろう。

THE BEGINNING

始まり

Fred Deakin I first got into graphic design through my clubs. I was DJing and running various club nights in Edinburgh, where I was at university doing an English Literature MA, and so I ended up designing publicity material and visuals for the events I was putting on. I wanted my clubs to blow people's minds as they walked through the door – a psychedelic wonderland kind of thing. After graduating I tried to start my own graphics company in Edinburgh but it wasn't really sustainable up there, so I moved to London to do an MA at St Martins and continued running my club nights. At the same time I got a job with Ian Swift aka Swifty, who was making great work as part of the acid jazz scene, creating identities for record companies like Talkin' Loud and Mo' Wax. He was a one-man band for a long time; then he tried expanding and employed me along with a cool little crew. We produced some good work and I learnt a lot, but his heart wasn't really into running a company and it didn't work out. However, I got a glimpse of what it would be like to create a community like that. I left and went freelance, but found it frustrating not being able to create the kind of work I wanted to. Nat was one of my best friends at university, and it was her who suggested we start a studio with this guy, Alex.

Alex Maclean The earliest common thread between the three of us is that we've all got a connection to Edinburgh. I'd met Nat there through friends, but I'd already left by the time Fred was running these infamous clubs; nonetheless I knew of Fred by reputation as all my friends were going to his nights. When I went to the RCA I bumped into Nat in the canteen. She was very experienced with digital interactive disciplines and I knew nothing, so she taught me a lot. We started working on projects together – I was involved in setting up a charity to put democracy on the internet with a project called The Virtual Parliament, and Nat and I worked on its interface in 1995.

After my MA I stayed on at the RCA as a research fellow for two years, but we ended up freelancing together at Pinewood Studios on feature films – Nat was doing special effects while I was doing websites. We worked for a company called Bionic and did work for films like *Mission Impossible* and *Lost in Space*. Because we were

フレッド・ディーキン 僕は、クラブの仕事をしているうちに、グラフィックデザインをやるようになった。エディンバラの大学で英文学の修士課程にいた頃、クラブでDJをやったり、いろいろなイベントをオーガナイズしたりしていて、宣伝用のデザインやイベントの映像を手がけるようになったんだ。クラブに来る人たちが、ドアを開けた途端、サイケデリックなワンダーランドに迷い込んだみたいに驚かせるのが、うちのクラブの狙いでね。卒業後、グラフィックの会社を始めようとしたけど、エディンバラではとても長続きしそうもなくて、ロンドンに移ったんだ。セント・マーチンで修士号を取ってから、引き続きクラブの経営を始めて、同時にスウィフティ、ことイアン・スウィフトのもとで働いた。彼は、アシッド・ジャズ・シーンに大いに貢献した男で、トーキング・ラウドやモ・ワックスなどのレコード会社のレーベルデザインを手がけたデザイナーなんだけど、長いこと1人で働いた後に、もう少し手を広げることにして、僕や他の面白いメンバーを何人か雇ったんだ。そこではいい仕事がで きたし、いろいろ学ばせてもらったけど、彼があまり経営に熱心じゃなくて、結局上手くいかなかった。でも、人が集って何かを創るっていうのがどういうことか、経験させてもらったと思う。それからフリーランサーになったんだけど、なかなか思うような仕事ができないことにフラストレーションを感じ始めた。そんな時、大学時代の親友だったナットが、みんなでスタジオを始めないかと、アレックスを紹介してくれたんだ。

アレックス・マクレーン 僕たちの一番始めの共通点は、3人ともエディンバラと繋がりがあるということ。友人を通してナットと知り合ったんだけど、フレッドがいくつかのクラブ経営で成功していた頃には、僕はもうエディンバラを離れていたんだ。でも僕の友達がみんな彼のクラブイベントに出かけていたから、フレッドの評判は耳にしていた。その後、RCA (ロイヤル・カレッジ・オブ・アート) に通い始めてから、偶然、学生食堂でナットと再会した。彼女はデジタル・インタラクティブの分野に精通していて、僕はまったく知らなかったから、いろいろ教 わったよ。やがて僕らはRCAで同じプロジェクトに携わることになった。僕は「バーチャル・パーラメント」という、ネット上で民主主義を広めるチャリティーの立ち上げに関わっていて、1995年に2人でそのウェブデザインを担当したんだ。

修士号を取ってから、僕は研究者としてもう2年、RCAに在籍した後、ナットと一緒にフリーランスでパインウッド・スタジオの長編映画製作に携わって、ナットは特殊効果を、僕はウェブ制作を担当していた。また、バイオニックという会社の依頼で「ミッション・インポッシブル」や「ロスト・イン・スペース」といった映画の仕事も一緒に取り組んだ。でも、誰かの下で働くか、自宅で独りっきりで働くような環境に、2人ともだんだんストレスを感じてきて「じゃあ、一緒にスタジオを持とうか」という話になったんだ。ちょうどその頃、フレッドを紹介してもらってね。僕らはみんな、パジャマ姿のまま家でノートパソコンを広げて仕事するより、インスピレーションを受けて、健全な社会生活を送ることのできる場所を探していたんだ。

1 Cover of acid house
fanzine *Gear*
Fred Deakin, 1989

アシッド・ハウス専門誌
「ギア」表紙
フレッド・ディーキン 1989

2 Avalanche Records
gig poster
Fred Deakin, 1989

アヴァランチ・レコーズ
ギグポスター
フレッド・ディーキン 1989

3 *Wild Life* mix tape
Fred Deakin, 1991

「ワイルド・ライフ」
コンピレーションテープ
フレッド・ディーキン 1991

4–5 *Straight No Chaser*
magazine spreads
Fred Deakin, 1995

「ストレイト・ノー・チェイサー」
雑誌見開きイラストレーション
フレッド・ディーキン 1995

6 *The Son Of Rococo*
club flyer
Fred Deakin, 1985

「ザ・サン・オブ・ロココ」
フライヤー
フレッド・ディーキン 1985

The Beginning

始まり

working together for other people or working alone at home and getting frustrated with both, we started talking about getting a studio. That's when I met Fred. We were all looking for a space where we could get some inspiration and also a social life, rather than just sitting at home in your pyjamas, working on your laptop.

——————— **Nat Hunter** I was the glue between these two. In Edinburgh I was studying Human Computer Interface Psychology while Fred was doing English Literature; then at the RCA I was doing an MA in Interactive Multimedia, and Alex was doing an MA in Interior Architecture. I freelanced for a while after the MA, creating fictitious futuristic computer interfaces on spaceships for the film industry and some other really nice jobs, but as a freelancer you're always at the bottom of the pile. Also, I couldn't find my niche – I couldn't find a job that would employ me on a multi-skilled level as a programmer, an interaction designer, and someone who wanted to really think about the brief and innovate on that brief. We're all a bit multi-skilled like that. Fred has to do his music and graphic design, while Alex needs to do the digital side, but also to be working with the design of spaces. I used to go into Swifty's and help Fred and the others out with their web and moving image projects, and I could see they were having a really nice time, but also that Fred needed to do his own thing. We hatched a plan that evolved to include various other people we knew who were all freelancing. The idea was we'd get a studio, invite loads of like-minded freelancers, give it one name and make it look like one big company. That way when a potential client walks in, they change the way they relate to you.

——————— **Fred** They think you're bigger than you are.

——————— **Nat** And it really worked. As a freelancer you turn up somewhere and the client keeps you waiting for an hour. After we set up the studio we were working for the same people, but they came to us and we kept them waiting! The whole balance of power changed. Rather than just doing the same work in a new building, suddenly we were perceived as a larger group and were able to take on bigger projects and be trusted in a different way. We knew we needed to get a big space and sublet desks to our friends, because that was the only way to fund it. We found our building in Islington because Alex had met a guy on the Trans-Siberian Express, who

8

7

7 *Cowgirl*
Fred Deakin, 1996

「カウガール」ポートレイト
フレッド・ディーキン 1996

8 *Still Life*
Fred Deakin, 2000

「静物画」
フレッド・ディーキン 2000

——————— ナット・ハンター　私が2人を紹介したの。エディンバラで人間=コンピューター間の心理学を学んでいた頃、ちょうどフレッドが英文学を学んでいて、その後、私がRCAでインタラクティブ・マルチメディア科の修士課程に在籍していたとき、今度はアレックスがインテリア建築科の修士にいたのね。修士号を取得してからは、映画向けに架空の宇宙船のコンピューターパネルをデザインしたり、しばらくフリーで仕事をしたわ。中にはいい仕事もあったけど、フリーランスだと常にピラミッドの底辺。それに、自分に相応しい場所が見つけられなかったのよ。マルチレベルのプログラマー兼インタラクション・デザイナーとして私を雇ってくれるような仕事がなかったし、知恵をしぼって何か革新的なことをしようとしている人たちにも出会えなかった。私たちは皆それぞれに、いくつか得意分野があるのね。フレッドは、音楽とグラフィックデザインの両方をやりたいし、アレックスも、デジタル系のことはもちろん、空間デザインもやりたいのよ。当時、私はスウィフティのところに出入りして、フレッドやみんなのウェブや動画プロジェクトを手伝っていて、みんなすごく楽しんで仕事をしていたけれど、フレッドが自分のプロジェクトをやりたがっているのも知っていた。そこで、知り合いのフリーランサーたちを巻き込む計画を練り始めたの。スタジオを借りて、うまの合うフリーランサーたちを招いて、ひとつの大きな会社のように共通の名前を名乗るっていうのが最初のアイデア。そうすれば、スタジオを訪ねてくるクライアントたちの態度も変わるでしょう？

——————— **フレッド**　フリーランスでいるより、一人前

knew the person who owned it. We came to see it, and fell in love with it.

——————— **Fred** When it came to choosing a name, we were all sitting around at my mum's house – I remember the orange wallpaper. Someone had the Oxford Dictionary of New Words, which listed all the words that had recently entered the English language.

——————— **Alex** We were looking for a domain that was still available in .com or .co.uk and we'd run out of obvious words we could buy a domain for. We came across Airside as we went through this dictionary. We started at the beginning of the book, and as soon as we found a name that resonated and was a domain that was available, that was pretty much it.

——————— **Nat** Airside is where you are when you've gone through passport control and before you get on the plane. Since then we've post-rationalised it and created a story about how we create connected spaces across the world.

——————— **Fred** "We'll transcend your boundaries... we're an international company... we'll help you take off". The real story is "A is for Airside". So we had a name and we had a space. But we needed

に扱ってくれるからね。

——————— **ナット**　それが本当に上手くいったのよ。フリーランスで働いていると、オフィスを訪ねてもクライアントに1時間も待たされるでしょ。ところが、スタジオを構えたら、同じクライアントがスタジオまで訪ねて来て、今度は私たちが彼らを待たせる立場になったわけ。力関係がまったく変わったわね。単に新しいビルに移って同じような仕事を続けたのではなく、突然まわりが私たちのことを大きな集団と見なすようになって、より大きなプロジェクトと、違った形の信頼を得られるようになった。まずは広いスペースを借りて、間借りしてくれる仲間を募ったんだけど、それが資金繰りをする唯一の方法だったのね。私たちが見つけたのは、イズリントンのとある物件。アレックスがシベリア横断鉄道の中で出会った人が、たまたまそこのオーナーと知り合いで、下見に行って、皆一目で気に入ったわ。

——————— **フレッド**　名前を決める時は、みんなで僕の母親の家に集まって話し合った。うちのオレンジ色の壁紙を今でも思い出すよ。誰かが、最近追加された言葉を掲載した「オックスフォード新語辞典」を持って来ていてね。

——————— **アレックス**　僕らは「.com」「.co.uk」が使えるドメインを探していたけど、使える単語がなかなか見つからなかったんだ。でも辞書を開いて「Airside」って単語を見つけた。辞書の最初から探し始めてピンと来た単語で、しかもドメインが有効だったから、一件落着というわけ。

——————— **ナット**　「エアサイド」というのは、空港で税関を通過してから飛行機に搭乗するまでの空間のこと。「世界中

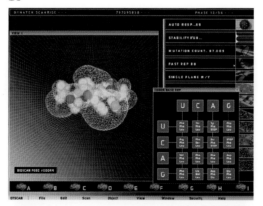

9　Visualisation of Virtual Parliament
Alex Maclean, 1997

「バーチャル・パーラメント」イメージ
アレックス・マクレーン　1997

10　*Mission Impossible* concept interface
Nat Hunter, 1997

「ミッション・インポッシブル」コンセプト・インターフェース
ナット・ハンター　1997

11　*Lost in Space* interface
Nat Hunter, 1997

「ロスト・イン・スペース」インターフェース
ナット・ハンター　1997

The Beginning

始まり

12

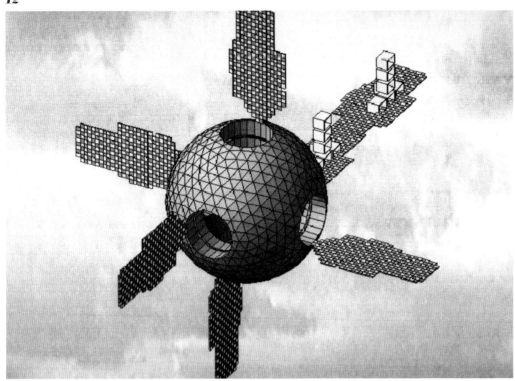

13

12 Sketch for
Virtual Parliament
Alex Maclean, 1997

「バーチャル・パーラメント」
スケッチ
アレックス・マクレーン 1997

13 Sketch for
Virtual Parliament
Alex Maclean, 1997

「バーチャル・パーラメント」
スケッチ
アレックス・マクレーン 1997

14 Airside's first job:
Future Nightclub for
Ministry magazine,
1998

エアサイド初仕事
ミニストリー・マガジン
見開きイラストレーション
「未来のナイトクラブ」1998

14

to pay the rent, so we kept on doing our freelance stuff. I was teaching at St Martins one day a week and running my clubs. Nat went and freelanced for Price Waterhouse Coopers for six months making a CD Rom about financial instruments. And Alex was doing his 3D stuff, building models of interiors for Conran. We were letting the rest of the studio space to other freelancers, and it was all very sociable. There was Anna Pank, who worked for art publishing house Bookworks but convinced them she should work in our studio instead of their office because she wanted to join in all the fun; the illustrator Paul Bowman; then Eben Halford and Tom Redfern – two digital developers who ran a company called Zesty; Mick Kent, an old mate from Edinburgh doing digital outputting; Sam Burford who was an experienced post-production artist; and Rosie Walford; a brand consultant and photo-journalist, as well as the three of us.

——————— **Nat** In that first year I had to make a choice about Airside. I was offered a job to go to Australia and head up the special effects unit for *Mission Impossible II* and I had to decide whether to stay and do Airside or go to Australia, and I chose to stay.

を繋ぐ空間を創造するのがエアサイドの仕事」という説明は、後から思いついたんだけど。

——————— **フレッド** 「僕らは国境を超えた国際企業。あなたの離陸をお手伝いします」って言えばカッコいいけど、実は、辞書の冒頭で見つけたから「Airside」。とにかく、名前も決まったしスペースも確保した。でも家賃を払わなければならないから、その後もしばらくフリーランスの仕事を続けた。僕は週1回セント・マーチンで教えながらクラブを経営し、ナットはプリンス・ウォーターハウス・クーパーズで半年間、金融商品に関するCD-Rを作り、アレックスはコンランの3Dインテリアモデルの制作を行った。スタジオは、僕ら3人のほかは、フリーランサーたちに貸し出していたけれど、みんな愛想のいい仲間ばかりだったな。ブックワークス出版で働いていたアナ・パンクは、僕らのお楽しみに加わりたくて、オフィスじゃなく、うちのスタジオを仕事場にするって職場に直談判してね。それからイラストレーターのポール・ボウマン。ゼスティを経営するデジタル技術の開発者のエバン・ハルフォードとトム・レッドファーンの2人。エディンバラ時代からの古い友人で、デジタル出力の仕事をしていたミック・ケント。ベテランのポスプロ・アーティストのサム・バーフォードに、ブランド・コンサルタントでフォトジャーナリストでもあるロージー・ウォルフォード。

——————— **ナット** 最初の年に、私はエアサイドに関して大きな決断を迫られたわ。オーストラリアで「ミッション・インポッシブル2」のスペシャル・エフェクト・チームを統率する大きな仕事のオファーが来てね。そのまま留まってエアサイドを続け

nat hunter
interaction designer
+44 (0) 171 354 9912
nat@airside.co.uk

airside

twenty four cross street
islington london N1 2BG

fred deakin

+44 (0) 171 354 9912
fred@airside.co.uk

airside

twenty four cross street
islington london N1 2BG

alex maclean
multimedia designer
+44 (0) 171 359 5529
alex@airside.co.uk

airside

twenty four cross street
islington london N1 2BG

Alex We'd always been employed by other people, but this was our first opportunity to do our own thing.

Nat But we never said "Let's start a business". We just did enough freelance work to get along. Towards the end of that year it was starting to get complicated; jobs began to come in that we were all working on together and we didn't have a company account or anything like that.

Alex That's when our accountant said: "You can't carry on like this. You can't call yourselves Airside and bill as individual people – the taxman doesn't like it."

Nat When we got the articles of memorandum for the business, and it said "You only exist for the profit of the shareholders" we were like "Who? What?" We were totally naïve about all that stuff and never saw ourselves as business people until much further down the line.

Alex Our first actual job as Airside was for a friend of mine, Rachel Leach, who commissioned me and Fred to do an illustration for *Ministry* magazine, a double page spread. The brief was to visualise 'The Nightclub of the Future'. We were paid about £100 for it. It was our first attempt to collaborate, and it was awful – we chucked the file back and forth, and it got worse and worse.

Fred But we had a very good time. The real turning point for Airside as a separate entity was our first birthday party. We held it in the studio and it was heaving; it went right off, like a club basically. Suddenly everyone went "Oh, you're Airside". We got a load of work out of that party.

Nat All our new business in the first five years came from who we knew. It was a big advantage starting when we were older and not when we were straight out of college because we had quite a few connections; lots of our friends were employed by bigger companies and gave us work to help us out.

Fred Our philosophy in those first few years was to make great work and tolerate being paid badly, because no one will give you the great work that pays well without a portfolio full of lots of other great work, so if all you ever do is bad work which pays well, then that's all you're ever going to do. It was a philosophy that served us well in the early years, but it was hard to move beyond that. You have to start there, but the key is to get to being paid properly for what you do as soon as possible.

るか、オーストラリアに行くか。で、結局ここに残ったの。

アレックス それまでみんな雇われる身だったけど、あの時が、初めて自分たちで事を起こすチャンスだったからね。

ナット それでも「さあ、ビジネスを始めるぞ」って感じではなかったわね。食べて行くのに充分なフリーランスの仕事を取っていただけ。その年の暮れから、徐々にややこしくなってきたんだけど。というのも、みんなで一緒に手がける仕事が来ても、会社の口座みたいなものがなかったから。

アレックス その時、会計士にこう言われたよ。「このままじゃダメだ。エアサイドと名乗っておいて、請求書をバラバラに出すなんて、そんなの税務署が認めないよ」

ナット 会社登録の書類を読んだら「あなたの役目は株主たちを儲けさせること」なんて書いてあって「誰が? 何ですって?」って感じ。私たち、ビジネスのことをほとんど知らなかったし、ずいぶん後になるまで、自分たちを起業家だなんて、考えたこともなかったのよ。

アレックス エアサイドとしての初の仕事は、僕の友人のレイチェル・リーチからの依頼で、ミニストリー・マガジン用にフレッドと僕が手がけた、見開きのイラストだった。テーマは「未来のナイトクラブ」の想像図で、100ポンドもらったよ。僕らの初めてのコラボレーションだったけれど、あれはひどかったね。やりとりすればするほど、どんどん冴えなくなっちゃって。

フレッド すごく楽しかったけどね。エアサイドに本質的な転機をもたらしたのは、1周年記念のパーティーだった。スタジオで開いたパーティーは、それはもうクラブナイトみたいに盛り上がってね。そうしたら突然、誰もが「あぁ、君たちがエアサイドか」ってことになって、その晩を境に、たくさんの仕事が舞い込んできた。あれは、僕たちが新しいビジネスの初めの一歩を踏み出した晩だった。

ナット 最初の5年間で手がけた新しいビジネスは、すべて知り合いからの仕事だったの。私たちが大学を出たてではなく、ある程度の年齢になって始めたのが、すごく有利だったと思う。それぞれ、既にたくさんの人脈があったし、大きな会社で働いている友達も大勢いて、協力的に仕事を振ってくれたわ。

フレッド 初めの頃の僕らの哲学は「予算は少なくても、とにかくいい仕事をしよう」ということだった。だって、ポートフォリオにいい作品がたくさんなかったら、誰も予算のあるいい仕事を振ってくれるはずがないだろう? 仮に予算は良くても、つまらない仕事を始めたら、その後も、ずっとそれを続けなければならない。初期の数年は、その哲学でうまく行ったけど、しばらくすると、それを続けて行くのが難しくなってきた。でも、まずはそこまで頑張って、そこから自分たちのやった仕事に見合うだけのお金をもらえるようになるまでが、勝負のしどころだね。

アレックス 僕は、アートカレッジに相当長いこといた。通算9年も! 少し長過ぎたかなとも思う。ファインアートから始めて、インテリア建築、そしてアニメーション、映像制作、ウェブデザイン、3Dモデリングなど、できることは何でも

15 Airside's first business cards, 1998

エアサイド初の名刺 1998

16 Nat in the Cross Street studio, 1998

ナット クロス・ストリートのスタジオにて 1998

The Beginning

始まり

Alex I had spent a long time at art college – nine years in the end! Probably too long. I had started in fine art, gone into interior architecture and ended up doing anything I could get my hands on: animation, filmmaking, web design, 3D modelling and so on. I had the sense that the disciplines were converging and that was where the excitement was.

Nat Mine and Alex's skills were in interaction design, interior architecture and creating websites while Fred's was in graphic design, music and running clubs, and somehow they lived very comfortably together. We had very varied backgrounds, but what united all of us was the way we thought about user experience. Fred thought about the experience of someone entering his clubs – what they would see and how to keep them surprised and entertained. For Alex as an interior architect, he was always thinking about how someone would perceive space. For me, with my human-computer psychology background, it wasn't just, someone's going to see this website, let's make it look pretty; we had to engage them on a deeper level than that. So we were always thinking about how people feel and how we could engage them from several different perspectives. That was what brought us together.

Fred As Airside developed I was still doing flyers and running clubs, which helped our profile and also acted as a social focus for what we were doing. *Impotent Fury* was a club night that I ran bi-monthly at the 333 in Hoxton, and everyone in the studio would chip in – Paul Bowman would help us out with visuals, Nat did interactive installations and I was doing the flyers. My background in clubs also inspired us to treat Airside a bit like a club in its promotion. Rather than advertise our services, we printed a calendar and gave it away for free so that people would have our artwork on their wall all year round.

Nat Except that it had the wrong phone number on it! The other thing we did which was quite club-like was the Airside T-Shirt Club, where you subscribe in advance and get exclusive T-shirts every month designed by us and other people that we rate. We started this right at the beginning of Airside and it's still going strong.

Alex People enjoyed the T-Shirt Club – being a member of something, and being able to identify with other people wearing the T-Shirts. The theme of self-initiated projects continues to this day – some projects happen just because we want to do them.

Fred It made us interesting, and for ages some people thought we were just a T-shirt company, whilst other people thought we just did websites. Other people thought we were an illustration company because of the flyers.

Nat One of the turning points was when Rosie, a brand consultant who was also freelancing in the studio, did some brainstorming with us in exchange for Photoshop lessons. She sat us down, made us put our values on the table and actually say what we wanted Airside to be. We came up with some really clear shared core values, for example using one of our websites should be as enjoyable as using a toy, and that you should never have that Sunday night feeling of dread about coming to work the next morning.

やった。いろいろ学んだことのすべてが融合するポイントにこそ、面白いことがあるような予感がしていたんだ。

ナット 私とアレックスは、インタラクティブデザインとインテリア建築、それからウェブ制作に、フレッドはグラフィックデザインと音楽とクラブ経営に、それぞれのスキルを活かしていたわけだけど、それがどうやら功を奏したのね。それぞれ違ったバックグラウンドをもっていても、私たちを結びつけていたのは「ユーザー体験」に関する共通の考え方だったと思う。フレッドは、クラブに入ってきた人に、何を見せるか、どうやって彼らを驚かせ、楽しませるかを考え、アレックスはインテリア建築の観点から、人々がどのように空間を認識するかを常に考えている。私は人間とコンピューター間の心理学を専攻した背景から、「ウェブサイトを見てくれる人がいるなら、素敵なデザインにしなきゃ」程度のことじゃ満足しないの。3人とも、より深いレベルで制作に携わる必要性を感じていた。つまり、受け手がどう感じるか、どうやったらユーザーを満足させられるかということを、それぞれ違う観点から考えることが、私たちをひとつに結びつけていたの。

フレッド エアサイドが成長してからも、僕はまだフライヤーを作ったり、クラブ経営を続けていたけど、それがエアサイドのプロモーションにもなったし、クラブに集って来る人たちに僕らのやっていることを知ってもらう役割も果たした。「インポテント・フューリー」という隔月のイベントをホクストンの333というクラブでやったよ。スタジオのみんなでお金を出し合ってね。ポール・ボウマンが映像を手伝ってくれて、ナットがインタラクティブ・インスタレーションを担当して、僕がフライヤーを作った。僕がクラブに関わっていた影響で、エアサイドのプロモーションは、ちょっとクラブのプロモーションみたいなんだ。提供できるサービスを宣伝するんじゃなくて、カレンダーをつくって無料で配ったり。そうすれば、みんな一年中僕らのアートワークを壁に飾ってくれるからね。

ナット 電話番号は間違っていたけどね! それと、もうひとつエアサイドが手がけたクラブ的なことといえば「エアサイド・Tシャツクラブ」。初回に購入手続きを済ませると、エアサイドや私たちの好きなアーティストがデザインした限定オリジナルTシャツが、毎月届くの。これは、最初の年からスタートして、いまだに根強く続けているわね。

アレックス みんなこの「Tシャツクラブ」を楽しんでくれてね。クラブのメンバーになって、同じTシャツを着ていることで仲間を認識できる。自分たちで始めたプロジェクトのテーマは、今も変わらないな。いくつかのプロジェクトは、単に僕らがやりたいからこそ続いているんだ。

フレッド だからこそエアサイドは面白いんだよ。長年僕らのことをTシャツ屋だと思っていた人もいれば、ウェブデザイン会社だと思っていた人も、フライヤーを見て、イラストレーションの会社だと思っていた人もいる。

ナット スタジオをシェアしていたフリーのブランド・コンサルタント、ロージーが、フォトショップの使い方を教えてあげる代わりに、私たちとブレインストーミングをしてくれたことがあって、あれも大きな転機だったわね。彼女は私たちを座らせると、それぞれの価値観を明確に出させて、実際エアサイドをどんなふうにして行きたいのか、話し合う機会を作ってくれた。そこで、オモチャで遊んでるみたいに楽しいウェブサイトを作りたいとか、翌日の仕事を考えて日曜の夜に憂鬱になったりしない環境を作りたいだとか、コアで明確なアイデアが出てきたの。

ロージー・ウォルフォード ひとりひとりがものすごい才能の持ち主だったんだもの。共通点は人生を楽し

scalating — *happy*

happening.

y job's an event

new

eg interactive
wheel of fortune

to use not
to look at

ful

using our work should
feel like using a toy
as pleasurable as

My — quote?

Rosie Walford They were all super-talented individuals. They had a common love of life, and their work was going in slightly different directions, but they sensed they could do something together. We sat down and used what I'd call a brand essence process to draw out their shared thinking, and morphed those ideas into a proposition that became Airside. One harmonising thought that came out was their determination to do work that was fun and playful and that they really loved. If they and the clients had fun doing it and people had fun interacting with the work then that was a success for them. It was a powerful, single organising theme. I remember Fred banging the table and saying, "We want to have fun with this!" It was the fun that brought them together.

Alex It touched on our core motivations – what did we want to achieve, how did we want to employ people, what kind of environment did we want to work in?

Nat Rosie was really valuable. She made us write down our dream client list, and within two years we'd worked for them all.

んでいること、そしてそれぞれ微妙に違った方向の仕事をしているけど、きっと何か一緒にできると感じていたのね。それで一緒に机を囲んで、私が「ブランド・エッセンス・プロセス」と呼んでいる方法を用いながら、彼らの共通の考えを浮き彫りにして、そのアイデアを「エアサイドとは何か」という定義に変換していく作業をしたわけ。そのとき全員に共通していた素晴らしい想いは「とにかく楽しく遊び心のある、愛せる仕事がしたい」という決意だった。彼らとクライアントが楽しみながら作り、見る人、使う人たちがそれを楽しんでくれたら、それこそが彼らの成功なの。それはものすごくパワフルな、みんなを繋ぎ合わせるのに充分なテーマだった。フレッドが机を叩いてこういったのを覚えているわ。「エアサイドで楽しいことをしたいんだよ!」あれで、みんながひとつになった。

　　　アレックス　僕らが何を達成したいのか、どのように人々を雇い、どんな環境で働きたいのか、という問いの答えには、いつもこの想いがあった。

　　　ナット　ロージーは、私たちの恩人ね。彼女の提案で、理想のクライアントリストを作ったら、2年後には、それが全部実現したんだから。

17　Airside mind map
Rosie Walford, 1998

エアサイド構想メモ
ロージー・ウォルフォード
1998

The Beginning
始まり

CALENDARS

カレンダー

Job name:	Airside Calendars
Client:	Airside
Media:	Print

Summary: Airside's annual calendar featuring the best published and unpublished work from the preceding year.

Airside's annual calendar has become a bit of an institution on the design scene. It was inspired by the calendar Fred gave away at his New Year's Eve club nights in Edinburgh as a thank you to all the party people who had supported him throughout the year: the Airside version is a similar thank you to friends, staff and clients who have helped Airside create much of the content. Over the years it has been a fruitful canvas for experimentation, especially around its format which continually morphs in search of new innovations.

As well as a place for the year's "greatest hits", the calendar also regularly features a selection of pitch work and experimental pieces that might not have found any other home over the last twelve months. Thus for fans it has become a must-have to complete their collection of all things Airside. From its humble beginnings as a promotional giveaway to a few lucky friends, to its life-saving role in capturing design guru Adrian Shaughnessy's attention, the Airside calendar is now a highly sought-after item sold in design stores all over the world. **Fiona Sibley**

作品名：	エアサイド・カレンダー
クライアント：	エアサイド
メディア：	印刷物

内容： 前年度の発表・未発表作品を掲載した、エアサイドの年間カレンダー

エアサイドのカレンダーといえば、デザイン界ではちょっと知られた存在である。そもそもエディンバラ時代に、大晦日のクラブイベントで、1年間支えたくれた人たちに感謝の気持ちを込めて、フレッドが贈ったカレンダーが、そのルーツ。エアサイド版も同様に、制作に協力してくれた友人、スタッフ、クライアントへのお礼として作り始めた。長年に渡り、このカレンダーは、実り多いデザインの実験結果を発表する場となっており、特にそのフォーマットに関しては、常に新たな形を求めて変化を繰り返している。

カレンダーには、その年の「ヒット作」のみならず、過去12ヶ月の間に、お披露目される機会のなかったプレゼン素材やその他の試作品も掲載されており、エアサイドの全作品を手に入れたいファンにとっては必須アイテムとなっている。ほんの数人の幸運な友人たちに贈ることから始まったこのカレンダーは、いつのまにかデザイン界のグル、エイドリアン・ショーネシーの目に止まってエアサイドの危機を救う役目を果たし、今では世界中のデザイン・ストアで引っ張りだこの商品となっている。(作品解説フィオナ・シブリー／以下、FS)

IMPOTENT FURY

インポテント・フューリー

Job name:	Impotent Fury
Client:	Impotent Fury / Fred Deakin
Media:	Print

作品名:	インポテント・フューリー
クライアント:	インポテント・フューリー／
	フレッド・ディーキン
メディア:	印刷物

Summary: Flyers and posters to promote *Impotent Fury* club nights.

内容: クラブイベント「インポテント・フューリー」の宣伝用チラシ、ポスター

——————— After years of running equally bizarre clubs in Edinburgh, *Impotent Fury* was Fred Deakin's big success in London and stayed loyal to his club philosophy – to combine music with madness, transcend expectations and blow the audience's minds. It was Fred's friend Laura Lees who suggested that he run a night at Hoxton's 333 club, which at the time featured some deeply fashionable nights but nothing left-field or eclectic. *Impotent Fury* reflected Fred's catholic tastes as a DJ: spinning a six foot high Wheel of Destiny determined the shift to the next genre, taking in techno, pop or even country and western – in fact with 12 musical genres the night wasn't easily categorisable except as eccentric and fun. Off the dancefloor clubbers engaged in a weird array of activities, such as dressing up in free second-hand clothes inside The Wardrobe Of The Stars (few realised at first that as they tried on clothes they were being filmed and screened to everyone outside). Airside evolved the visual and interactive content for the club, and the monthly night provided a social focus that brought the studio and their friends together. The flyers provided a canvas for Fred's continued experimentation with vector graphics, and as the club continued, he used this pop medium to evolve his aesthetic. **FS**

——————— エディンバラで奇抜なクラブを何年も運営したフレッド・ディーキン。ロンドンに移ってから始めたクラブイベント「インポテント・フューリー」でも「期待を上回る音楽と狂気で、オーディエンスを圧倒したい」という彼のクラブ哲学は健在で、大きな成功を収めた。そもそもフレッドの友人であるローラ・リーズが、ホクストンの333クラブでイベントを開催したらどうかと持ちかけたのが始まり。当時333クラブでは、かなりファッショナブルなイベントは開催していたものの、奇抜で幅広い音楽のイベントは行われていなかった。インポテント・フューリーは、DJとして様々なジャンルに精通しているフレッドのテイストが反映されており、ルーレットを回して次にかける曲のジャンルを決めた。テクノやポップ、さらにはカントリー＆ウェスタンまで、12のジャンルの音楽が流れるこのイベントは、カテゴライズすることが難しく、ただエキセントリックで楽しいとしか言いようがない。ダンスフロアーを離れても、好き勝手に古着に着替えておめかしできる「スターの衣装部屋」（着替えの様子が撮影されていて、外のスクリーンでみんなにお披露目されていることに、はじめはほとんどの人が気づかない）など、一風変わった遊びが用意されていた。エアサイドはクラブのビジュアルとインタラクティブ・コンテンツを制作し、毎月定期的に開かれるこのイベントは、メンバーと友人たちが集う格好の場となった。またチラシは、フレッドがベクター・グラフィックスを追究するよい機会となり、クラブの成長とともに、このポップ・メディアを通じて彼のスタイルも進化していった。(FS)

impotent
FURY

at
333
Old Street

on
Friday
8TH October

Admission
£5 b4 11, £10 after.

FEATURING:
THE WHEEL
OF DESTINY
BOOZY ANGELS
The Cuban Brothers
BOLLOX FACTORY
THE WARDROBE OF
THE STARS

The Beginning

始まり

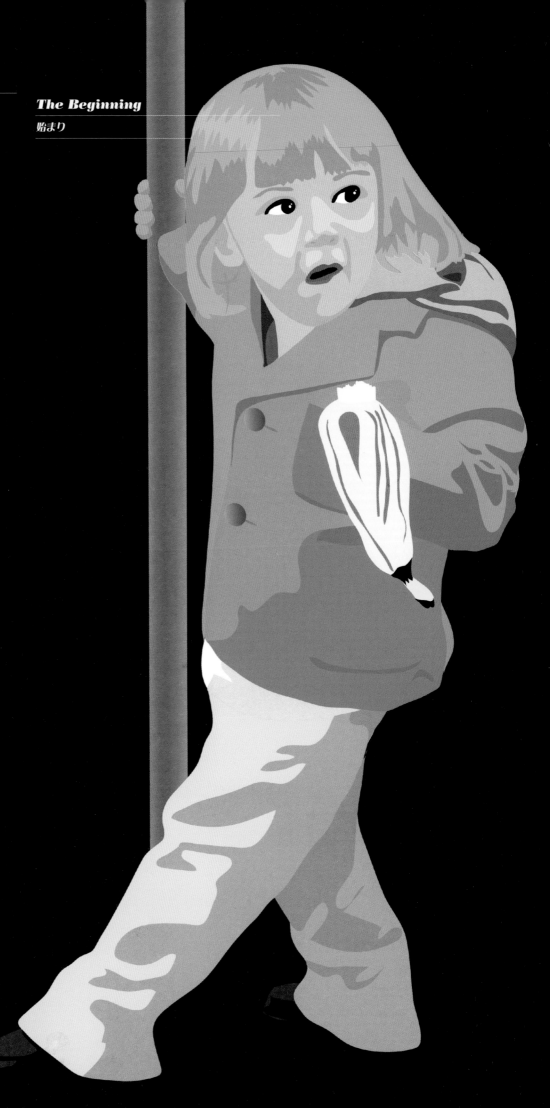

THE AIRSIDE AESTHETIC

エアサイドの美学

Fred Club flyers were my route into graphic design; having an ongoing dialogue with an audience is a great training ground. Make a bad flyer and your club is empty, so you learn fast. The 1930's and 1940's transport posters of Tom Purvis and Frank Newbould, and the US West Coast psychedelic poster art of the late 1960's were the two key influences on my early style. Those transport posters were all about holidays and going to the seaside, showing you Nice and the Riviera in these amazingly rich colours that draw you right in. The US West Coast posters are similar: they're all about that eye freakery – having the reds and the blues set at exactly the right intensity that makes your eyes pop out. I like things to go 'boing!' My style is very punchy and happy, as though I've eaten too many sweets and someone's just given me a glowstick.

Both of those poster styles were produced by screen-printing. It lends itself really well to big washes of flat colour and also to gradients. Before I went to St Martins, I enrolled at the Edinburgh Printmakers Workshop to learn how to do it for myself. I remember the first time I tried to make an old-fashioned gradient: I put one blob of ink of each colour at either end of the squeegee, and watched them slowly merge as the ink travelled across the screen to form a transition from one colour to the other. It had such emotion to it, that big sexy swathe of ink. And because of the gradient changing over time, every print was slightly different, which excited my collector instinct. At St Martins I finally nailed the art of screen-printing.

My breakthrough was making a Kylie print in the style of the transport posters. It was a real struggle to get the colours clean and keep it all pristine, but I managed to get a few perfect copies done before everything collapsed into chaos. Before that my flyers had used flat colours a lot, but they'd been created with a colour cartridge photocopier in just red, blue and black so there wasn't this scope of colour or tactility. Suddenly I was playing with these great big washes of colour and it was a revelation. I showed my Kylie print to David Law, a fellow student that I respected, and he told me it was great. Then he told me that my type was shit. That was when I knew I was onto something.

Alex Fred's stuff is very graphic whereas mine is usually more figurative. I've always

フレッド 僕の場合、クラブのフライヤー作りがグラフィックデザインへの入り口だった。クラブにやってくる人たちとの尽きない会話から、たくさんヒントを得たよ。冴えないフライヤーを作った日には、閑古鳥が鳴いてしまうから、上達は速かったね。初期の頃の僕のスタイルに影響を与えたのは、1930~1940年代にトム・パーヴィスとフランク・ニューボウルドが手がけた交通機関のポスターと、1960年代後半アメリカ西海岸で作られたサイケデリックなポスターアートの2つ。交通機関のポスターは、どれも休暇や海辺に誘うものばかりで、驚くほど眩い豊かな色彩でニースやリヴィエラが描かれていた。アメリカ西海岸のポスターも同様で、目の錯覚を引き起こすような、絶妙で強烈な赤と青が使われているんだ。バーンと目立つものが好きだから、パンチが効いていてハッピーなのが僕のスタイル。お菓子を山ほど食べてハイになってたら、誰かが輝くネオンスティックまでくれたみたいな気分さ。

影響を受けたこれらのポスターは、どちらもスクリーン印刷によるもので、これは輪郭のはっきりした配色やグラデーションにはぴったりの手法なんだ。セント・マーチンに通う前に、僕はこの技術を学びたくて、エディンバラ・プリントメーカーのワークショップに参加した。初めて古典的なグラデーションを試みた時のことを、今でも覚えているよ。ゴムべらの両端に、それぞれ違う色のインクを一滴ずつ垂らして、双方からインクがゆっくりとスクリーンの上を移動し、混じり合ってグラデーションを作るんだ。あの色っぽいインクのうねり、それは情緒があるんだよ。それに時間をかけてグラデーションが変化していくから、どの印刷も少しずつ違った味に仕上がるのが、僕のコレクター魂に火を点けたね。その後、セント・マーチンで、スクリーン印刷の技術を完全にものにした。僕の突破口になったのが、交通機関ポスターのスタイルで作った、カイリーのポスターだった。色が混ざらないように美しく保つのは至難の業だったけど、カオスに陥る前に、なんとか完璧なのを数枚刷ることができた。それまで僕のフライヤーといえば、ベタな色使いで、しかも赤・青・黒しか

ないカラーコピー機を使っていたから、これほどの色のバリエーションもニュアンスも出せなかったんだ。突然山ほど色が使えるようになって、まさに新天地が開けたよ。セント・マーチンで尊敬していた友人のデビッド・ロウに、カイリーのポスターを見せたら「これは凄い。だけどタイポグラフィーはヒドいね」って。あれがきっかけで、僕は何かを掴んだと思う。

アレックス フレッドの作品がグラフィック的なのに対して、僕のはもっと写実的だね。僕のドローイングはかなりアカデミックで、今でも写生をするし、休暇にはスケッチブックを持っていくんだ。エアサイドに職を求めてくる人たちのスケッチブックを見るのは、今でも楽しみだね。中でもリチャードは、誰よりも多くのスケッチブックを持ってきたっけ。僕は、近代建築や初期モダニストの時代の、あのグラマラスな魅力に取り憑かれているんだ。ヒーローは、ミース・ファン・デル・ローエとアルネ・ヤコブセン。とりわけ楽観的な人々で、彼らの建築やプロダクトは、機能性と魅力をバランスよく備えて設計されている。

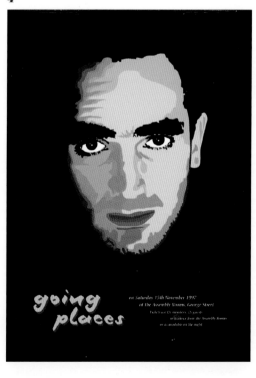

The Airside Aesthetic
エアサイドの美学

5

been quite academic about drawing and so I still do life drawing and take my sketchbook on holiday. I still love to see sketchbooks from people who apply to us for jobs. When we first employed Richard he got through more sketchbooks than anyone I've ever seen! I am obsessed with modern architecture and the glamour and excitement of that early modernist era. My heroes are Mies van der Rohe and Arne Jacobsen; they are so optimistic. Their buildings (and products) embodied balanced proportion, fitness for purpose and glamour. They created a clean canvas for life, with generous spaces containing broad strokes of simple colour and line, doing away with fussy ornamentation or tradition. The appearance of these designs is very graphic in itself; you have the feeling that the architects must have conceived them with just a few simple strokes of the pen. This genre of architecture has influenced a lot of my illustration work and many of the prints and T-shirts I have produced for the shop.
————— Henki Leung I like to pare down my design; that's how my illustration style is different to Fred's and Alex's. That's why the *Battle Royale* girl (page 170) doesn't have a face. I always think about simplicity, breaking it down to its bare essentials.

仰々しい装飾や伝統様式を排除し、広々とした空間に大胆かつシンプルな色やラインを用いて、優雅な生活風景を創出した。こうしたデザインの中でもとくに優れた作品は、それ自体が極めてシンプルなんだ。まるで建築家がささっとペンを走らせて描いたようにね。僕はイラストレーションやショップ用にデザインしたポスター、Tシャツを作る上で、こういう建築に多大な影響を受けているよ。
————— ヘンキ・レウン 僕はデザインを削ぎ落とすのが好きだから、そこがフレッドやアレックスのイラストレーションと違うところかな。バトル・ロワイヤルのポスター（170ページ参照）で、女の子の顔が描かれていないのも、そういう理由からなんだ。シンプルであること、必要最小限まで取り払っていくことをいつも念頭に置いている。
————— リチャード・ホッグ エアサイドの美学は、シンプルであること、そしてルールに従うこと。つまり、自分で課題を設けて、それを達成していく。例えば白を含む3色しか使わずに描こうと決めたら、女性の髪の毛を、背後に描かれた要素に対して、どうやって目立たせるか？ ルールにこだわることで、よりエレガントなデザインを用いなければならない。シンプルであることは、エアサイドがこれまで手がけてきたすべての作品に通底する信念なんだ。例えば僕らは「間」を活かした陰画の技法をよく使う。僕の作品「紅茶とケーキ」の中では、3~4人の女性たちが互いに淫らな振る舞いをしているんだけど、彼女たちは白地に白で描かれているんだ。何をしているかはっきりと描けば、いやらしさも増すだろうけど、そこは見る

人に想像力を働かせてもらわないとね。
————— アレックス エアサイドの初期の頃に、ちょうど世に出てきたFlashは、当時フレッドがフライヤー作りに用いていたベクターグラフィックスの構造と、完璧にマッチする技術だった。ベクタースタイルとフレッドがイラストレーションで培ってきたシンプルな色づかいを、Flashで簡単に動画にできたのは、嬉しい発見だったね。
————— フレッド DAB（38ページ参照）のプロジェクトは、初期のFlashアニメーションの典型的な例だね。古典ジャズの雰囲気を醸し出す青の濃淡を使ったシンプルな作品。均一色で塗り分けられた単純なベクターアウトラインのアニメーションで、データ速度を低く保つことが、初期の回線容量では不可欠だったからね。
そうして僕らはこのフラットなベクタースタイルを確立したわけだけど、そのうち誰もが同じことを始めたから、すぐに次の段階に進まなければならないと感じた。僕はレモン・ジェリーのアルバムジャケットのために、抽象的なパターンを追究し始め、その後キャラクター、風景、パターンの3つをテーマに、日本で展覧会を開催したよ。
————— ナット アレックスの建築的ドローイングはとてもダークで雰囲気があって、そこにフレッドがレモン・ジェリー用に作ったパターンを加えたの。キャラクターに関しては、それまでたくさん作っていたけれど、長いことひとまとめにしていなかったわ。3つとも異なる領域に共存していて、それらに統一感を与えていたのは、私たちの色のセンスだった。多くのスタジ

Richard Hogg Airside's aesthetic is about simplicity and following rules: you set yourself problems and then solve them. If I have to create a whole scene using only three colours and one of those is white, how am I going to make the woman's hair stand out against those background elements? You have to use more elegant design than you would have otherwise. That belief in simplicity is at the core of everything Airside has ever done. We use a lot of negative space. In my *Tea and Cakes* picture which features three or four women doing rude things to each other, they're white on a white background. If you could see what they were doing it would be even ruder, but your imagination has to do the work.

Alex When Flash came along in the very early days of Airside, its technology worked perfectly with the form of vector graphics that Fred had been creating with his flyers. It was a happy coincidence that we could take the vector style and big washes of colour that Fred had developed in his illustrations and make them work easily in Flash.

Fred The DAB project (page 38) was typical of our early Flash animations, just using a few tones of blue to echo the classic jazz feel.

Having clear vector outlines with flat colour inside kept the data rate low which was essential for those primitive bandwidths.

So we'd established this flat vector style which then started popping up everywhere: pretty soon we knew we had to move beyond it. I'd started experimenting with abstract patterns for the Lemon Jelly sleeves and we did an exhibition in Japan where we divided our work up into characters, landscapes and patterns.

Nat Alex's architectural drawings were very dark and atmospheric; then there were Fred's Lemon Jelly patterns. We had this whole other category of character work and for a long time we didn't put them together: they co-existed as different strands. What united them was our sense of colour. We create our illustrations in-house rather than focusing on type and layout and then bringing in freelance illustrators, as many studios do. For example, traditionally when publishers commission book covers they always want one person working as the illustrator and then another as the typographer, whereas we've always believed that the two elements will work better together when they are conceived together. It's a model that's much more

7

The Airside Aesthetic

エアサイドの美学

8

Japanese in spirit and not very typical of British graphic design studios. We've always felt we had an affinity with Japan.

——————— **Fred** Japan gets it – they understand our philosophy. They talk about 'creators' not designers or illustrators. The average person has a much higher degree of graphic awareness, and they're really into British alternative culture. When we first went out there on tour, just as many people knew who Airside were as knew about Lemon Jelly. Stylistically, Manga and that cute kawaii thing were really up our street, so it was an instant attraction from both sides.

——————— **Alex** The caricature has existed since the 14th century in Japan. They would use cartoons in depictions of famous characters or situations and they blur the boundaries really successfully between graphic design, typography and illustration.

——————— **Fred** The Airside style evolved as individual people came into the studio. Ian Stevenson had a very quirky sense of humour and his stuff was always either very happy or very dark. Around the time that we employed him lots of characters started popping up. The characters came out of a

9

love we all had of cartoons and animation, Japanese Manga and toys, and the whole concept of creating a little world. Characters are fun to play with – you can give them a personality and a whole environment to live in. Back then there were a few people making plastic toys, but generally it was regarded as too childish. You'd never see characters in client work; now you have adverts that are packed with them.

——————— **Ian Stevenson** I got into character design at Airside. It just came out of experimentation and what was in my head. It worked so well for the Jam website, and I really got into that world.

——————— **Fred** We were never afraid to play, and characters immediately said playtime. They're fun to make, but you have to have a certain warped imagination. The point where they really come alive is finding that unique characteristic. The adoption thing gave the Stitches (page 182) that edge, while all the Dot Com Refugees (page 104) had wonky eyes and stupid job titles.

——————— **Nat** There are other darker design groups exploring the world of the tortured artist and making some great work. We don't have that mentality, but we do have a slightly twisted sense

オがやっているように、タイポグラフィーとレイアウトを決めたら、後はフリーランスのイラストレーターに任せるというやり方でなく、私たちはすべてインハウスでイラストレーションを仕上げているから。例えば、出版社が装丁デザインを依頼する場合、従来イラストレーターとタイポグラファーを別々にお願いするけど、私たちは両方の要素を分けずに考えたほうが、より良い効果が発揮されると信じてきたの。これは英国のグラフィックデザインスタジオでは稀な考え方で、どちらかというと日本的な精神だと思う。日本には、常々何か通じるものを感じるわ。

——————— **フレッド** 日本は僕らの哲学を理解してくれる。彼らはデザイナーだ、イラストレーターだと分けずに、皆「クリエイター」と見なす。一般の人でもグラフィックに対する意識が高く、英国のオルタナティブ文化にとても興味を持っているんだ。ツアーで初めて日本を訪れた時、レモン・ジェリーを知っているのと同じくらい多くの人々が、エアサイドを知っていた。スタイル的にも、マンガやいわゆるキュートで可愛らしいものは、まさに僕らの得意分野だから、日本と僕らは初めから相思相愛だったね。

——————— **アレックス** 日本では、14世紀から風刺漫画が存在していて、有名な人物や名場面を漫画で描写することで、グラフィックデザイン、タイポグラフィー、イラストレーションの境界線を易々と見事に超えてきたんだ。

——————— **フレッド** エアサイドは、新しいメンバーが加わる度に、進化してきた。イアンは、ひねりの利いたユーモア

の持ち主で、彼の作品はいつも、すごくハッピーか、でなければすごくダークだった。彼を雇った頃から、いろんなキャラクターたちが、次々と生み出された。アニメや日本の漫画、オモチャへの僕らの愛と、小宇宙を自分たちで作り出そうというコンセプトから、このキャラクターたちが生まれたんだ。性格を吹き込んで、住む世界まで創造できるんだから、キャラクター作りの楽しみは尽きないよ。当時、プラスチックのオモチャを作っている人はいたけど、大概、子供っぽいとみなされて、クライアントとの仕事に、キャラクターを用いるなんて、もってのほかだった。今じゃ、どの広告もキャラクターだらけなのにね。

——————— **イアン・スティーブンソン** 僕はエアサイドで、キャラクターデザインに目覚めたんだ。試しにあれこれ作っているうちに、思い描いていたものが形になった。ジャムのウェブサイトが本当に上手くいって、ますますキャラクター作りにのめりこんだね。

——————— **フレッド** 僕らは遊ぶのを恐れなかったし、キャラクター作りといえば、すぐに遊びの時間になった。制作は楽しいけど、ひねりの利いた想像力も必要だ。ユニークな性格を吹き込んで初めて、キャラクターが本当に生き生きとしてくるからね。スティッチィズ（182ページ参照）は「養子縁組み」というアイデアでユニークになったし、ドットコム・レフュジーズ（104ページ参照）は、あの虚ろな瞳とバカげた肩書きが個性になった。

——————— **ナット** 苦悩の芸術家の世界を追究して素晴らしい作品を生み出している、さらにダークなデザイナー

10

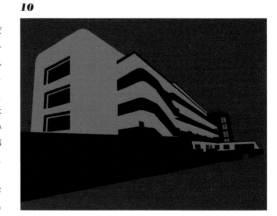

11

of humour hiding behind it all. We like to think that we lure people in with the bright colours and then shock them with the darkness.

——————— **Fred** I didn't personally relate to much contemporary graphic design back when we started out; I've got enormous respect for people like Tomato and David Carson, but it wasn't what I wanted to do. It was designers from a lot earlier that gave us the confidence to pursue our own style when no one else was making work like us. We got our inspiration from what our contemporaries weren't doing. When great people like Rinzen in Australia popped up and clearly had similar influences, it was a validation.

——————— **Richard** I found a lot of popular graphic design in the early 2000's very aggressive, masculine and unfriendly. When I came across Airside it was the opposite – friendly, cheerful and not trying to be cool. There was a spirit of generosity to it. I don't want to say colourful because that's too restrictive, but it's unapologetically cheerful. And it's fun. A lot of fashionable illustration and design work has to be sinister or subversive, but Airside is the reverse of that. It's often disarmingly nice.

たちもいるわね。そういったメンタリティーはないけど、私たちの作品には、ちょっと歪んだユーモアのセンスが潜んでいるの。明るい色でみんなを惹きつけておいて、ダークな部分を見せて驚かすのが好きなの。

——————— **フレッド** 結成当初、僕は現代のグラフィックデザインには個人的にそれほど関わりがなかった。トマトやデヴィッド・カーソンといった人たちのことはすごく尊敬していたけど、僕がやりたいことはまた違っていたんだ。僕らのような作品を制作している人がいなかった頃、自分たちのスタイルを追究していく自信をくれたのは、かなり初期のデザイナーたちだった。同時代のデザイナーたちが、誰もしていなかったことから、インスピレーションを受けていたね。オーストラリアのリンゼンのような面白い人たちが登場した時、明らかに僕らと同じ所から影響を受けているとわかって、これはイケると確信したよ。

——————— **リチャード** 2000年代初頭に目立っていたグラフィックデザインは、ほとんどが攻撃的で男っぽくて、無愛想だった。ところがエアサイドは、まったく逆。フレンドリーで元気で、クールを装ったりせずに、寛大な精神すら感じられた。月並みだから「カラフル」という言葉は使いたくないけど、とにかく堂々とした明るさに満ちていたんだ。それに楽しいしね。流行のイラストレーションやデザインは、不吉で破壊的なのが主流だろうけど、エアサイドはその逆を行く。拍子抜けするくらい素敵なんだよ。

The Airside Aesthetic

エアサイドの美学

12

Alex You've got to practise what you preach. We're trying to have fun in our work and most of the time that comes through – you see that we are really enjoying ourselves.

Guy Moorhouse We don't respond well to humourless, chin-stroking design. This is because as people, we like having fun. We prefer to laugh than to be bogged down with seriousness.

Fred It's a bit of a Christmas mentality. When we started out, we said that using one of our websites should feel like playing with a toy. The same goes for running clubs or doing Lemon Jelly gigs. There should be a sense of surprise. We want to blow people's minds and give them a pleasurable rush from looking at our work, a real reward for having bothered to take time to engage with the stuff we've produced. It's not necessarily thinking about the meaning of life or getting people into a buying frenzy – ultimately we're just trying to push the orgasm button in the middle of people's brains. In this busy modern world with all its different proliferations of media you really have to reward people if you want to engage them.

Alex It would be harder choosing a muted colour palette for one of our projects.

13

12 *Band*
Richard Hogg, 2006

「バンド」
リチャード・ホッグ 2006

13 *Sidecar*
Malika Favre, 2007

「サイドカー」
マリカ・ファーヴ 2007

―――――― **アレックス** 人に説く前に、自ら実践しないとね。僕らは仕事を楽しいものにしようと努力していて、大抵は上手くいくんだ。僕らが本当に楽しんでいることが伝わるだろう？

―――――― **ガイ・ムーアハウス** ユーモアのない、真面目くさったデザインにはあまり興味がない。僕らは、楽しむのが好きな人種だから。深刻になって行き詰まるより、笑っていたいからね。

―――――― **フレッド** 言ってみれば、クリスマス精神みたいなもんだよ。仕事を始めたばかりの頃、僕らのウェブサイトは、オモチャで遊ぶような感覚で使ってもらいたいと話し合った。クラブの経営も、レモン・ジェリーのギグも同じ気持ちでやっている。そこには一種の驚きがあるべきなんだ。作品を見た人たちをびっくりさせて、満足感を味わってほしい。わざわざ時間を作って、僕らの作品を見てくれるんだから、そのお返しにね。べつに人生の意味を考えたり、人々を熱狂させたいわけじゃなくて、要は、僕たちは人々の脳の中枢にある快感ボタンを押そうとしているだけなんだ。あらゆるメディアが増殖するせわしない現代社会で、人々の関心を引くためには、本当に見る価値のあるものを作らないといけない。

―――――― **アレックス** 僕らが手がけるプロジェクトで、控えめな色彩を選ぶことはまずないね。もっとも、Tシャツをデザインする時は、僕がベージュや砂っぽい色しか選ばないって仕事場でひやかされるけど、味のある色が好きなんだ。エアサイドは、そういう渋い色も使っているよ。

―――――― **フレッド** 実際、ピンクやオレンジを着るのは、僕だけだね。とはいえ、去年Tシャツクラブ用に蛍光色のTシャツを作ったけど、印刷から戻ってきたものを見たら、僕でさえ引いてしまうほど派手だったな。

―――――― **ナット** ビジネスの観点から言えば、レモン・ジェリーの世界観を創り出した集団として知られていることには、利点と難点がある。たくさんの人々と知り合えたのは事実だけど、かなり固定したイメージを持たれているわ。自分たちでは、幅広く多様な作品を手がけてきたと思っているんだけど。

―――――― **フレッド** 僕らの存在を知ってもらい、覚えてもらうためには、独自のスタイルを打ち出さなければならず、独自のスタイルを打ち出せば今度は、固定観念を持ってカテゴライズされるという矛盾がある。でも人はどこかで必ず一歩先に踏み出さなければならない。エアサイドは多彩なメンバーで構成されているから、常にいろいろな個性が出入りしているんだ。

―――――― 仕事を依頼してくれそうなクライアントがやってきて「よし、あの『Ducks』（76ページ参照）のミュージックビデオと同じアニメーションCMを制作してくれ。どこから動物たちを登場させて、どこから浮浪者の体にラバ・ランプみたいな水玉を投影しようか？ 浮浪者はべつに登場しなくてもいいんだけど…」などと言われると、ちょっと待てと言いたくなるね。あの作品で重要なのは、彼らの言うところの動物やら何やらの登場するアニメーションスタイル自体ではなく、あのブリーフに僕らがあの手法で応えたという点なんだから。

14

Although when I'm designing T-shirts the joke in the office is that I only ever choose colours like beige and sand. I like those tasteful colours – they're not absent from Airside.

——————— **Fred** I'm the only one who actually wears pink and orange. Having said that I did this great dayglo T-shirt for the T-shirt Club last year and when it came back from the printers it was too bright, even for me.

——————— **Nat** From a business point of view, being known as the people who created the Lemon Jelly aesthetic has been both a good and a bad thing. It's brought lots of people to us, but we've been pigeon-holed a bit. From our point of view we think our work is very diverse.

——————— **Fred** There's a paradox in that you have to develop a house style to get noticed and for people to identify you, and there's no doubt that some people associate us with a certain kind of aesthetic. But then at some point you have to be able to move on. Airside is made up of lots of different people, so there are always different flavours coming in and out of the company.

——————— We get some potential clients coming to us and saying: "Great, make us an animated ad that's exactly like the *Ducks* video (page 76). So when are the animals going to come out, and when is the lava lamp fill going to wipe through the tramp's body? Not that we want a tramp, obviously, but…" We have to say hang on a second, the point of that piece of work wasn't that we were doing a particular animated style of animal or whatever other detail they have in mind, it was that we were approaching the brief in a particular way.

——————— **Alex** TV commercials are particularly bad – some ad agencies can turn around and say: "I've shown the client your previous work and that's exactly what they want". The key is to get an educated client who's buying into our process rather than looking to rip off our previous work. The Orange idents (page 128) were a good example of that, and the titles for *The No. 1 Ladies' Detective Agency* (page 254), where Anthony Minghella was open to almost anything we came up with.

——————— **Mark Swift** That level of humour, quirkiness and boldness in our early work was really refreshing and clients wanted it; the danger was that the illustration style was so bold that people came for that and nothing else. The motion graphics work has helped Airside to move on and let people

15

14 *Thumbnails*
Richard Hogg, 2006

「サムネイル」
リチャード・ホッグ 2006

15 *Wizards*
Jamie Wieck, 2007

「魔法使い」
ジェイミー・ヴィエック 2007

16

see their humour working in a different medium. The breadth of output for motion graphics makes it a bit easier for your style to change – one minute you could be doing an advert for Yakult, the next a film for Live Earth. People now understand Airside's work isn't just about funny, quirky illustration – it's about pushing the client to stand out from the crowd and be a bit daring.

————— **Nat** Every couple of years we sit down and consciously consider how to push our style forward, and it's that internal effort which moves it on more than any particular client or job.

————— **Fred** But to move on you either have to have complete control or complete trust. Both of those are very hard to get. That's why our self-initiated projects are so exciting – they're crucial to the evolution of our style.

————— Kerin Cosford I don't think Airside really does have any one particular aesthetic; although they are closely associated with Lemon Jelly's visuals and identity, there are actually many different distinctive voices within Airside. Everybody's work is their own, and identifiably so – the T-shirts were always a good example of the different styles and sensibility of each designer. Unlike many other agencies, where designers seem to converge on one house style, Airside values the plurality of disciplines and the various aesthetics of the team.

————— **Fred** I remember the illustrator Ian Wright accosting me on the tube and saying: "It's your fault! You're the reason all these graphic design students are doing this bloody vector style!" I always say that if you're getting imitated then you must be doing something right, but you do have to move on. Hopefully what sets us apart is that we always try to integrate some concept or meaning into our designs. There's always a backstory.

————— **アレックス** テレビCMは特にひどいね。中には「君たちの過去の作品をクライアントに見せたところ、これこそ彼らの望むものだと返事をもらった」と言ってくる代理店もある。大事なのは、過去の作品の焼き直しを求めるクライアントではなく、むしろ制作の過程に重きを置いてくれる賢いクライアントに出会うこと。オレンジ（128ページ参照）のCMはその良い例だね。それにNo.1レディーズ探偵社（254ページ参照）のタイトル制作もそう。アンソニー・ミンゲラは、僕らが思いついたことをほとんど採用してくれた。

————— **マーク・スウィフト** 初期の作品にみられる、あのレベルのユーモア、独創性、大胆さは、すごく新鮮で、クライアントはそれを欲していた。問題は、イラストレーションのスタイルがあまりに大胆だったから、みんなが同じスタイルばかり求めてきたことだね。モーショングラフィックスの仕事をするようになったおかげで、一歩進んで、異なったメディアでもエアサイドのユーモアが通用することを人々に理解してもらえるようになった。モーショングラフィックスは表現の幅が広いから、スタイルに変化をつけやすいんだ。ヤクルトの広告を制作したかと思えば、ライブアース用の映像を制作したりね。今では誰もが、エアサイドの仕事は、面白くて奇抜なイラストレーションだけでなく、クライアントが他の企業から頭一つ抜け出せるように、もう少し大胆に押し出すことだと理解してくれている。

————— **ナット** 2〜3年に1度は、自分たちのスタイルを今後どうやって前進させていくか、意識的に話し合っているの。スタイルを進化させているのは、特定のクライアントや仕事というより、内部の努力によるものね。

————— **フレッド** 進化するには、完全にコントロールするか、完全に信頼しなければならないわけで、どちらもなかなか難しい。だからこそ、自分たちで始めたプロジェクトほど面白いものはないんだよ。僕らのスタイルを進化させるには、不可欠だね。

————— **ケリン・コズフォード** エアサイドがひとつの美学しか持ち合わせていないとは、到底思えない。確かにエアサイドと言えば、すぐにレモン・ジェリーのビジュアルやロゴを連想するけど、実際エアサイドには、実に多彩で際立った個性が共存していると思う。メンバーがそれぞれ独自のスタイルを持っているから、誰の作品か見分けがつくし。Tシャツは、各デザイナーのスタイルやセンスの違いがわかる良い例だね。デザイナーたちを集めて、ひとつの決まったスタイルでデザインさせる多くの代理店と違って、エアサイドは互いの個性を認め合い、チームに多様な美意識が混在することを尊重しているんだよ。

————— **フレッド** ある時地下鉄の中で、イラストレーターのイアン・ライトが僕に近づいて来て「まったく、君のせいでグラフィックデザイン専攻の学生たちが、憎たらしいベクタースタイルしか描かなくなっちまったじゃないか!」と言ったのを憶えているよ。僕はいつもこう言っているんだ。誰かが模倣し始めたら、君のやっていることは正しいに違いないけど、君自身はそこからさらに前進しなくちゃいけないって。僕らが他と違うのは、常に、ある種のコンセプトや意図をデザインに融合させる努力をしているからだと思いたいね。そこにはいつも根拠があるんだ。

17

18

19

THE EARLY YEARS

初期

Alex When we started Airside at the end of the nineties, website design was a black art. There were no rules; we were inventing them as we went along. It was the start of the dotcom boom, and we were one of the first to discover that websites could be entertaining and not just pages of brochureware. We tried to make them much more interactive and engaging in a way that few websites were at that time. Our basis was that we didn't work with just the graphic design or the technology. We also explored the experience – what someone would be feeling, what they would take away from it, how they were going to engage with it and what would keep them there. Not many people were asking those fundamental questions. It was an innovative way of thinking about websites. Whereas other people might have thought about the technology or just about beautiful design; we thought about the user experience as well.

Nat There were only a handful of other people doing anything similar at the time, like the London-based collective Antirom for example. Everyone else was making sites that had hideous bevelled buttons as the only navigation device.

Fred We were playing, discovering how the internet worked. There wasn't much imagination in web design – a lot of it was technologically driven and didn't understand the issues of aesthetic or emotional design. We felt there was a big gap in the market for a company that could deliver something that worked but also addressed those other factors.

Alex Nat's background in Human Computer Interface Psychology and programming taught us a lot, and we'd done a lot of work on film websites where we'd had to get people to enter competitions and take part in challenges online. I had also spent two years establishing a charity that provided a forum for political discussion online which involved all the party leaders in 1997 – a pre-web 2.0 political networking site. We carried that knowledge through with us.

アレックス 90年代の終わりにエアサイドを始めた頃、ウェブサイトデザインは、まだ未開の分野だった。ルールも何もなかったから、制作しながら自分たちで決めていった。ちょうど「ドットコム」ブームの先駆けの頃で、僕らはウェブサイトというのは、企業パンフレットの内容をそのまま掲載するのではなく、エンターテイニングであるべきだって最初に思いついたうちの1組なんだ。そこで、当時ではあり得ないくらい、はるかにインタラクティブで魅力的なサイトを作ることにした。単なるグラフィックデザインや技術だけのサイトは作らないと決めて、主に、サイトを見た人が何を感じるか、何を得ることができるか、何が人を惹きつけて、どうすればユーザーをサイトにつなぎ止めておけるのか、といった「ユーザー体験」を探求した。そういった根本的な問いを持つ人は、まだ少なかったね。僕らのウェブサイトに対する考え方は、革新的だった。多くの人たちが、技術的なことや、美しいデザインのことだけ考えていた頃、僕らは、すでにユーザー体験について考え始めていたんだ。

ナット その頃、私たちと同じようなことをしている人は、ごく僅かだったわ。例えばアンチロムとか。他のサイトはどれもこれも、ナビゲーションといったら悪趣味な3D風のベベルボタンだもの。

フレッド 僕らは楽しみながらインターネットの活用法を発見していった。当時は、想像力に長けたウェブデザインがなくて、ほとんどが技術を見せつけるものばかり。美しく、人の心に響くようなデザインをしようなんて発想がそもそもなかったんだ。単に機能するウェブサイトを提供するだけでなく、それ以上の何かを提案できるエアサイドのような会社にとって、それこそ市場はチャンスだらけに見えた。

アレックス 人間＝コンピューター間のインターフェース心理学に造詣の深いナットからは、多くのことを教わった。おかげでサイトを訪れた人がコンペに参加したり、オンライン上でゲームに挑戦することのできる映画のウェブサイトをたくさん作ったよ。僕は、1997年から2年間を費やして、全党首が集うオンライン政治討論フォーラムを提供するチャリティーサイトを構築した。web2.0以前の政治ネットワークサイトだったけどね。こうして得た多くの知識が、エアサイドに今も活かされているよ。

1

2

1   Visualisation of Virtual
Parliament project
Alex Maclean, 1997

「バーチャル・パーラメント」
イメージ
アレックス・マクレーン 1997

2   Sketch of Virtual
Parliament project
Alex Maclean, 1997

「バーチャル・パーラメント」
スケッチ
アレックス・マクレーン 1997

JOHN PAUL JONES

Nat One of our earliest websites was for John Paul Jones, Led Zeppelin's multi-instrumentalist, who had a new album to promote called *Zooma*. True to our lack of new business policy, we got the job because he lived next door to a friend from my school. He was up for doing something quite experimental, so we made a website where you don't really get it first time and you're rewarded by exploring. We referred to it as 'user-grumpy' – everyone else was trying to make sites that were user- friendly so it was a reaction to that. The navigation was a star map of 20-30 lights that you had to follow around, forming a timeline. It was a more interesting way of finding out about his life. You were playing with it, basically.

Alex It wasn't a bad budget either – £9k was about four times what we were paid for anything else back then.

Nat At that point there was pretty much no online content worth looking at – you didn't browse the internet for long before you got bored.

Alex Innovation was coming from people like Daniel Brown, who was doing all this algorithm-based programming that created animations and interactivity under the name of Noodlebox. It was very geeky and very beautiful, a combination of good programming skills and aesthetic quality. It was all experimental artistic work at that point – corporate clients couldn't get their heads round that kind of interactivity. With John Paul Jones we were lucky to find a client who was open to a more adventurous approach.

Nat At the beginning the web industry was made up of either graphic designers or technologists – on the graphic designers' sites the navigation was terrible, and the technologists' sites all looked awful. We were trying to be both.

Fred One of things I used to say to pitch Airside in meetings was that a website needed three things: to look great, to work properly, and to be engaging in a psychological way. We said that with any other company you'd get two of those things at best. We could do all three.

SERPENTINE

Nat An early job we pitched for was the Serpentine Gallery, who didn't have a website and were told they needed one by Bloomberg, their sponsors. We told them they needed to spend £35k on a database-driven site. We really put the work in for our pitch – we wanted to do it properly. We had to explain what the internet and the world wide web were: "It's a matrix of interconnected computers", and so on: that's how 'dark ages' it was.

Alex We took the directors to Bloomberg, and did a whole presentation about art on the web. We got a lot of material from our friend, the artist Carey Young. We were in the land of the blind, but because we'd done a lot of research and knew our stuff we certainly had at least one eye.

Nat But despite all our work they just didn't see the possibilities. When it came down to it, they said we've got £1,000 and we need something online in a week. So we did a very basic but functional site instead, which we manually updated for them for eight years before they went and hired someone else to do what we'd recommended originally. If they'd had a database from the outset it would have kept an archive of every exhibition.

ジョン・ポール・ジョーンズ

ナット 初期の頃に制作したもののひとつが、レッド・ツェッペリンのベーシストで、当時ニューアルバム「Zooma」の宣伝をしていたジョン・ポール・ジョーンズのウェブサイト。私たち、新規ビジネス獲得のポリシーに欠けていたでしょ、この時もジョンが私の学生時代の友人の隣に住んでいたことから、仕事をもらったのよ。ジョンが斬新なものを作るのに乗り気だったから、ユーザーが1度訪れただけでは全貌が掴めないけど、何度も探索していくうちにだんだんわかってくる仕組みを作ったわ。名付けて「ユーザー無愛想サイト」。誰もがこぞって、ユーザーフレンドリーなサイトを制作していたから、その反動ね。ナビゲーションは、星座みたいに並んだ20~30個の光点で、ユーザーがその光を辿って行くと、内容が時系列に並んでいって、楽しみながらジョンの人生の軌跡を辿れるの。基本的に、遊びのサイトなのよ。

アレックス 予算も悪くなかった。9,000ポンドなんて、当時手がけた他の仕事のほぼ4倍だよ。

ナット あの頃は、見るに値するオンライン・コンテンツは存在してなくて、飽きるまでネットサーフィンなんてこともなかったわね。

アレックス ダニエル・ブラウンのような人たちの登場で、改革が始まったんだ。彼はアルゴリズムベースのプログラミングをつくった人物で、ヌードルボックスという名前で、アニメーションやインタラクティブ・コンテンツを作っていた。優れたプログラミング技術と美的センスの融合は、すごくマニアックで、同時にすごく美しかった。でも当時は、それが実験的アートとみなされて、企業のクライアントたちは、そういったインタラクティビティを理解できなかった。僕らは、ジョン・ポール・ジョーンズのプロジェクトで冒険的な手法にオープンなクライアントと出会えて、ラッキーだったんだ。

ナット 初期のウェブ業界を担っていたのは、グラフィックデザイナーか、技術者のいずれかだった。前者のサイトはナビゲーションがまるでなっていなかったし、後者のサイトは見るに耐えなかった。私たちはその両方に長けたサイトを作ろうとしていたの。

フレッド ミーティングでエアサイドを売り込むときに、僕はよくこう言った。「ウェブサイトには3つの要素が必要だ。見映えが良く、機能的で、心理的にユーザーを惹きつけること。他社に頼んだら、よくても2つしか満たしてくれないけど、うちなら、3つとも実現できるよ」って。

サーペンタイン

ナット 初期の頃、サーペンタイン・ギャラリーのウェブ制作のコンペに参加したのね。彼らはそれまでウェブサイトを持っていなくて、スポンサーのブルームバーグから作るように言われていたの。私たちは、35,000ポンドかけてデータベース主導型のサイトを作ることを薦めたわ。きちんとやりたかったから、プレゼン用の素材には、ものすごく力を入れた。インターネットとは何か、から始めて、ワールド・ワイド・ウェブとは「相互に接続したコンピューターのマトリックスであり...」ということまで説明して。それくらい「暗黒時代」だったの。

アレックス 僕らはディレクターを率いてブルームバーグに出向き、ウェブアートに関する一大プレゼンテーションを行ったんだ。友人のアーティスト、ケアリー・ヤングから膨大な素材を手に入れてね。右も左もわからない中だったけど、準備に時間を費やし、専門的なリサーチもしたから、僕らは自分たちの提案しているものを知り尽くしていた。

ナット でも、あれだけ頑張ったけど、クライアントは可能性に目を向けようとしなかった。結局のところ、サーペンタインは1,000ポンド用意するから、1週間以内に何か仕上げてオンラインにあげてほしいと言ってきたの。だから私たちはとてもベーシックだけど機能的なサイトを38時間で完成させたわ。それから8年間、手作業でアップデイトを手伝った挙げ句、彼らはようやく人を雇って、私たちが初めに提案した方法を採用したの。はじめからデータベースを作っておけば、過去の全展覧会のアーカイヴが保存できたのにね。

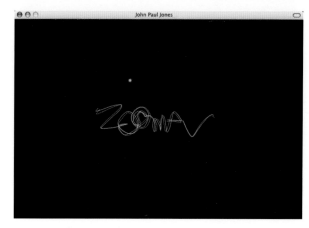

3 Screens from the John Paul Jones website, 1999

ジョン・ポール・ジョーンズ
ウェブサイト 1999

The Early Years

初期

DAB

Fred DAB (Digital Audio Broadcasting) was one of our first real Airside projects, and gave us a proper chance to innovate. It was for the BBC, who wanted to make a regular digital radio broadcast but with visuals – at one point DAB radios were conceived as having small screens.

Nat It was very ahead of its time. It went out as a test transmission, because no one had the technology in their homes – it was a concept to see if there was a market for this type of broadcast. Flash was a new technology, and we persuaded the BBC to use it although they were resistant at first. It was a chance to really think about the project from the ground up. They initially asked us to make a still image sequence that changes every sixty seconds, but we said, look, you can use this new thing called Flash which will reduce your file size so much that you can transmit much more interesting information.

Fred The broadcast featured Evan Parker, the legendary avant-garde saxophonist. We generated some figurative animated loops from footage of Evan and his musicians playing; then we created some more abstract pattern loops, and put the two elements together.

Alex Evan is an intense character. He'd been playing the saxophone one night and cut his lip, and as the blood dripped down through his saxophone onto the floor it had created this pattern of blood on the floor. He showed us some photographs, and we based our abstract visuals on it. The loops were animated to match the audio during the broadcast. Amazingly, it was one of those projects where we talked to the commissioners at the BBC, the boffins in their lab, the production company Somethin' Else and even the artists themselves.

Nat You still don't get these jobs very often where you get to truly innovate; where you say, we're not going to do that thing you asked us to do, we're going to do better than that, and then go on to really understand the technology and make something you didn't think was possible. It won an Innovation in Radio award.

Fred It was really useful for Airside. It was one of the first moving image projects we did that had a degree of professionalism about it. We designed this unique experience that interacted with an audience in a completely new way. With that and Lemon Jelly, the exploration of relationship between music and visuals began, and it's one we're still exploring to this day.

Nat We've always questioned the brief from the very beginning. We'd say, you can come asking for a website but we might give you an umbrella. Although that hasn't actually happened yet.

DAB

フレッド DAB（デジタル音声放送）はエアサイドにとって初の、本格的なプロジェクトのひとつで、僕らが一歩先へ踏み出すのにうってつけの仕事だった。クライアントはBBCで、彼らは映像つきデジタルラジオの定期放送を実現したいと考えていた。DABラジオに、小さな画面を付けて売り出す案もあったんだ。

ナット 当時としては、すごく画期的なことだったのね。これに対応するシステムがどの家庭にも備わっていなかったから、伝送テストという形で放送されたの。この種の放送に見合う市場があるかを調査する目的でね。そこで、まだ登場したてだったFlashを使うようBBCを説得したのだけれど、最初は嫌がってね。あれがプロジェクトを根本から考え直す転機だった。彼らは初め、60秒ごとに差し変わる静止画を依頼してきたけれど、「ちょっと待って。このFlashというものを導入すれば、ファイルのサイズを大幅に軽減できて、もっと画期的な情報を発信できるんですよ」って。

フレッド 放送内容は、伝説のアヴァンギャルド・サックス奏者、エヴァン・パーカーを特集したものだった。僕らは、エヴァンと仲間たちが演奏している映像からいくつかの図形のループを作成し、僕らの作った抽象模様のループと組み合わせたんだ。

アレックス エヴァンは激しい性格の持ち主で、ある晩サックスを吹いていたら唇が切れて、血がサックスから地面に滴り落ち、床に模様を描いたっていうんだ。その時の写真を何枚か見せてもらって、それをもとに抽象的な映像を制作した。放送中、ループ映像が音とシンクロするようにアニメーション化してね。このプロジェクトは、驚いたことに、BBCのコミッショナーやラボの専門家、制作会社のサムシングエルス、さらにはアーティスト自身と直接話し合って進めることのできた、類い稀な仕事のひとつだった。

ナット こんなに革新的なことに挑戦できる仕事は、今でもそう多くないわ。頼まれたことをやらずに、それ以上に凄いことをすると宣言して、技術に関する理解をとことん突き詰めて、実現不可能だと思われていたことを実現できた。このプロジェクトでラジオ革新賞をもらったのよ。

フレッド エアサイドにとって、すごく貴重な体験だった。ある程度プロの専門知識が必要な、初めての動画プロジェクトだったからね。オーディエンスと触れ合うこのユニークな体験を、現代的な新しいやり方でデザインしたんだ。この仕事やレモン・ジェリーの活動から、音楽と映像の関係性の探求が始まって、今でも僕らはそれを探し続けている。

ナット 私たちは常に、依頼概要の根本から疑問を持つようにしているの。だから例えば誰かがウェブサイト制作を依頼しにやって来たとしても、私たちが提供するものは傘かもしれない。まぁそんなケースは、まだ実際には起きてないけどね。

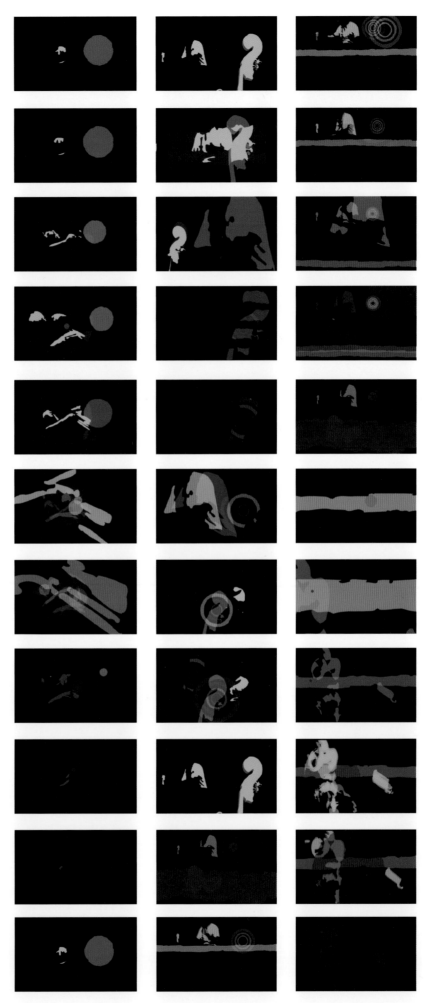

4   Development work for
BBC DAB project, 1999

BBC DAB
アニメーション制作過程
1999

5

WHITE CUBE

Fred The White Cube were moving into Hoxton Square and needed a new website. Jay Jopling had given me my first DJ job in Edinburgh and they had seen our work for the Serpentine so they got us in to do both the website and their new identity. The direction we came up with was very kaleidoscopic and full of motion; we had to create something with a strong look and feel which could also showcase a wide variety of aesthetics without overshadowing them. Jay liked the Bloomberg site with its live feel and a tickertape running underneath so we made the whole thing very dynamic.

Nat The web was still the wild west in those days and pretty much anything went, so we were inventing navigation with moving menus, making text enlarge as you rolled over it, creating transitions that enhanced the interface – we enjoyed making websites that were fun to use.

Alex Even back then our work was all about animation and movement. It was obvious where we were going.

Fred Frieze magazine said it was the best fine art site they had ever seen.

Nat With several exciting projects

8

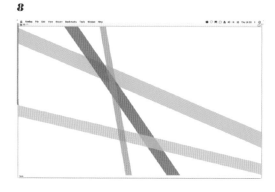

ホワイト・キューブ

フレッド ホワイト・キューブがホクストン・スクエアへの移転を機に、新しいウェブサイトを作ろうとしていた。ジェイ・ジョプリングはエディンバラ時代、僕にDJの初仕事を振ってくれた人物で、僕らが作ったサーペンタインのウェブサイトを見て、ホワイト・キューブのサイトと新しいIDの制作を依頼してきたんだ。そこで、インパクトがあって個性的でありながらも、多種多様な作品を邪魔しない、万華鏡のような、動きのある方向性を思いついた。ジェイが、画面下に絶えず帯状に速報の入るライブ感のあるブルームバーグのサイトが気に入っていたので、僕らもダイナミックな動きを演出した。

ナット その頃はまだ、ウェブサイトが未発達な時代だったから、何でもできたのよ。ナビゲーションのメニューを動かして、ポインタを合わせると文字が大きくなる工夫をしたり、インターフェイスを使いやすくする方法をいろいろ編み出しながら、使いやすいサイトを考えるのは、楽しかったわ。

アレックス その頃からすでに、僕らの仕事はアニメーションと動画ばかりだったから、進みたい方向は明白だった。

フレッド 「今まで見た現代美術のウェブサイトの中で一番」って、雑誌フリーズで評されたよ。

ナット いくつかの刺激的なプロジェクトを経験したところで、そろそろエアサイドの規模を拡大すべき時が来ていた。すでにビジネス・デザイン・センターの一角で開かれた「新人デザイナー卒業制作展」で物色済みだったんだけれど、まずインタラクティブ・デザイナー兼プログラマーとして、初めて採用したのがマーク・スウィフト。1年後の2000年にはアンソニー・ブリルの推薦を受けて、イアン・スティーヴンソンにも入ってもらったの。イアンもまたマルチスキルの持ち主で、イラストからウェブデザインまでこなすのよ。それからタイポグラフィーに精通している人も必要だったから、当時新卒だったヘンキ・レウンを迎えたの。次に、スタジオ管理のために、アン・ブラーシェィを雇ったんだけど、今ではPRや新規ビジネスも任せている。こうして段階的に人を採用したわけだけど、私たち自身はまだディレクターとして、すべてのプロジェクトに携わっていたわ。

マーク 初期の段階から関わることができて、とても恵まれていたと思う。ディレクター3人対、雇われ人1人ということで、しょっちゅうおじけづいていたけどね。僕はインスタレーションとインタラクティブ・デザインに強い大学の出身だけど、エアサイドには多様なスキルの持ち主がいて、興味も幅広いから、ある時はTシャツのデザインをしたかと思えば、ある時はアニメーションやウェブサイトを制作したり。初めはかなり技術寄りだった僕も、あっという間にメディアの枠を超えたクリエイティブに対応できる能力を身につけたよ。

5	Flyposters advertising launch of White Cube website, 1999	6–12	Screens from White Cube website, 1999
	ホワイト・キューブ サイト開設告知ポスター 1999		ホワイト・キューブ ウェブサイト 1999

6

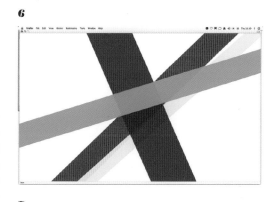

under our belt we'd reached a point where we needed to expand our staff. We had already been shop-
ping at *New Designers*, the graduate show around
the corner at the Business Design Centre, and we
employed Mark Swift, our first employee, as an
interaction designer and programmer. A year later
in 2000 came Ian Stevenson, following a recommen-
dation by Anthony Burrill. Ian was another multi-
tasker – good with illustration, and also able to
do web design. Henki Leung followed, also a new
graduate, as we needed someone with typography
skills. Anne Brassier came next, initially to manage
the studio but then taking on PR and new business.
There was a gradual hiring of people, but as directors, we still had a hand in everything.

——————— **Mark** I was blessed with the fact
I was there from the very beginning, although it
was always going to be a bit daunting with three
directors and one employee. I came from a strong
college background of designing installations and
interactions. Yet because of the diverse skillset
and interests at Airside, one minute I'd be designing a T-shirt, the next, an animation or a website.
My skills soon changed drastically from being quite
technical to being creative across a broad range
of media.

7

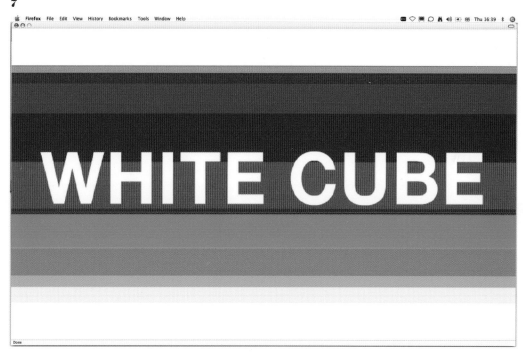

9

10

11

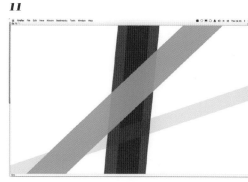

12

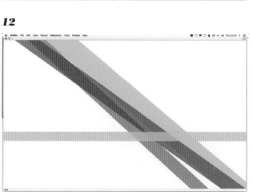

JAM:TOKYO–LONDON

ジャム：東京ーロンドン

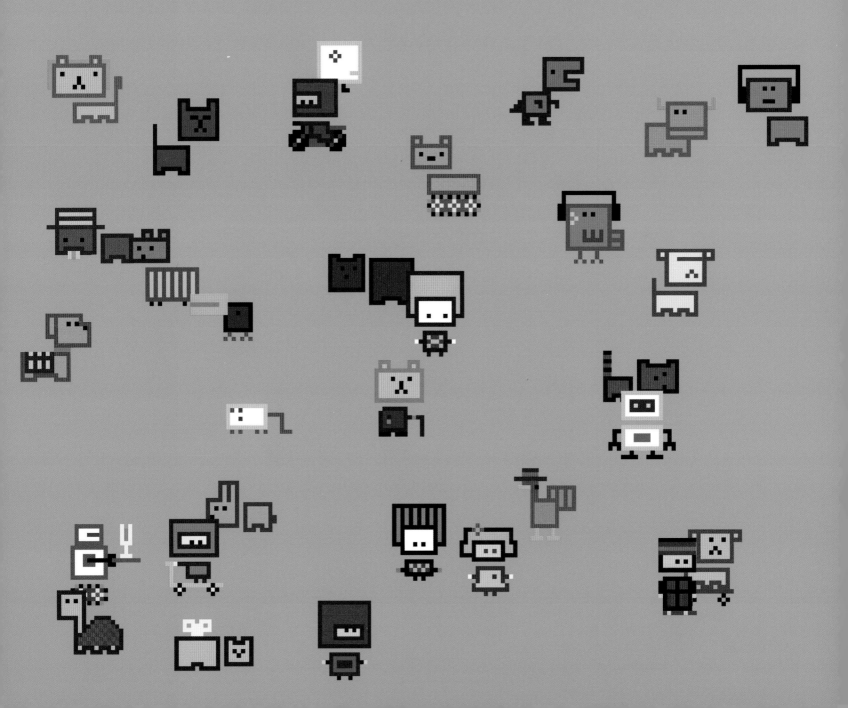

Job name:	JAM:Tokyo–London
Client:	The Barbican Art Gallery, London
Media:	Digital
Awards:	D&AD, Design Week Awards 2002 – Interactive Media

Summary: A website to serve both as an information point and as an exhibit in the exhibition itself.

——————— Airside and Japan have a mutual appreciation for each other, and so it was fitting that Airside were selected by the Barbican Centre to participate in *Jam: Tokyo–London*, an exhibition celebrating the contemporary cultural influences shared by the two cities. Airside were invited to produce an engaging exhibition website that also served as their personal gallery exhibit for the show; a deeply challenging brief to say the least! Airside's approach unified several strands of its design thinking: the creation of a playful experience, even in the nascent days of web design; a focus on interaction which gives the user more than just straightforward information; and a vibrant, engaging aesthetic. A gaggle of pixellated characters representing the exhibitors reacted to an interactive menu in various ways depending on their particular disciplines, thus replicating the functionality of a standard drop-down menu in a highly entertaining manner. This website demonstrated how artistic innovation could be applied to any website to deliver information effectively in the context of an entirely new form of user experience. **FS**

作品名：	ジャム：東京—ロンドン
クライアント：	バービカン・センター、ロンドン
メディア：	ウェブサイト
受賞歴：	D&AD賞、デザイン・ウィーク賞2002／インタラクティブ・メディア部門

内容： 展覧会の情報を提供するサイト兼展示作品

——————— 何やら、お互いにウマの合うエアサイドと日本。バービカン・センターで開催された「ジャム：東京—ロンドン」展の参加者にエアサイドを選出したのは、まさに大正解。「ジャム」とは、刺激し合う２都市の現代カルチャーを讃える展覧会。エアサイドは、魅力的な展覧会の告知ウェブサイトであり、同時に各参加アーティストの作品ギャラリーの機能も兼ね備えたサイトの制作を依頼された。これは、控えめに言っても、かなりの難題！そこでエアサイドは、いくつものデザイン構造を統合することにした。当時、ウェブデザインといえば、まだ未開分野だったが、遊び心あふれる場を創り出し、ただの情報告知ではない、ユーザー参加型のインタラクション機能を備えた、賑やかで魅力的なデザインに仕上げた。参加アーティストたちを表すピクセル・キャラクターたちが、カテゴリーごとの様々なインタラクティブ・メニューの命令に従って動き回り、従来のドロップダウン型メニューの機能をはるかにエンターテイメントな方法で表現した。このウェブサイトは、まったく新しいユーザー体験を提案することで、情報を効果的に発信するのに、いかにアーティスティックで斬新なアイデアが応用できるかを示す、良い見本となった。（FS）

The Early Years

初期

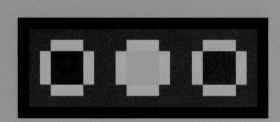

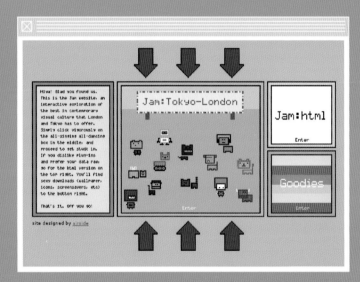

Hiya! Glad you found us. This is the Jam website, an interactive exploration of the best in contemporary visual culture that London and Tokyo has to offer. Simply click vigorously on the all-singing all-dancing box in the middle, and proceed to get stuck in. If you dislike plug-ins and prefer your data raw go for the html version on the top right. You'll find sexy downloads (wallpaper, icons, screensavers, etc) to the bottom right.

That's it. Off you go!

site designed by airside

Jam:Tokyo-London

Jam:html
Enter

Goodies
Enter

Enter

Photographers | Graphics/Illustrators | Art

Motion | Music | Performance | Fashion

Airside

Projects: 1 2 3 4 5 6 7 8 9

Airside are driven by the prospect of creating innovative and exciting experiences for their contemporaries via a diverse array of media. They relish the democratic opportunity that digital technology offers and think a lot about how to make interaction with a computer both accessible and fun; simultaneously they are quick to step outside the box when appropriate in search of an alternative means of communicating with their audience. Fred Deakin, Nat Hunter and Alex Maclean who run the company are committed to a quest for excellence in both design and process.

Though their website is animated and patterned with primary colours, it's not just eye candy: the directors have fused their talents from extensive backgrounds of music and clubs, human-computer psychology and architecture to champion a range of truly interactive projects that charm and surprise.

From the user-friendly portfolio of artists at White Cube gallery to a dark and sophisticated game that begrudgingly delivers data in tantalising packets for John Paul Jones, Airside's websites are unique in their creative approach. They are uncompromising on quality but for the right clients. Incredibly versatile in

The Manny Manny Airside crew 2000

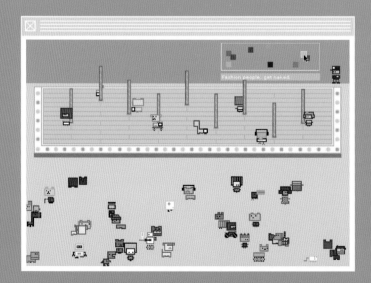

Fashion people, get naked

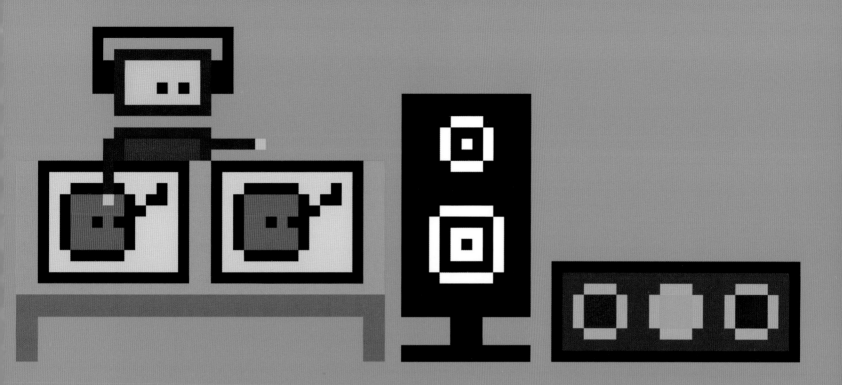

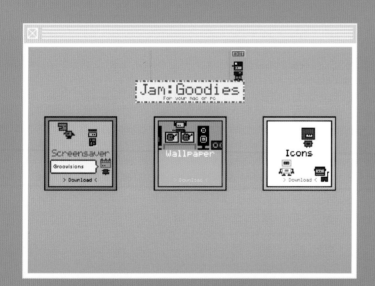

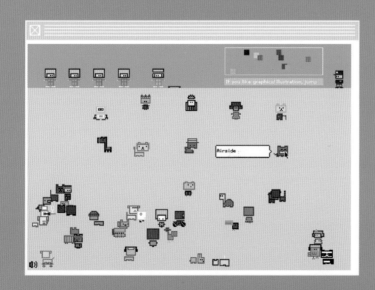

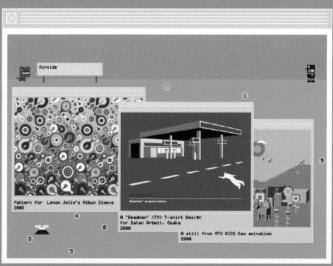

JAM

——— **Nat** One of our star projects was for a Barbican exhibition called *Jam: Tokyo–London*, featuring 20 artists from Tokyo and 20 artists from London. We were asked to design the website for the exhibition, and then they asked if the website could also be our exhibit in the show. We created this world where you could boss around all these characters, each of which represented one of the artists. You could choose the command 'If you're from Tokyo, dance' and then the DJ would come out and all the Japanese characters would dance. That's exactly the same as a pull-down menu – it allowed you to see all the Japanese exhibitors. By clicking a different command, the fashion people took off all their clothes and went pole dancing – but because they're babies they left their nappies on. At that time potential clients didn't understand the idea of doing a non-traditional, experimental website as they had no way of conceptualising what was possible. So for years afterwards we used this site to inspire clients to be more adventurous.

——— **Mark** We were keen to make it a really playful experience for people who couldn't get to London or Tokyo and see the exhibition, so they could still get involved by going online and playing with the content. We tried to give a bit of playfulness to the work in a way that also encouraged people to explore more of the content. People were navigating around to see all the artists' work because they wanted to click on the man in the little monkey suit, or the sheep that had a gas mask on. It was breaking down people's inhibitions to interact with the content, and trying to engage them enough so they would explore in depth. Normally with a website you get two or three clicks before the user leaves – the trick is to get them to see the whole of the piece, and for them to have a nice, playful time while they're doing it.

——— **Fred** A lot of the concepts behind *Jam* were developed with us all around the table. We operate in this group brain kind of way; everything goes in the pot. We ended up creating this crazy world for Ian's surreal characters to run around in. Everyone loved it, and it was eventually nominated for a Bafta, as well as winning a Design Week award – the first time we'd won anything significant.

——— **Ian** I was already quite into character design and really got into that world at Airside. Characters were a good vehicle for the web – it made it more fun, and people could represent themselves as a little character and walk around. With that pixelated aesthetic, the challenge was being able to animate a bunny and get it to do as much as possible whilst keeping the file size small so it wouldn't slow everything down. It was a good way

ジャム

——— **ナット** バービカンで開催した「ジャム:東京—ロンドン」っていう展覧会は、私たちの中でもハイライトのひとつよね。東京、ロンドンの両都市から、それぞれ20人のアーティストを紹介する展覧会で、もともと私たちは、そのウェブサイト制作を依頼されていたの。その後ウェブサイトも展示品として出展されることになったわ。ユーザーは各アーティストをモデルに作られたキャラクターを思い通りに動かすことができるの。例えば「東京のアーティストたちよ、踊れ!」と命じると、DJが登場して日本人アーティストのキャラクターたちが一斉に踊りだすとかね。もちろんプルダウンメニューから日本人アーティストを選出することも同様に可能なのよ。他にも「ファッション関係の人、ぜんぶ服を脱いで!」なんていう命令もあって、そうするとキャラクターたちが服を脱いでポールダンスを始めるの。と言っても、みんな赤ん坊だから、脱いでもオムツ姿。あの当時は、クライアントになり得る企業はどこも、紋切り型のウェブサイト以外の実験的サイトを作るという発想を持ち合わせていなかったの。ウェブサイトで何ができるかを思い描く方法がなかったのね。だから私たちは、この後長いこと、クライアントの冒険心をそそるのに、このサイトを見せていたわ。

——— **マーク** ロンドンや東京の展覧会を訪れることができない人たちのためにも、本当に面白い体験をしてもらえるようなサイトにしたかったんだ。会場に足を運べなくても、オンラインでコンテンツに触れることで、充分参加できるんだよってね。それから、ユーザーがもっとコンテンツを見たくなるような遊びも仕掛けた。猿のコスプレをした男や、ガスマスクを付けた羊など、思わずクリックしてみたくなるようなキャラクターを配置することで、結果的にユーザーがアーティスト全員の作品を見て回るようになっている。コンテンツに触れる際の、ユーザーの抵抗感を緩和して、彼らを惹きつけることでもっと深くまで探索できるようにしたんだ。通常、ユーザーはひとつのウェブサイトを訪問し、2,3度画面をクリックしたら去ってしまう。惹きつけるコツは、ユーザーがサイト全体を見たくなるような、楽しく遊び心があるサイトを作ること。

——— **フレッド** ジャムを支えるコンセプトの多くは、全員で話し合って構築した。ブレインストーミングを繰り返すような感じで、みんなのアイデアをひとまとめにして。その結果、イアンが作り出したシュールなキャラクターたちが走り回る、クレイジーな世界を作ることになった。そしてそれがみんなに愛され、遂にはBAFTA(英国映画テレビ芸術アカデミー賞)にノミネートされ、デザイン・ウィークでは賞も獲得したんだ。僕らにとって、初めての大きな賞だった。

——— **イアン** 僕はもともとキャラクターデザインには興味があって、エアサイドで本格的にのめり込んだ感じ。キャラクターは、ウェブにとって格好のツールだった。ウェブをさらに盛り上げてくれるし、ユーザーは自分を小さなキャラクターに見立てて動き回れるからね。ピクセルキャラクター作りでの挑戦は、例えばウサちゃんのキャラクターを自在に動かすだけでなく、ファイルサイズを小さく保って画面全体の速度を落とさないようにすることだった。情報を提供するのにキャラクターを使

The Early Years

初期

14

15

of presenting the information, rather than using buttons. All the characters move around randomly like they're alive – it's as though they're making their mind up where they want to go.

— **Nat** The music for *Jam* was composed by an old Edinburgh friend, Philip Pinsky, one third of the band Finitribe. The brief was mad Japanese gaming music, with a different version playing depending on what you'd told the characters to do.

— **Philip Pinsky** I've worked for Airside on soundtracks for cereal bars, underground trains, shoes, photographers, science museums, yoghurt drinks, tourist boards, film websites, TV channels and art exhibitions, all accompanied by a huge cast of bizarre animated characters. A shared sense of humour and love of the grotesque has made for a symbiotic collaboration.

— **Fred** Our first proper animation job for TV happened soon after – an animation for MTV for Aids Day. It starred a pixelated penis moving across the screen like a Space Invader icon, with the message that you should wear a condom. MTV's lawyers freaked out a bit but fortunately we managed to get it through. It was probably the first time we made a storyboard before beginning work on the animation.

— **Nat** We pitched for the job with a pretty hardcore idea and to our surprise won it. Fred's sister Ellen did a lot of the graphics with Ian. That was the first time we'd taken the Flash skills that we'd developed on websites and used them to create an animation for TV.

うっていうのは、ボタンを使うよりもずっといい方法で、どのキャラクターもまるで生きてるみたいに無作為に動き回るんだ。まるで自分の意思でどこへ行くか決めているみたいにね。

— **ナット**　ジャムの音楽は、エディンバラ時代の古い友人で、フィニトライブという３人組のバンドで活動している、フィリップ・ピンスキーが作ってくれたの。奇抜な日本のゲーム音楽のような感じで、キャラクターに与える指示内容によって、違った趣の音にして欲しいと頼んだわ。

— **フィリップ・ピンスキー**　僕はこれまでエアサイドのウェブ作品に、あらゆる音を提供してきた。地下鉄、靴メーカー、フォトグラファー、科学美術館、ヨーグルト飲料、観光振興会のウェブサイトから、映画、シリアルバー、TVチャンネル、展覧会のウェブサイトまで。いつも奇抜なアニメーションキャラクターのオンパレードだからね。僕らに共通したユーモアとグロテスクなものに対するセンスが、互いを活かし合うコラボレーションを可能にしているんだ。

— **フレッド**　それから間もなく、僕らは初めて正式なTVアニメーションの仕事を任された。MTVで流すエイズ・デイのためのアニメーションで、ピクセル画のペニスが、スペースインベーダーのアイコンみたいに画面上を動き回り「コンドームをつけましょう」というメッセージが現れる。MTVの弁護士たちはビビッてたけど、幸運にもなんとかこの案を通すことができた。アニメーション制作を開始する前に、絵コンテを準備したのは、確かあの時が初めてだったと思う。

— **ナット**　相当ハードコアなアイデアでコンペに挑んだら、驚いたことに勝っちゃったのよね。フレッドの妹のエレンが、イアンと一緒にほとんどのグラフィックを担当してくれたの。私たちがウェブ制作で培ったFlash技術を駆使してTVアニメーションを制作したのは、あれが最初だったわね。

16

17

18

19

NADAV KANDER

ナダブ・カンダール

Nadav Kander

i - Chernobyl, The Parade | Recent   MENU

Job name:	Nadav Kander Official Website	**作品名：**	ナダブ・カンダール オフィシャル・ウェブサイト
Client:	Nadav Kander, Photographer	**クライアント：**	ナダブ・カンダール、写真家
Media:	Digital, moving image	**メディア：**	ウェブサイト、動画
Awards:	D&AD, Design Week Awards 2002 – Interactive Media	**受賞歴：**	D&AD賞、デザイン・ウィーク賞2002／インタラクティブ・メディア部門

Summary: A portfolio website which allows the user to browse the photographer's entire body of work without clicking the mouse once.

内容： マウスを1度もクリックせずに写真家の作品全体を見渡すことのできるポートフォリオ・ウェブサイト

――――――― When faced with showcasing his portfolio of photography online, Nadav Kander wanted a minimal, image-led site that would offer an overall view of his artistic work without the use of categorisations, long descriptions or a complicated site structure. His needs were understood and translated by Airside to produce an online gallery so simple to use that it almost belies its sophisticated, bespoke design. The navigation was pared down and refined extensively until the interface was a single, intuitive portfolio page, which after a few minutes of mouse movement, would introduce the user to all of Nadav's work. Single click-throughs enlarged pictures beyond their thumbnail size and revealed minimal descriptions, but everywhere the photography was allowed to reign. Nadav's work is harrowing and realistic, and Airside created a dark, atmospheric framework to offset these powerful shots, resulting in a site that was beautifully aligned to its content. The project revealed Airside to be skilled in user interface innovation, and moreover, able to implement that in any given aesthetic style. **FS**

――――――― 作品のオンライン・ポートフォリオを作るにあたって、ナダブ・カンダールが希望したのは、カテゴリー分けや長い解説文、複雑なサイト構成を用いずに、彼の作品全体を見渡すことのできる、ミニマルでイメージ主導のウェブサイトだった。その願いを聞き入れエアサイドが制作したのは、洗練された独自のデザインでありながら、非常にシンプルなオンライン・ギャラリーである。ナビゲーションを大幅に簡素化し、インターフェースは、直に作品を見せるポートフォリオページのみ。わずか数分マウスを動かすだけで、ナダブの全作品を閲覧することができる。小さな写真をクリックすると拡大され、短い説明文が表れるが、一貫して写真が主役であることに変わりはない。悲痛で現実的なナダブの写真。エアサイドは、これらのパワフルなショットを補完する、ダークで情緒のある環境を演出し、結果として美しく作品を活かしたサイトに仕上がった。このプロジェクトを通じ、エアサイドは、革新的なユーザー・インターフェースを創り出す技術と、さらにそれをいかなる美的様式にも応用できることを示した。（FS）

The Early Years

初期

20 Screens from Nadav
Kander's website,
2001

ナダブ・カンダール
ウェブサイト 2001

NADAV KANDER

Fred We reached a point where we needed to do some stuff that wasn't cheerful and happy like all our other work, and along came a couple of photography websites for Burnham Niker and Nadav Kander.

Alex My friend Rachel Leach (who had given us our first commission) was now working at a photographic agency called Burnham Niker who represented the photographer Nadav Kander. We designed the Burnham Niker website and then got a call from Nadav. He had such a great portfolio of photography that it was a fantastic opportunity to do his website. He wanted a site where you could very easily browse his archive and quickly get an idea of the breadth of his work.

Mark Without clicking or going to any other sections, just from rolling your mouse around the home page for a few minutes, you could get a really good sense of his whole portfolio. It was one of the first photography sites that moved away from the work being split into categories like landscape and portraiture. A lot of Nadav's work was solemn and morbid, like pictures of prostitutes in Cuba, but there were also beautiful Marlboro country landscapes, so the site being dark and eerie really showcased his work well. And it was one of the first experiential Flash sites out there. This site used technology in a way that enhanced the experience and allowed people to interact quickly with the content.

Nat The only thing on the front page was the photographs, so no text-based navigation would distract from them. Clicking on any picture brought it up on a bigger canvas, with a subtle way of returning to the home page exactly where you had left it. It was the result of a lot of very delicate tuning of an interface. The process worked really well, in that we really thought about what he needed and worked with him to get inside his head, although it consequently took a great deal of time. A very original result came out of it, not in the same vein as what Airside had done before. Work like this in our portfolio acted as a counterbalance to *Jam* and Lemon Jelly, which was the kind of work we were getting known for: bright and shiny and jumping up and down.

Alex In the same year we made the Nadav Kander and Jam sites, and entered them in the Design Week Awards. We won awards for them both, but at the ceremony they were announced together in the very first category, so after five minutes our night was over. We got very drunk!

Fred With clients like the Serpentine Gallery, White Cube, Bute Fabrics and Nadav Kander, we made great work on a small budget for people who wanted to be on the web, and in return they gave us some freedom to play. It was a very good trade – we got a sexy portfolio and they got a sexy website, and that's how Airside built up. There had to be a lot of trust, because the industry was so new. They were intelligent clients running small companies, and they trusted us with their vision. In those days we couldn't have interfaced with bigger companies because we were so small ourselves, but we didn't care – we were happy with what we were achieving creatively.

ナダブ・カンダール

フレッド そのうちに僕らは、今まで仕上げてきたような元気でハッピーな作品とは異なったプロジェクトも手がけてみたくなって、バーナム・ナイカーやナダブ・カンダールといった写真家たちのウェブサイト制作を担当した。

アレックス 僕の友人であるレイチェル・リーチ(僕らに初めて仕事を依頼してくれた人物)が、その頃ナダブらが所属しているバーナム・ナイカーという写真家のエージェンシーで働いていたんだ。僕らはまずバーナム・ナイカーのウェブサイトをデザインして、それからナダブから連絡をもらった。彼のポートフォリオはほんとうに素晴らしかったから、彼のウェブサイトを任されたことは光栄だったね。アーカイブが検索しやすく、素早く作品の全貌を捉えてもらえるようなサイトを、というのが彼の希望だった。

マーク そこで、どこかをクリックしたり別のセクションに移動したりせずに、ホームページ上でマウスを数分動かすだけで、彼のポートフォリオ全体の印象を掴むことのできるサイトを作ったんだ。風景やポートレイトというように、写真をカテゴリー別に分けない、初めてのサイトのひとつだった。ナダブの写真はキューバの売春婦たちを撮った作品をはじめ、ほとんどが厳かで陰鬱なんだけど、同時にマルボロ広告の風景のように美しい作品もある。このダークで不気味なサイトは、彼の作品にうってつけだったと思う。こうして、Flashを実験的に使用した初のサイトが出来上がった。ユーザー体験をさらに高め、よりスピーディーにコンテンツと触れ合うことのできる技術を用いたんだ。

ナット フロントページに掲載したのは写真だけで、余計なナビゲーション関連の文字は一切なし。どの写真も、クリックひとつで拡大して見ることができて、そこからまた速やかに元の場所に戻る仕組みになっているんだけど、これはインターフェースの変換をものすごくデリケートに調整した成果なの。ナダブが必要としているものを考え、一緒に作業しながら彼が考えていることを引き出すには、結果的にかなりの時間を要したけど、おかげで本当にいい仕事ができたと思ってるわ。それまでエアサイドが手がけたものとはまったく違う、独自の結果を出せた。こういった作品は、私たちのポートフォリオの中でも、例えばジャムやレモン・ジェリーみたいな、明るくてキラキラ飛び跳ねてる感じの、多くの人が「エアサイド的」だと考えている作品と対照をなして、うまくバランスを取ってくれているわ。

アレックス ナダブ・カンダールとジャムのウェブサイトはどちらも同じ年に制作して、両方ともデザイン・ウィーク・アワードに出品したんだ。そしてなんと2つとも賞を獲得した。授賞式では僕らの部門の発表が一番最初だったから、始めの5分で輝かしい夜は終わってしまったけどね。後はとことん酔っ払ったよ!

フレッド サーペンタイン・ギャラリー、ホワイト・キューブ、ビュート・ファブリクス、ナダブ・カンダールといった、ウェブに進出したいと考えていたクライアントの仕事は、少ない予算で引き受けるかわりに、クリエイティブ・フリーダムをたくさんもらった。すごくいい取引だったな。僕らはセクシーなポートフォリオを手に入れ、彼らはセクシーなウェブサイトを手に入れる。こうしてエアサイドは成長してきたんだ。何せ新しい分野だったから、信頼して僕らに任せるのは、大きな賭けだったと思う。だけど、小さな会社を経営している知的なクライアントたちが、しっかりとしたビジョンをもって信頼してくれた。当時の僕らは本当に小規模だったから、きっと大企業とは折り合わなかっただろう。それでも全く気にならなかったね。クリエイティブな面から見て、僕らは自分たちの達成したことに心底満足していたから。

LEMON JELLY

レモン・ジェリー

Job name:	Lemon Jelly
Client:	Lemon Jelly / XL Recordings
Media:	Print, moving image, digital

Summary: A truly multi-disciplinary client with projects ranging from music packaging and merchandise to music promos and live visuals.

As Fred Deakin is a key member of both Airside and Lemon Jelly, it stands to reason that this downtempo electronic band's visual identity is produced exclusively by Fred and Airside. This project began with a series of striking vinyl sleeves, influenced by Fred's love of 1940s screen-printed posters and 1960s op-art abstract patterns, and went on to incorporate live visuals, merchandise, TV promos and a full-length animated DVD to accompany the album '64-'95. As a result, Lemon Jelly became one of the most uniquely packaged bands of its generation.

Fred has always been interested in the relationship between music and art, and used this project as a laboratory to test those ideas and aesthetics. Fred's distinctive graphic style, as seen on the early Lemon Jelly sleeves, became a foundation for much of Airside's prominent aesthetic of drawing pared-down illustrations using vectors, which can be traced through much of their work. What unites all the Lemon Jelly artwork is its on-the-button accuracy in representing the buoyant, fun, celebratory personality of Lemon Jelly's music, and this is also divested in most of Airside's design work.

Lemon Jelly gave Airside ample opportunity to build and showcase its skills in graphic design, illustration and animation: the video for *Nice Weather For Ducks* became the calling card that led to much of Airside's work in advertising. It has also influenced Airside's philosophy of taking time to produce self-initiated work, and setting goals to stretch themselves creatively. **FS**

作品名:	レモン・ジェリー
クライアント:	レモン・ジェリー／ XLレコーディングス
メディア:	印刷物、動画、ウェブサイト

内容: パッケージ、関連グッズをはじめ、ミュージックビデオやライブ映像に至るまで、実にマルチなクライアントの要望に合わせた多種多様なプロジェクト

フレッド・ディーキンがエアサイドとレモン・ジェリーの主要メンバーであることを考えれば、このダウンテンポなエレクトロニック・バンドのビジュアルを、フレッドとエアサイドが専属で手がける理由は説明するまでもないだろう。プロジェクトの始まりは、フレッドがこよなく愛する1940年代のスクリーン印刷のポスターや1960年代のオプ・アートの抽象パターンに影響を受けて制作された、人目をひく一連のレコードジャケット。続いて、ライブ映像、関連グッズ、テレビ用プロモーション映像、果てはアルバム「'64–'95」の全曲をアニメーション化したDVDも手がけた。こうして、レモン・ジェリーは、同時代のアーティストの中でも、最もユニークなビジュアルイメージを持つバンドへと成長した。

音楽とアートの関係に常に興味を抱いてきたフレッドは、このプロジェクトをそれらのアイデアやスタイルを試すラボラトリーと位置づけた。初期のレモン・ジェリーのジャケットに見られるような、フレッド独特のグラフィック・スタイルは、後にエアサイドを特徴づける、ベクターベースの無駄のないイラストレーションの基礎となり、多くの作品にその影響を見ることができる。また、楽天的で、楽しく人生を謳歌するようなレモン・ジェリーの音楽の持ち味を、正確なまでに視覚化したアートワークも、エアサイドの他の作品に反映されている。

レモン・ジェリーのおかげで、エアサイドはグラフィックデザイン、イラストレーション、アニメーションといった様々な技術を身につけ、披露する機会を多く得た。また「ナイス・ウェザー・フォー・ダックス」のミュージックビデオの成功により、多くの広告制作の依頼を受けることになった。そしてなにより、創造性を伸ばすような目標を設定して、自主制作に取り組むという、エアサイドの哲学にも大きな影響を与えた。(FS)

Airside by Airside

エアサイド バイ エアサイド

Lemon Jelly

レモン・ジェリー

Fred I'd been running these crazy clubs in Edinburgh and London, that were very successful and enjoyable but had no longevity to them. One of the main factors behind my desire to DJ and run clubs was my vinyl habit. I would spend every spare penny I had on records so I had to find a way to make them earn their keep. I saw people like DJ Shadow taking weird old records and making new music out of them; I was buying a lot of similar records and building up a library of my own samples. In the meantime I had bumped into Nick Franglen, who I had known a bit back in our teenage years and who had become master of all things musical since then, and thus Lemon Jelly was born. Nick and I tried a few musical experiments that really clicked, and very quickly we were

both hooked. We would be in Nick's studio in Kentish Town for three or four days at a time making our bizarre soundscapes. There was a comment on our website that said: "This record is music for summery evenings and blissful open skies, made by the two of us in a dark basement with no light."

Nick Franglen Fred and I worked away at it in our spare time at first, doing three EPs over three years. It was a personal project up until *Lost Horizons* when we went into the studio full-time.

Fred The Lemon Jelly visual aesthetic was always very abstract. My theory was that repeating abstract patterns of an op-art nature created a visual metaphor for the loops and beats of the music, so it made sense to feature them on the outer sleeves as an indication of what you

would find inside. Victor Vasarely and Bridget Riley made all their work by hand, yet you can now make similar patterns to the op art classics very quickly with a computer, so then where do you go?

Anyway, very soon we had three tracks finished and the next logical step was to release an EP. When it came to designing the sleeve I knew that I wanted to create an artefact, something that had the feel of an old record even though it was new. So I hand-printed all 200 of the first EP sleeves at the Edinburgh Printmakers Workshop where I had learnt to screenprint. It nearly killed me – it was definitely a one-off experience.

フレッド 僕はかつてエディンバラとロンドンで、クレイジーなクラブを何軒か経営していた。どれも盛り上がったし楽しかったけど、長続きはしなかったね。DJとクラブ経営に僕を駆り立てた要因のひとつは、僕のレコード収集癖で、とにかくありったけのお金をレコードにつぎ込んでいたから、元を取る方法を見つけたかったんだ。DJシャドウとかが古い変なレコードを見つけてきては、そこから新しい音楽を作り出すのを見てきたから、僕も似たようなレコードをたくさん集めて、サンプリングのアーカイブを作っていたよ。その頃、ニック・フラングリンとばったり再会した。10代の頃は、顔見知り程度だったけど、彼が当時の音楽シーンにめっぽう強いことがわかって、レモン・ジェリーが誕生したんだ。ニックと僕で、実験的なセッションをしたら、あっという間に意気投合して、お互いこれだ、と思った。

ケンティッシュ・タウンにあるニックのスタジオに、毎回3〜4日こもっては、何やら突飛な音作りをしたもんだよ。僕らのウェブサイトには、冗談めかしたこんなコメントがある。「この音楽は、光のない真っ暗な地下室で、僕ら2人が、夏の夕暮れやこの上なく広い空を想って作りました」って。

ニック・フラングリン はじめのうち、フレッドと僕は、時間を見つけては作業を進め、3年で3枚のEPを制作した。フルタイムでスタジオ入りするようになったのは「ロスト・ホライズンズ」からで、それまでは自主プロジェクトだったんだ。

フレッド レモン・ジェリーのビジュアルの世界は、いつもすごく抽象的だった。オプ・アート的な抽象パターンの繰り返しは、音楽のループやビートの視覚的メタファーを創り出す、というのが僕の持論。だから、中身の音楽を示唆するもの

として、ジャケットにそういったパターンを施すのは理にかなっているんだ。ヴィクトル・ヴァザルリやブリジット・ライリーは、すべて手作業で作品を仕上げていたけど、今や、古典的オプ・アートもどきのパターンなんか、コンピューターでいとも簡単に作れてしまうわけで、じゃあ次は一体、何をすりゃいいんだ？

まぁとにかく、僕らはすぐに3曲完成させたから、当然次はEPをリリースすることになった。ジャケットのデザインは、新作だけど古いレコードのような印象を与えるアートワークにしたいと思っていたから、かつてスクリーン印刷を学んだエディンバラ・プリントメーカーズ・ワークショップで、今度はEPのジャケットを200枚、手作業で印刷したんだけど、死ぬほど辛い作業だった。もう2度とできない経験だね。

1   *The Bath EP*
Impotent Fury
Records & Tapes, 1998

EP「バス」
インポテント・フューリー
レコーズ&テープス 1998

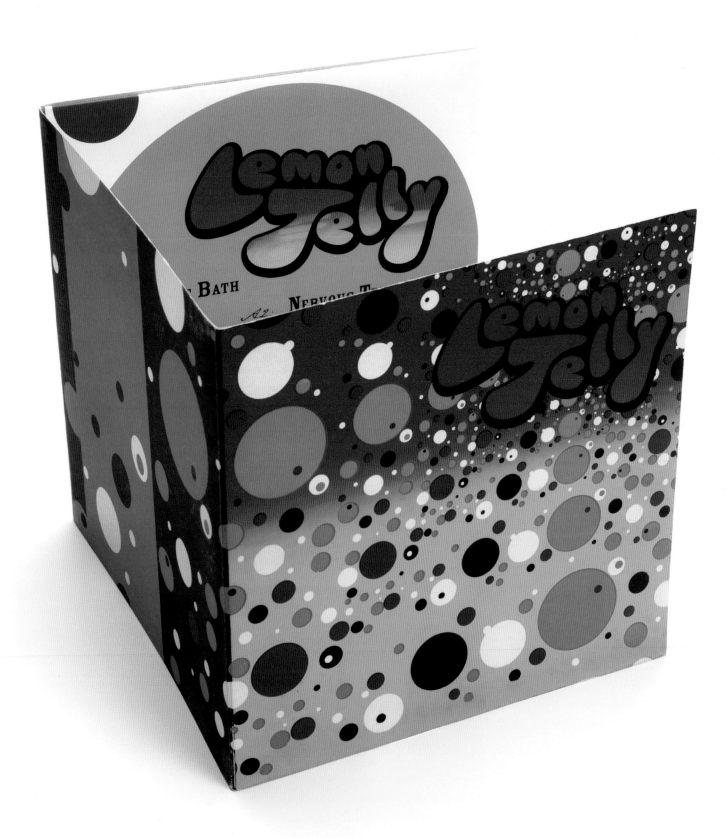

Airside by Airside

エアサイド バイ エアサイド

Lemon Jelly

レモン・ジェリー

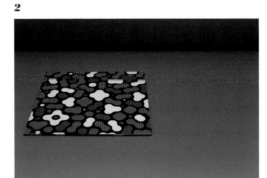

——— **Nick** Then we discovered the problems of releasing music yourself. The sleeves were complicated double gatefolds and we thought we'd glue them together ourselves, so we got hold of some glue, a scalpel and a metal ruler, and got stuck in. After an hour we had managed to complete three sleeves between us. So in the end we took them to a professional folding company and they said it was the hardest job they'd ever had to do. It was typical of Lemon Jelly, in that we ended up making it in the most complicated way possible.

——— **Fred** The first EP was the only time any type ever appeared on the outside of a Lemon Jelly sleeve. When I saw it, I realised it would be much better without the logo because then you wouldn't necessarily know it was a record sleeve. It could simply be a piece of art.

——— With the complicated construction of the record sleeves for the three early ten inch vinyl EPs – *The Bath EP, The Yellow EP* and *The Midnight EP* – I was trying to insert value and meaning into new places. In that moment between want-

2–4 *The Yellow EP*
Impotent Fury
Records & Tapes, 1999

EP「イエロー」
インポテント・フューリー
レコーズ&テープス 1999

——— **ニック** つまり、自分たちでレコードをリリースすることが、いかに大変かに気づいた。ジャケットは複雑な左右の見開き構成で、自分たちで作れると思ったから、接着剤とカッターと金属定規を握って格闘したけど、1時間頑張って、2人で3枚仕上げるのがやっとだった。結局、プロの製本業者に持ち込んだわけだけど、彼らにまで、今まで手がけたどの仕事よりも厄介だったと言われたよ。あらゆる方法の中でも、とりわけ複雑なものを選んでしまうところが、レモン・ジェリーらしいよな。

——— **フレッド** この最初のEPは、レモン・ジェリー史上、唯一、ロゴをあしらったジャケットになった。仕上がりを見て、ロゴさえなければ、レコードジャケットだと気づかれずに、立派なアートワークになったのにって、後悔したよ。

——— 初期の3枚のEP、「バス」「イエロー」「ミッドナイト」用に、複雑な構造のレコードジャケットを作ることで、僕はこれまでと違った形で、価値と意味を加えたいと考えていた。レモン・ジェリーの曲を聴きたいと思い立ち、レコードをジャケットから取り出してターンテーブルに乗せる。この間に、何かセンセーショナルな出来事が起きてもいいんじゃないかと

思ったんだ。2枚目のジャケットには切り抜き窓がついていて、内側のジャケットをひっぱり出すと、小窓にロゴが現れるようになっている。3枚目の「ミッドナイト」では、内側のジャケットに銀箔のパターンをデザインして、夜空をイメージした外側のジャケットには小さな穴をいくつも開けた。レコードを取り出す度に、星がキラキラ輝く仕組みにしたんだよ。手の込んだレコードジャケットは好きだけど、やはり魅力や意味があってこその話。無意味な装飾ではなく、全体のコンセプトにきちんと融和したものでないとね。

——— **ニック** 僕は、それまで音楽のデザイン面には関心がなかったけど、フレッドとやってきて、細部への徹底的なこだわりを学んだ。作品を取り巻くオーラを創造することで、人々が音楽を聴く前に、どんな音楽なのかを伝えることは、とても重要だね。

——— **フレッド** それから、XLレコーズとの出会いがあった。A&Rのレオ・シルバーマンが、過去にアヴァランチーズとも契約を交わしていたことが決め手になったね。それから、アイランド・レコーズで10年間代表を務めたマーク・

ing to hear Lemon Jelly and putting the record on the turntable, something else could happen that could be part of your experience. The second sleeve had these cutout shapes positioned so that as you pull out the inner sleeve our logo appears in the windows. The third sleeve, for *The Midnight EP*, had a metal foil pattern on the inner sleeve and tiny holes all over a night sky design on the outer sleeve, so that when you took the record out the stars twinkled. I love complicated record sleeves, but only if they have some traction or meaning; they have to be well integrated into the whole package rather than just being a bolt-on for no reason.

——————— **Nick** I'd never been into the design side of music previously. I learned about that attention to detail entirely through working with Fred. It's critically important to create an aura around something and let people know what your music is about before they've listened to it.

——————— **Fred** So then XL Recordings popped up. Leo Silverman was their A&R man and having previously signed The Avalanches he really under-

stood us. Then Marc Marot, who had been head of Island Records for 10 years, became Lemon Jelly's manager.

——————— **Leo Silverman** I started off liking the music, which was cute and bubbly, and then it became very apparent the design was great too. It stood out a mile in the shops and created a fanbase for them to grow from. Fred probably had quite a lot of fans of his design work who went and bought the first album just for the cover because it was so striking, then went home, put it on and discovered they liked the music as well.

——————— What you look for in artists or bands is a really strong sense of identity, and Lemon Jelly had that in spades with the combination of the music and the design. I'm sure it was part of Fred's unique dayglo vision of the world. It was both a blessing and a curse that all the design had to be by Airside – Fred wouldn't let our in-house people touch anything so he was kept very busy.

5

6

5–7 *The Midnight EP*
Impotent Fury
Records & Tapes, 2000

EP「ミッドナイト」
インポテント・フューリー
レコーズ&テープス 2000

7

マローがマネージャーになってくれた。
——————— **レオ・シルバーマン** はじめはキュートで陽気な音楽が気に入ったんだ。それから、デザインも素晴らしいことに気づいた。彼らのジャケットはショップでひときわ目立っていたから、デザインに惹かれてファンになった人々がレモン・ジェリーを育てたとも言える。おそらく、フレッドのデザインのファンだという人がたくさんいただろうね。印象的なファーストアルバムのカバーに惹かれてCDを買い、家に帰って聴いてみると、音楽も劣らず良いことに気づくんだ。アーティストやバンドに何が必要かって、自分たちが何者かという強い主張で、音楽とデザインを見事に融合させたレモン・ジェリーにはそれがあった。フレッドが手がけたユニークな蛍光色の世界観のおかげもあるだろうね。すべてのデザインをエアサイドが手がけたのは、素晴らしいことでもあったし、厄介なことでもあった。僕ら社内のデザイナーには指一本触れさせなかったから、フレッドは大忙しだったよ。

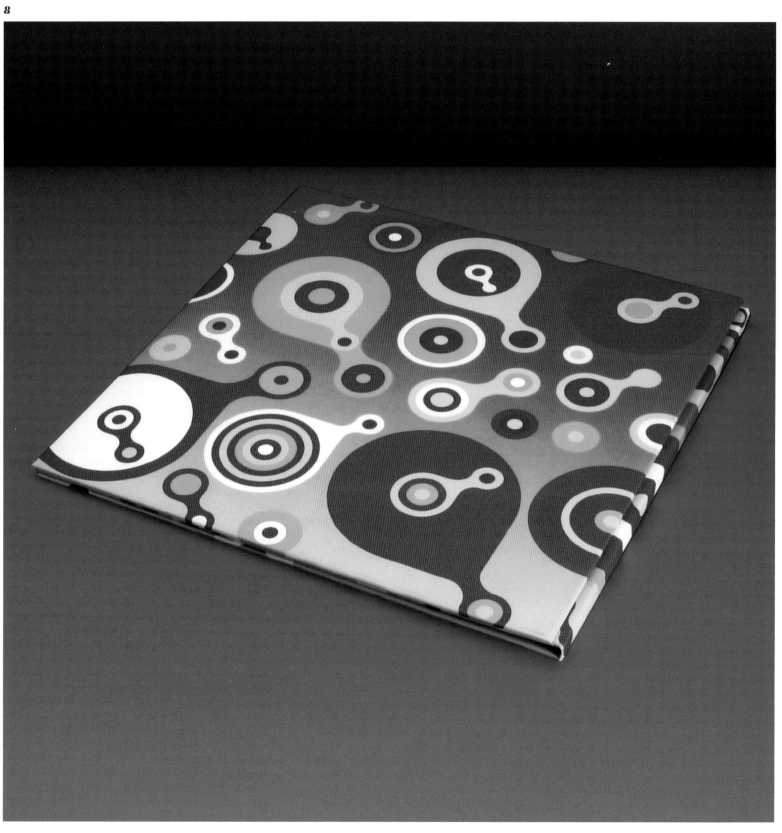

9

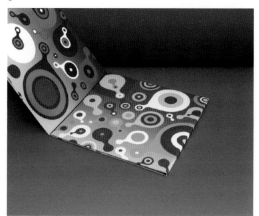

10

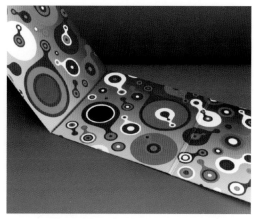

11

12

This and next page:
本頁＆次頁

8–
13

lemonjelly.ky
Impotent Fury
Records & Tapes/
XL Recordings, 2000

「lemonjelly.ky」
インポテント・フューリー
レコーズ＆テープス／
XLレコーディングス　2000

LEMONJELLY.KY

———— **Fred** We compiled the first 3 EPs into an album, *lemonjelly.ky*, and I came up with a blobby psychedelic pattern spread over a grid. It was a triple gatefold cardboard sleeve with six sections, and on each section there's a different direction to the pattern – north-east or south-west – so they're always crossing each other, giving that idea of rhythm and repeating elements. At the last minute Nick suggested we put the gradient in the background which really lifted it, and that became a Lemon Jelly visual signature.

———— **Leo** Lemon Jelly didn't really figure on anyone's radar when we put *lemonjelly.ky* out, but even unpromoted it sold about 1,000 copies per week for two years. By the time we released *Lost Horizons*, they'd already sneakily sold about 70,000 copies of the first album without anyone noticing, and set up an audience for the follow up which had a chart hit.

LEMONJELLY.KY

———— **フレッド**　僕らは最初の3枚のEPを「Lemon-jelly.ky」という1枚のアルバムにまとめた。その時に、グリッド状に広がるサイケデリックな斑点パターンを思いついたんだ。ジャケットは観音開きで、各6面のパターンが、それぞれ、北東、南西といった方向を向きながら、互いに交錯していて、あたかも音楽のリズムや反復を思わせるデザインになっている。完成間際に、ニックの提案で背景をグラデーションにしてみたら、ぐっと良くなって、以来これがレモン・ジェリーのトレードマークになった。

———— **レオ**　このアルバムをリリースした時、レモン・ジェリーは、まだほとんど誰にも知られていなかったんだけど、それでも宣伝なしで、2年間、毎週1,000枚も売れたんだ。「ロスト・ホライズンズ」を発表する頃には、知らぬ間に7万枚も売り上げて、次のアルバムを待つファン層が出来上がっていたから、見事チャート入りを果たした。

Lemon Jelly

レモン・ジェリー

This and next page:
本頁＆次頁

14–
17
Lost Horizons
Impotent Fury
Records & Tapes /
XL Recordings, 2002

「ロスト・ホライズンズ」
インポテント・フューリー・
レコーズ＆テープス／
XLレコーディングス 2002

LOST HORIZONS

——————— Fred *Lost Horizons* was our biggest record; it was nominated for the Mercury Music Prize which was definitely a moment. We stuck with the triple gatefold cardboard sleeves – XL were very good about that. From the beginning I said that I never wanted one of our albums in a plastic CD case – I still really dislike them. After we had sold about 60,000 we compromised, but all the original ones were cardboard. The sleeve for *Lost Horizons* was based on a 3D model I designed in collaboration with Sam Burford; the idea is that in the daytime the city is boring and the countryside is the place to be, but at night it's the other way round. Sam built the city model in 3D – I was clear that I wanted a very flat aesthetic so it looks like an illustration, but actually it's a virtual 3D model. The gradient over the fields was crucial, even though it is the least realistic element - the red, yellow, and green puts it squarely in our vernacular. At the end we priced up the job out of curiosity, and worked out that if we'd been charging a client on a sensible day rate that sleeve would have cost £40,000.

——————— Leo A lot of things they did were similar to the famous New Order *Blue Monday* single.

After we had been selling *Lemonjelly.ky* for a year and a half, some bright spark at Beggars Banquet had a look at the money side of it and realised we'd been losing money with every CD we sold because the sleeves were so elaborate.

——————— Nick During *Lost Horizons* I noticed that the rest of Airside were getting much more involved with the design, which had a lot to do with the scale of the work we were embarking on. It was a very seamless transition from the homegrown way that Fred had created the early sleeves on his own to the more ambitious work we did with Airside.

ロスト・ホライズンズ

——————— フレッド 「ロスト・ホライズンズ」は最も売れたアルバムで、マーキュリー音楽賞にノミネートされた時は、本当に嬉しかったな。このアルバムでも、観音開きのジャケットにこだわった。XLも理解してくれてね。はじめから、僕はプラスチックのCDケースはごめんだと主張していて、いまだにあれが嫌いなんだ。6万枚ほど売れた頃に、やむなく妥協したけど、オリジナル盤はすべて紙ジャケットで作った。「ロスト・ホライズンズ」のジャケットは、友人のサム・バーフォードと一緒にデザインした3Dモデルがもとになっていて、日中、都会は退屈で、田舎こそ理想的な場所に見えるけど、夜になるとそれが逆転する、というのがアイデア。サムが3Dで都市のモデルを制作した。僕ははじめから平面的な仕上がりを念頭においていたから、イラストレーションのように見えるけど、実際あれはバーチャルな3Dモデルを元に作られている。赤、黄、緑の野原なんて、現実とはほど遠いけど、野に広がるこのグラデーションこそが、レモン・ジェリーらしさの鍵なんだ。最後に、これがクライアントからの仕事だったら、幾らくらい請求することになるのか、好奇心から僕らがこのジャケットにつぎ込んだ労力を計算してみたら、なんと 40,000 ポンドになった。

——————— レオ ニュー・オーダーが例の「ブルー・マンデー」のシングルを作った時と同じような状況さ。「Lemon-jelly.ky」を売り出してから一年半ほどして、ベガーズ・バンケットにいた頭のキレる奴が、アルバムの収入面に目を向けたところ、ジャケットに凝り過ぎたために、1枚売るごとに赤字を出していることに気づいたんだ。

——————— ニック 「ロスト・ホライズンズ」の頃には、僕らが手がける仕事のスケールも大きくなっていたから、エアサイドとの結びつきも益々深くなった。フレッドが家内作業でジャケットを作っていた初期の頃から、エアサイドと取り組んだ意欲作まで、継ぎ目のない自然な流れでここまで来たと思う。

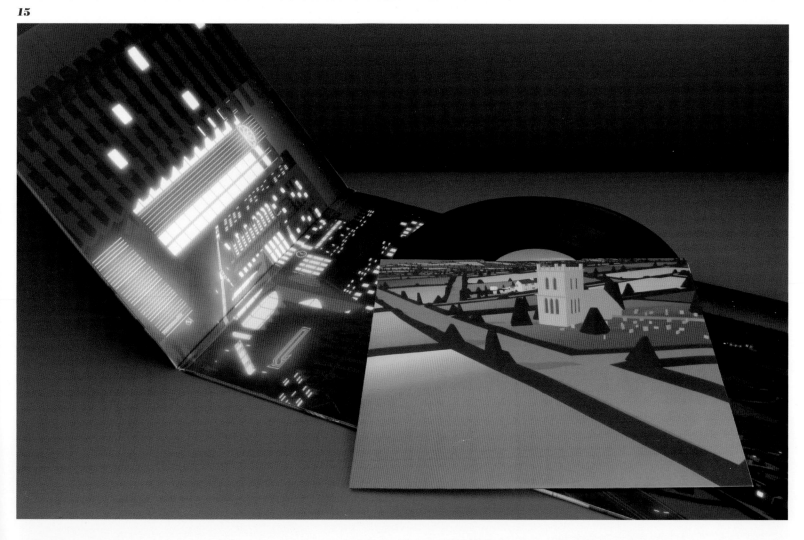

Lemon Jelly
レモン・ジェリー

18

LIVE SHOWS

——————— **Fred** After *Lost Horizons* we had to put a live show together. It was quite a challenge but was also a chance for Airside to do some more animation. Nat got very involved in creating the visuals and ended up VJing at a lot of the gigs. Nick and I aren't really pop stars in the traditional sense, so the visuals are the star in the live arena, although they have to be ambient and complementary to the show rather than overwhelming the audience which creates a passive cinema-like experience.

——————— We loved to explore new ways to interact with our audience. For our first live shows the tickets were T-shirts that you had to wear to get in. Once the audience was inside the venue they formed a giant repeating pattern that mimicked the album artwork, and the punchline came halfway through the gig when we turned on a UV light to

19

20

ライブ

——————— **フレッド** 「ロスト・ホライズンズ」を発表してから、僕らは一緒にライブを行う必要があった。相当なチャレンジだったけど、エアサイドにとっても、アニメーションにより力を入れるいいチャンスだった。ナットが全面的にビジュアル制作に関わってくれて、最終的にはあちこちのギグでVJまで担当してくれた。ニックも僕も、いわゆるポップスターという感じではないから、会場ではビジュアルが主役なんだ。それでいて、観客を圧倒して映画を見ているような受け身な気持ちにさせるものではなく、むしろ音楽を補完してくれるようなアンビエントなものでないと。

——————— 僕たちは、オーディエンスと関わる新しい方法を見つけるのに凝っていて、最初のライブでは、Tシャツがチケット代わりだった。ギグに入場するには、そのTシャツを着て来ないといけない。お客さんは会場に近づくにつれ、同じTシャツを来た人々と出会う。そしてギグが始まると、観客が同色のヒューマンパターンを形成していて、それは素晴らしい光景だったね。中盤から、UVライトを点灯して、みんなのTシャツにUV

18–26 Photographs from various Lemon Jelly gigs, Marc Marot, 2002–05

レモン・ジェリー
ギグの様子
マーク・マロー 2002–05

21

22

23

24

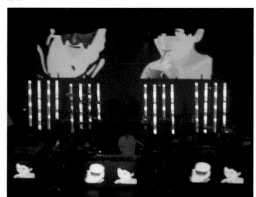

25

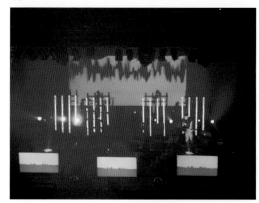

reveal the T-shirt's secret pattern. People would be wearing the T-shirt weeks later and someone else who had also been there would recognise it and say hello. It really broke down people's barriers and made them feel they were part of one big gang. It's the difference between "Come and look at me being a star on stage", and "Come and help us create something great". I'm not into that egotistical star thing; I'd rather give people the chance to participate. That's why we started having bingo and treasure hunts at our gigs.

————— **Leo** They were insane to work with. When they headlined three nights at the Forum, it was quite a big deal. Most bands would roll up in their tour bus or a limousine. They took the 134 bus. I always liked that. They just made everything into an event because Fred was so into design, and after all those strange clubs he did, he wanted to make things as fun as possible.

————— **Nick** When we play live we bounce around on stage quite a lot – I'm jumping from the guitar to the keyboards, while Fred is playing some bongos or scratching up a record. Our live shows have the same sense of fun as the music. People come along thinking they're just going to hear this lulling, soporific thing; they don't expect to be jumping up and down madly. It surprises people.

————— **Marc Marot** The intensity of the workload was so much greater than with your usual band. In the case of those first live gigs at 93 Feet East in East London we posted every T-shirt and logged every ticket sale from my tiny management office. For the Forum children's matinee, we were sourcing bingo cards, pencils and balloons, and then my kids and I were handing out sweets to people as they entered. But it was never less than a pleasure every day I worked with them. There was a real sense we were doing something different.

インクで印刷してあった別の模様が浮かび上がる、というオチまでつけた。かなりインタラクティブな試みだったけど。何週間かして、誰かがそのTシャツを着て街を歩いていると、同じギグに参加していた別の誰かが声をかける。人々の見えない壁を取り払って、大きな集団の一員であるかのような感覚をもたらした。毎回僕らはギグをクラブのように考えているんだ。「僕がステージに上がっているのを見に来てよ」というんじゃなく「一緒に楽しい時間を過ごそうよ」ってね。エゴイスティックなスター気取りは好きじゃないからね。それより、来てくれる人たちが参加できるような場を生み出したかった。だからビンゴや宝探しをギグに盛り込んだんだ。

————— **レオ** 一緒に働いてみて、奴らがどれほど「普通じゃない」かが分かった。フォーラムという会場で3晩に渡って、レモン・ジェリーがヘッドライナーを務めたことがあるんだけど、かなり大きなイベントでね。たいていのバンドならツアーバスとかリムジンで会場入りするのに、なんと彼らはルート134の公共バスでやって来た。そういう心意気が気に入ってね。フレッドが猛烈にデザインに入れ込んでいて、奇抜なクラブイベントの経験があったおかげで、彼らは何でも「ハプニング」に変え

てしまう。何をやるにも、できる限り楽しくしたいってわけ。

————— **ニック** ライブの時、僕らはステージの上を、絶えず跳ね回ってるね。僕がギターからキーボードに移ると、フレッドはボンゴを叩いたり、レコードをスクラッチしたり。だから僕らのショーは、曲そのものと同じくらい楽しい空気に満ちている。お客さんは穏やかでゆったりしたサウンドを聴くつもりでやって来て、誰も狂わんばかりに飛んだり跳ねたり、なんて想定していないから、実際ライブに来た人たちは驚くんだ。

————— **マーク・マロー** 仕事量の多さといったら、他のバンドとは比べ物にならないくらい、半端じゃないよ。93 Feet Eastのギグでは、みんなで僕の小さな事務所からチケット代わりのTシャツを発送し、チケットセールスの記録を付けた。フォーラムで開催した子供向けの昼の部では、ビンゴカードや鉛筆、風船を調達して、うちの子供と僕が、入り口でみんなにお菓子を配った。でも、彼らと一緒に仕事をしていて楽しくなかったことなんて1度もないんだ。他とは違うことをやっていると、みんなが確信しているからね。

26

Airside by Airside

エアサイド バイ エアサイド

Lemon Jelly

レモン・ジェリー

28 *Rolled Oats* – limited
edition vinyl bootleg
Impotent Fury
Records & Tapes, 2003

「ロールド・オーツ」
限定版レコードジャケット
インポテント・フューリー
レコーズ&テープス 2003

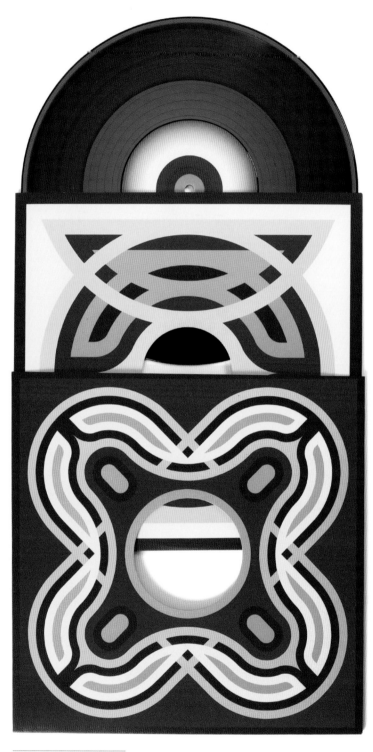

29   *Spacewalk –*
10" vinyl
Impotent Fury
Records & Tapes /
XL Recordings, 2002

「スペースウォーク」
10インチ・レコード
インポテント・フューリー
レコーズ&テープス／
XLレコーディングス 2002

30   *Stay With You –*
10" vinyl
Impotent Fury
Records & Tapes /
XL Recordings, 2004

「ステイ・ウィズ・ユー」
10インチ・レコード
インポテント・フューリー
レコーズ&テープス／
XLレコーディングス 2004

31   *Nice Weather For*
        Ducks – 7" vinyl
        Impotent Fury
        Records & Tapes /
        XL Recordings, 2003

        「ナイス・ウェザー・フォー・
        ダックス」7インチ・レコード
        インポテント・フューリー
        レコーズ&テープス／
        XLレコーディングス 2003

32   *The Shouty Track* –
        7" vinyl
        Impotent Fury
        Records & Tapes /
        XL Recordings, 2005

        「ザ・シャウティ・トラック」
        7インチ・レコード
        インポテント・フューリー
        レコーズ&テープス／
        XLレコーディングス 2005

33   *Make Things Right* –
        7" vinyl
        Impotent Fury
        Records & Tapes /
        XL Recordings, 2005

        「メイク・シングズ・ライト」
        7インチ・レコード
        インポテント・フューリー
        レコーズ&テープス／
        XLレコーディングス 2005

Lemon Jelly

レモン・ジェリー

34 *Spacewalk –*
CD single
Impotent Fury
Records & Tapes /
XL Recordings, 2002

「スペースウォーク」
CDシングル
インポテント・フューリー
レコーズ&テープス／
XLレコーディングス 2002

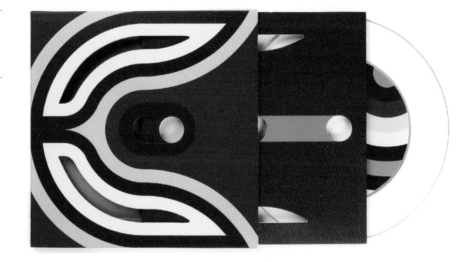

35 *Nice Weather For*
Ducks – CD single
Impotent Fury
Records & Tapes /
XL Recordings, 2003

「ナイス・ウェザー・フォー・
ダックス」CDシングル
インポテント・フューリー
レコーズ&テープス／
XLレコーディングス 2003

36 *Nice Weather For*
Ducks – DVD
Impotent Fury
Records & Tapes /
XL Recordings, 2003

「ナイス・ウェザー・フォー・
ダックス」DVD
インポテント・フューリー
レコーズ&テープス／
XLレコーディングス 2003

37 *Stay With You* –
CD single
Impotent Fury
Records & Tapes /
XL Recordings, 2004

「ステイ・ウィズ・ユー」
CDシングル
インポテント・フューリー
レコーズ&テープス／
XLレコーディングス　2004

38 *Stay With You* –
DVD
Impotent Fury
Records & Tapes /
XL Recordings, 2004

「ステイ・ウィズ・ユー」
DVD
インポテント・フューリー
レコーズ&テープス／
XLレコーディングス　2004

39 *The Shouty Track* –
DVD
Impotent Fury
Records & Tapes /
XL Recordings, 2005

「ザ・シャウティ・トラック」
DVD
インポテント・フューリー
レコーズ&テープス／
XLレコーディングス　2005

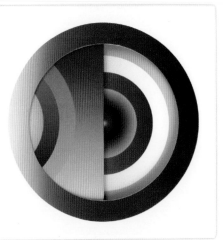

40 *Make Things Right* –
CD single
Impotent Fury
Records & Tapes /
XL Recordings, 2005

「メイク・シングズ・ライト」
CDシングル
インポテント・フューリー
レコーズ&テープス／
XLレコーディングス　2005

Lemon Jelly

レモン・ジェリー

DUCKS

———— **Nat** The video for *Nice Weather for Ducks* was the beginning of Airside making moving image. Fred had always been very much in control of the design for Lemon Jelly and created all the print work himself, but that first video was very much an Airside job.

———— **Fred** Nick and I came up with the story. The tramp is telling you the meaning of life and all these amazing secrets you need to know, but it sounds like he's just saying: "All the ducks are swimming in the water". A magic raindrop falls from the sky and takes him away from his hum-drum world into this magical kingdom. The raindrop falls on you in the last frame.

———— **Alex** I was very excited about the opportunity of doing a music promo. Fred and Nick had loads of ideas, and there was a very strong aesthetic already in place, but Airside was taking a big leap out of our comfort zone. Eventually Fred and I went and sat in a café and talked through the ideas, and I then drew them as storyboards. Once the ideas were on paper we could see that it would be achievable. It had live action elements as well as animation so we began looking for an actor to play the tramp. We wanted Brian Blessed – his agent was keen but sadly he was not available at the time. Instead, we got this guy whose only real acting experience had been playing a corpse at the Royal Shakespeare Company.

———— **Fred** It was an attempt to take the aesthetic conventions we'd evolved previously and make them move as part of a coherent narrative. The gradients, colour washes, flat colour graphics and patterned fields: we threw it all into the pot with the narrative and hoped it worked. And it did – I look at it now and it's a bit creaky round the edges, but it's stood the test of time.

———— **Nat** Leo at XL knew an animated video would be less of a pull for MTV than a live action promo, so he said: "You can take it on, but it'll have to be brilliant". It was a lot of pressure.

———— **Nick** Fred and Airside had really discovered the visual identity of *Lost Horizons* by this time. There is this real tie-in between the *Ducks* video and the album sleeve. That is one of Lemon Jelly's strengths; the music and the visuals are all coming from the same place. We are not going outside of this artistic core to bring things in, whether it's the T-shirts or the record production, so automatically it is true to the feel of Lemon Jelly.

ダックス

———— **ナット**「ナイス・ウェザー・フォー・ダックス」のミュージックビデオは、エアサイドの動画作りの始まりだった。それまでレモン・ジェリーのデザインといえば、フレッドがすべてコントロールしていて、印刷物も全部彼が制作していたけれど、あの初めてのミュージックビデオは、エアサイドの作品と言えるわね。

———— **フレッド** ニックと僕で、あのストーリーを考えたんだ。主役の浮浪者が、人生の意味とか、知っておくべき驚きの秘密なんかを教えてくれるんだけど、まるで「カモがそろって、水中を泳いでいる」と言っているようにしか聞こえない。魔法の雨粒が空から降ってきて、浮浪者を退屈な世界から魔法の王国に連れて行く。そして最後にその雨粒が、見ている人々に降り注ぐんだ。

———— **アレックス** ミュージックビデオを作れることに心が躍ったね。フレッドとニックにはたくさんのアイデアがあって、すでに明確な世界観が出来上がっていたけど、エアサイドにとってそれは、今まで手がけた領域から大きな飛躍を遂げる経験だった。結局、フレッドと僕でカフェに座ってアイデアを一通り話し合って、僕がストーリーボードを描いた。アイデアを出して、言葉を絵にしてみたら、みんなこれなら出来ると感じたんだ。アニメーションだけじゃなく、実写の撮影も必要だったから、浮浪者役を探し始めた。ブライアン・ブレストにやってもらいたくて、彼のエージェントも興味を示してくれたけど、残念ながらスケジュールが合わなくてね。代わりに、かつてロイヤル・シェイクスピア・カンパニーで、1度だけ死体役を演じたことのある男性に頼むことになった。

———— **フレッド** この映像で、僕らは今まで作り上げてきた美的世界観を存分に詰め込んで、ひとつのストーリーに沿って動かしてみようと試みた。グラデーションや色彩配色、平面カラーグラフィックスや抽象パターンを施した風景など、すべてを物語に盛り込んで、上手くいくよう願ったら、本当に上手くいったんだ。今見ると、さすがにもうとんがった感じはないけど、それでも時を越えて印象に残る作品だと思うよ。

———— **ナット** XLのレオは、MTVではアニメーションのミュージックビデオが実写のものより人気がないことを知っていたから、私たちにこう言ったの。「作ってもいいけど、やるからにはとにかく素晴らしいものでなくちゃね」って。かなりプレッシャーを感じたわ。

———— **ニック**「ロスト・ホライズンズ」の頃には、フレッドとエアサイドは、すでにビジュアル・スタイルを確立していた。この「ダックス」のビデオとアルバムのジャケットも、ちゃんと一貫性がある。そこがレモン・ジェリーの強みだと思う。音楽と映像がすべて同じところで創られているというのがね。Tシャツであろうとレコード制作であろうと、何を創ろうとも、ある種の美意識から外れることはない。自然とレモン・ジェリーらしいものが出来上がるんだ。

41–60

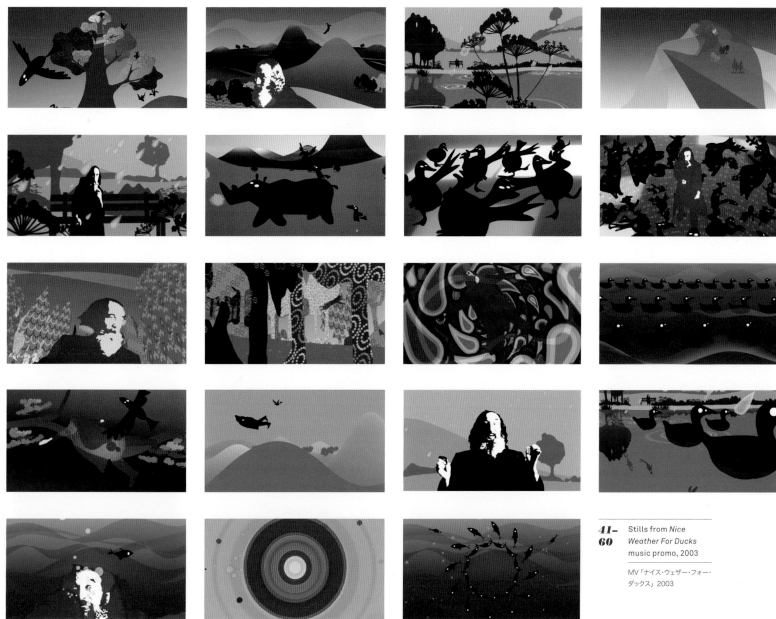

Lemon Jelly

レモン・ジェリー

'64–'95

Fred The next album, '64–'95, was about exploring as many musical genres as possible by creating all of the tracks around various diverse samples. Leo had the idea to do a full length animated DVD to accompany the album, so we agreed to make nine individual six-minute animations, all very different in style to echo the theme of the album, which added up to just under an hour of animation in total. It was the first proper animation project we had taken on and Airside created its first showreel overnight.

Nick The record took a really long time to make, and at the end there were lots of issues around clearing the samples. It's a complicated record; it deliberately bounces around the genres, from post-punk to funk to soul, but it's got its core. The DVD goes through all of these different styles by getting different Airsiders involved

in each video, and so the eclecticism really comes across. It's to their credit that they just embraced it and delivered such a great partner to the album. It was slightly mad.

Nat It was something that everyone at Airside got involved in. The record company said to us, okay if you really want to do this, we've got £60k and we need 60 minutes. It was a ridiculous schedule – we had three months to make it – and a ridiculous budget. We knew we wouldn't make money and in fact as we suspected we ended up losing a little, but we had to do it purely as a creative stretch.

Fred Everyone got a chance to get their hands dirty and the company grew and blossomed as a result. It was a case of saying, "Who wants to direct a music video? We have got three months to learn a new trade." It was animation boot camp for everyone at Airside. Alex particularly really came into his own: he discovered a hitherto

dormant talent for directing moving image and he's been on fire ever since.

Alex There was a very clear brief from Nick and Fred about what the music meant narratively, but then the visual style and implementation were completely up for grabs. It was a case of learning animation direction on the job. The metaphor we used was the digital album sleeve; what is the visual element of music in the 21st century, now that people consume most of their music by downloading?

Nat It was a lot of fun. I remember being really pleased that everyone in the studio was enjoying themselves so much.

Fred XL very generously funded us to do the DVD, then regretted it because it didn't sell very well. It wasn't really marketed as a separate entity. It worked a lot better in Japan where they packaged it with the album and it boosted overall sales as a result.

'64–'95

フレッド 次のアルバム「'64–'95」では、ありとあらゆるサンプルを用いて楽曲を作り、できるだけ多くのジャンルの音楽を模索した。レオは、アルバムとともに全編フルアニメーションのDVDを作りたいと考えていたから、僕らは全9曲、各6分のアニメーションを制作することに同意したんだ。アルバムのテーマに合わせて、アニメーションのスタイルも多種多様にして、全部で1時間に収まるようにした。僕らにとって、正式なアニメーションプロジェクトはこれが初めてで、短期間で一気に初のショーリールを完成させたみたいなもんさ。

ニック アルバムのほうは、とんでもなく時間がかかった。結局、サンプル素材の権利処理の問題が山のようにあってね。これは、複雑なアルバムで、ポストパンクからファンク、ソウルまで、ジャンルをあえて混ぜているけど、ちゃんとアルバム自体の軸があるんだ。DVDでは、曲ごとに、異なったエアサイドのメンバーによって作られた異なったスタイルのア

ニメーションを見ることができて、折衷主義が上手く昇華されている。このアイデアを受け入れて、アルバムにあれほど相応しい作品を提供してくれたエアサイドの功績は、まったく称賛に値するよ。相当の入れ込みようだったからね。

ナット エアサイドの全員が、制作に携わったわ。レコード会社から「もし本当にやりたいのなら、予算は60,000ポンドで、尺は60分だけど」って言われてね。制作期間は3ヶ月。時間もなければ、予算もなかった。儲けにならないばかりか、懸念したとおり若干の赤字まで出してしまったけど、それでも創作の幅を広げるために、やるしかなかったのよ。

フレッド 全員が苦労して制作に関わったおかげで、会社が成長し、開花したんだ。「ミュージックビデオを監督してみたい人？ 3ヶ月あるから、新しい事にチャレンジしてみよう」ってノリで、さながらエアサイドのメンバーによるアニメーション・ブートキャンプみたいだった。特に本領を発揮したのがアレックスで、今まで眠っていたアニメーション・ディレクターとしての才能に目覚めて、以来夢中になっているよ。

アレックス 楽曲の物語性については、ニックとフレッドからすごく明確な説明があったけど、映像スタイルや手法については、まったく制約がなかった。音楽的な感覚だけではあまりに抽象的だったから、この制作は、ある程度の尺の演出を学ぶのにいい機会だったよ。僕らが比喩として用いたのは「デジタル・アルバム・ジャケット」。つまり、人々が音楽をダウンロードして購入するのが当たり前になった今、21世紀の音楽には、どんな視覚的イメージが相応しいだろうかと考えたんだ。

ナット ものすごく楽しい作業だった。スタジオにいるみんなが楽しんでるのがひしひしと伝わってきて、本当に嬉しかったわ。

フレッド XLは、ものすごく気前よくDVD制作費を出してくれたけど、売り上げが芳しくなくて、ひどく後悔していた。CDと別売りじゃダメだったんだよ。日本ではアルバムとセットで販売したから、結果的に総売上がずっと伸びたんだ。

Following four pages:
次4頁

61 '64–'95 – 10" vinyl box set
Impotent Fury Records & Tapes / XL Recordings, 2005

「'64–'95」10インチ・レコード・ボックスセット
インポテント・フューリー
レコーズ&テープス／
XLレコーディングス 2005

62– 63 Stills from '64–'95 DVD
Impotent Fury Records & Tapes / XL Recordings, 2005

「'64–'95」
DVD収録映像
インポテント・フューリー
レコーズ&テープス／
XLレコーディングス 2005

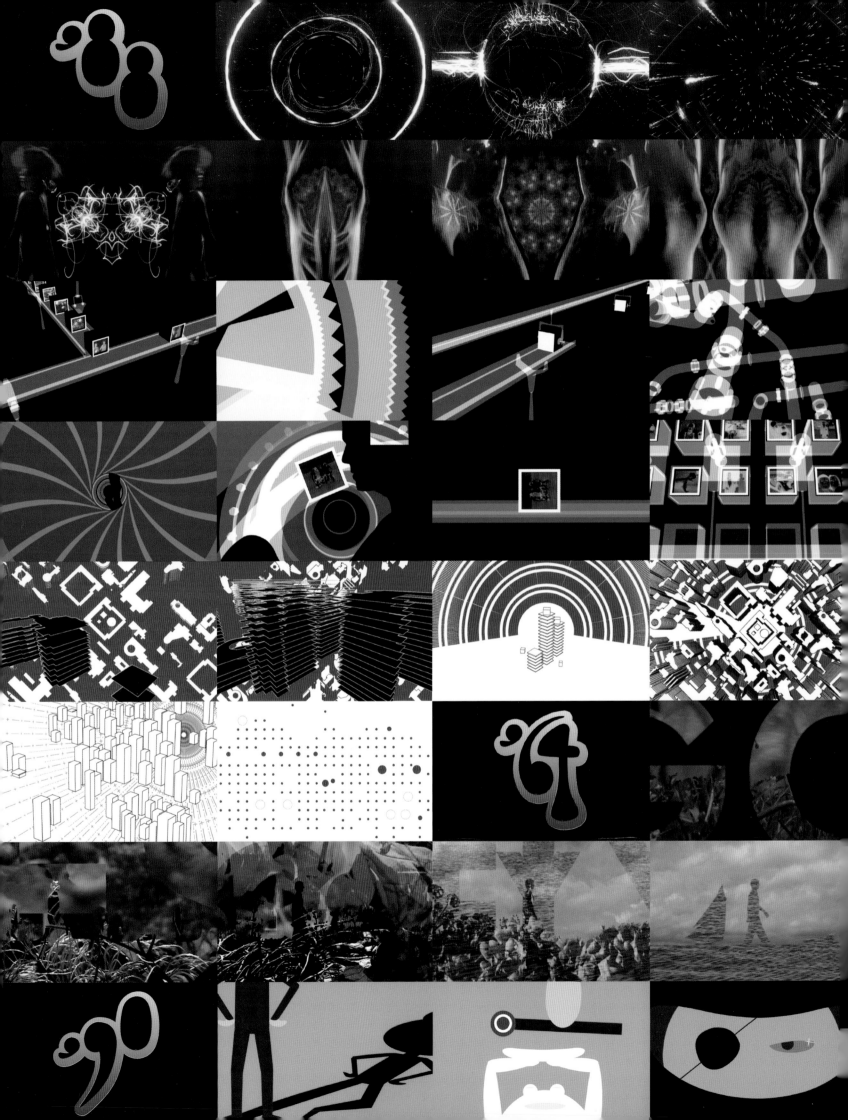

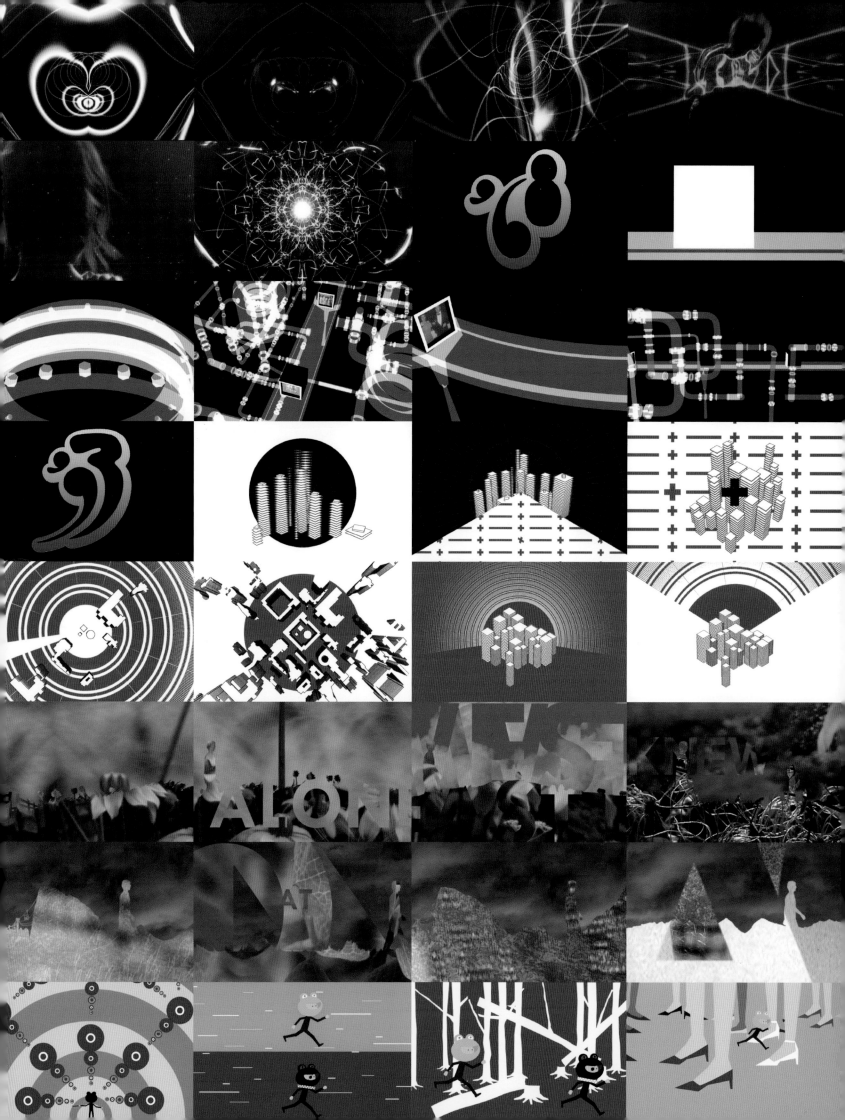

Airside by Airside
エアサイド バイ エアサイド

Lemon Jelly
レモン・ジェリー

IOTA

IOTA

Job name:	Inventions of the Abstract		**作品名:**	インヴェンションズ・オブ・ジ・アブストラクト
Client:	Lemon Jelly		**クライアント:**	レモン・ジェリー
Media:	Moving image		**メディア:**	動画

Summary: Abstract visuals for Lemon Jelly's one-off performance at London's IMAX cinema, as part of the BFI's *Optronica Festival*.

内容: BFI（ブリティッシュ・フィルム・インスティテュート）のオプトロニカ・フェスティバルの一環として、ロンドンのIMAXシネマで開かれた、一夜限りのレモン・ジェリーのコンサート用に制作された抽象ビジュアル

When the BFI's *Optronica Festival* commissioned a brand new piece of work from Lemon Jelly to be screened at the IMAX Cinema in London, a call to Airside was inevitable. The core concept behind this project, named *Inventions Of The Abstract*, is the exploration of minimal abstraction, both sonically and aesthetically. Fred and Nick realised this concept through close collaboration with Airside and a crack squad of their talented freelancers; uniquely, this team developed the separate audio and visual elements of the performance simultaneously, informing and reacting to each other at regular stages in their evolution. The end result is an intense hour long sensorial experience that has at the time of writing only been experienced by the 600 people who attended the March 2007 IMAX performance. **FS**

BFIのオプトロニカ・フェスティバルから、ロンドンのIMAXシネマでの上映を兼ねた新作を依頼されたレモン・ジェリーが、次にすることと言えばエアサイドに連絡すること以外考えられない。「抽象芸術の発明」と名付けられた、このプロジェクトの中心的なコンセプトは、音と映像の両面から、ミニマルな抽象芸術を探求するというもの。フレッドとニックは、エアサイドおよび、才能溢れるフリーランサーたちとの密接なコラボレーションによって、このコンセプトを実現した。ユニークなことに、チームは、オーディオと映像の要素を別々に展開し、ライブで定期的に互いのタイミングを見計らいながら、シンクロするパフォーマンスを成し遂げた。現時点で、このセンセーショナルでユニークな1時間を体験できたのは、2007年3月にIMAXシネマのパフォーマンスに来場した600人だけである。（FS）

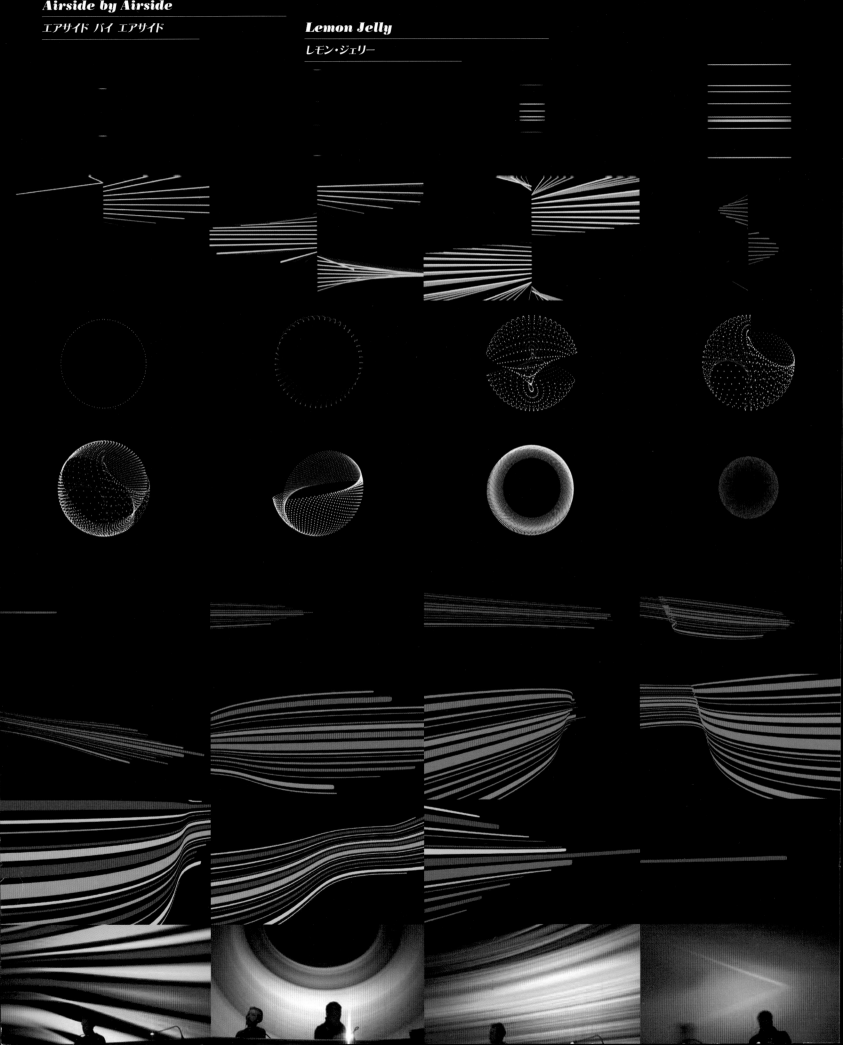

Lemon Jelly

レモン・ジェリー

65

CONCLUSION

———— **Leo** *Lost Horizons* sold 200,000 albums, which is pretty amazing for an electronic album. Maybe only Daft Punk has managed that. Some people called them the English Air, but Air were always about jazz whereas Lemon Jelly were much more electronic and whimsical; they were influenced by people like the Kinks and Cream, rather than Serge Gainsbourg.

———— **Marc** There was a sticker on the front of the first album, which said: "This is a compilation of our first three EPs – if you own those there is no reason for you to buy this album." That is unique in a world where everyone is happy to flog the same album five times over in slightly different packaging with an extra bonus remix. I think their fan-base noticed things like that and

came to expect those value-added things from Nick and Fred.

———— **Neil Simpson [fan]** I first heard them on Mary Anne Hobbs's BBC Radio 1 show, *The Breezeblock*, and was immediately taken by the distinctive musical style – a combination of crisp beats with melodies and samples from an age long past. The artwork for the covers always had this same intriguing quality. Many bands strive for an identity which Lemon Jelly had right from the start. Those bright, primary colours in a style reminiscent of earlier times but with a modern slant proved eye-catching and immediately recognisable. The packaging reached its zenith with their two unofficial releases, *Soft Rock* and *Rolled Oats*. These two records went to the very limits of presentation and showed the lengths Lemon Jelly were prepared to go to provide something memorable.

———— **Fred** It's really good to have a visual consistency throughout everything we do. That is quite rare. It was always our intention that Lemon Jelly should be perceived as more than just music. Sure, music is at very the core of it, but there is no reason it can't encompass all this other stuff. The gig we did at Somerset House – where the visuals were projected onto all the surrounding buildings – and more recently the IOTA show at the IMAX, where we had created abstract oscillating patterns and ambient music working in tandem with each other; it is all about trying to do something where there is a genuine integration between the music and the visuals.

———— In the end it was a win-win: Airside got to experiment and won a lot of work out of Lemon Jelly's success, and Lemon Jelly got a shit-hot visual identity at a rock bottom price.

結論

———— **レオ** 「ロスト・ホライズンズ」は20万枚を売り上げた。エレクトロニックのアルバムとしてはかなりの快挙だ。他に成し遂げたのはダフト・パンクくらいかな。レモン・ジェリーを、英国版エールだと言う人もいるけど、エールがジャズ寄りなのに対して、レモン・ジェリーはもっとエレクトロニックで風変わりだからね。セルジュ・ゲンズブールよりも、キンクスやクリームに影響を受けているんだ。

———— **マーク** ファーストアルバムの表には、「これは僕らの最初のEP3枚をまとめたアルバムだから、もう持っているのならわざわざ買う必要はないよ」と書かれたステッカーが貼られていた。同じアルバムのパッケージをちょっと変えて、ボーナス・リミックスを付けたくらいで、5回以上も新作みたいに宣伝するのが当たり前の世界では珍しいよね。レモン・ジェリーのファンたちも気づいているみたいで、ニックとフレッドには、そういった心意気を期待するようになった。

———— **ニール・シンプソン [ファン代表]** 僕がレモン・ジェリーを初めて耳にしたのは、BBCラジオ1でメアリー・アン・ホブスがDJを務めるブリーズロックだった。独特の音楽スタイルに、たちまち虜になったね。メロディーと快活なビート、古いレコードからのサンプリングが絶妙に合わさっていた。アルバムジャケットのアートワークも、いつもクオリティーが高く魅力的なんだ。多くのバンドが、アイデンティティーを模索して奮闘するけど、レモン・ジェリーにはそれが最初から備わっていた。懐かしさを感じさせながらもモダンなスタイルで用いられる鮮やかな原色は、パンチが効いているから、すぐに人目につくんだ。彼らのアルバムのジャケットは、2枚の非公式リリースレコード「ソフト・ロック」と「ロールド・オーツ」で頂点を極めたね。どちらも枚数限定で発売されて、レモン・ジェリーが記憶に残るものを作ろうとした努力が、伝わってくるよ。

———— **フレッド:** 僕らの関わるすべての活動に視覚的統一感があるのはいいことだと思う。滅多にないことだよね。レモン・ジェリーを音楽以上の何かとして認識してほしいという想いはいつもあって、勿論、基本は音楽なんだけど、その他の要素を含んでいてはいけない理由なんかないだろ？ たとえばサマセット・ハウスで開催したギグでは、周辺の建物に映像を投影したし、最近IMAXシネマで開催したIOTAのショーでは、抽象的な振動パターンとアンビエントな音楽をシンクロさせた。つまり、僕らの目指すところは、何をおいても音楽とビジュアルのリアルな融合なんだ。

———— 結局、レモン・ジェリーとエアサイドのコラボレーションは、双方にメリットがあった。エアサイドにとってはいい実験の場になったし、レモン・ジェリーの成功のおかげでたくさんの仕事を得た。一方レモン・ジェリーも、とことんお金がない中で、えらくイカしたビジュアル・アイデンティティーを得られたからね。

GROWING PAINS

成長期の苦しみ

Fred The first few years of Airside were very exciting. Somehow we had managed to achieve the one thing we had all wanted when we left art school; a great place to go to every day to work with our friends on projects that excited and stretched us. It was even more exciting when the industry started taking notice of us.

D&AD

Nat In previous years the design for the D&AD Student Awards campaign had been very abstract, so when we were asked to design it we thought we'd try a more hard-hitting approach. The call for entries was the most important part, as entry fees are a big source of income for D&AD, but we realised students didn't really understand the importance of winning a yellow pencil. We came up with the idea of bunnies representing students, with an art college like the Titanic going down in the background. The yellow pencils were depicted as life-savers : a life jacket or a parachute. It said, a yellow pencil is a golden ticket into a job in the industry.

Richard For the annual, I had the idea of making a series of illustrated landscapes featuring various anthropomorphic rabbit figures drawn in silhouette. It was quite stylised and very storybooky. But it was so overambitious – it needed thirty drawings which meant finishing more than one a day to meet the deadline. Alex was saying, it's a great idea - you'll never do it in the time we've got. But they let me try and I got away with it. I felt I'd proved that I fitted in there and I became properly part of the team.

フレッド　エアサイドを立ち上げてから最初の数年間はとにかくエキサイティングだった。アートスクールを卒業してから僕らが望んでいたものを何とか形にできたわけだからね。毎日飽きることなく仲間と働ける場所で、楽しくプロジェクトを手がけながら、世界を広げてきた。しかも業界の中で僕らの存在が知られてきたのが嬉しかったね。

D&AD

ナット　それまでのD&AD（デザイン&アートディレクション）ステューデント・アワードのキャンペーンは、とても抽象的なデザインばかりだったから、依頼を受けた時、もっとパンチのあるものにしようと思ったわ。中でもD&ADでは、学生たちの参加料が収益の大部分を占めているから「作品募集のお知らせ」は一番重要だった。とはいえ、最高賞のイエロー・ペンシルを受賞することが、どれほどの価値を持つのかが、いまひとつ学生たちに浸透していないことに気づいたの。そこでアートカレッジを沈みゆくタイタニックみたいに背景に描いて、ウサギの姿をした学生たちがそこから脱出する場面を思いついた。イエロー・ペンシルを、救命胴衣やパラシュートといった救命道具に見立てて、メッセージは「イエロー・ペンシルは、業界へのゴールデンチケット」ってね。

リチャード　年鑑カタログ用のイラストには、擬人化したウサギのシルエットをモチーフにした風景を思いついた。独特の世界観があって、まるで絵本みたいなんだ。かなり野心的な提案で、30枚のイラストを仕上げるには、締め切りまでに1日1枚以上は完成させないといけなかった。アレックスが、「アイデアはすごくいいけど、時間内に仕上がらないと思うよ」って。それでもやらせてくれて、なんとかやり遂げたんだ。僕はエアサイドでうまくやっていけることを証明できたと感じたし、実際これで正式にチームのメンバーになったんだ。

D&AD STUDENT AWARDS 2004
CALL FOR ENTRIES

Growing Pains

成長期の苦しみ

D&AD

D&AD

Job name:	D&AD Student Awards campaign	作品名：	D&AD
Client:	D&AD		ステューデント・アワード・キャンペーン
Media:	Print	クライアント：	D&AD
		メディア：	印刷物

| **Summary:** | A commission to devise and design the Student Awards campaign to encourage more students to enter the awards. | 内容： | より多くの学生に応募を呼びかける、ステューデント・アワード・キャンペーンのプランニングおよびデザイン |

——————— For two years in a row, the British design and advertising industry body, D&AD, commissioned Airside to create all the campaign materials for its annual Student Awards. Realising that not all students understood that winning an industry award was a ticket to a job, Airside set about illustrating a set of scenarios in which students were represented by anthropomorphic rabbits, being rescued on their ejection from art college by yellow pencils (the format in which the awards are handed out) fashioned as life-saving devices. This idea became established as the theme for the whole event, and such was the success of the design that entries to the competition grew by 25 per cent. The project encompassed a range of outputs from the call for entries print campaign, the exhibition and awards interior design, to the design of the final book of winning work. **FS**

——————— 英国のデザインおよび広告産業団体、D&ADから2年にわたって依頼を受け、ステューデント・アワードのキャンペーン素材の制作すべてを手がけた。この賞を受賞することで業界への道が開けることが、思いのほか学生たちに知られていないことに気づいたエアサイドは、学生たちを擬人化したウサギで表し、アートカレッジからの脱出後、救命胴衣に見立てられたイエロー・ペンシル（受賞者には黄色い鉛筆型のトロフィーが授与される）のおかげで、ウサギたちが命拾いをする、という場面を描いたイラストレーション・シリーズを展開した。このアイデアはイベント全体のテーマにも採用され、応募も前年に比べ25％増加するという成功を収めた。応募告知ポスターキャンペーン、展覧会および表彰式インテリアデザイン、受賞作を集めた年鑑カタログのデザインに至るまで、エアサイドが幅広く手がけたプロジェクトとなった。（FS）

Page 94
Airside by Airside
エアサイド バイ エアサイド

Growing Pains
成長期の苦しみ

2 D&AD Student Awards
The Annual, 2004

D&ADステューデント・アワード
年鑑カタログ 2004

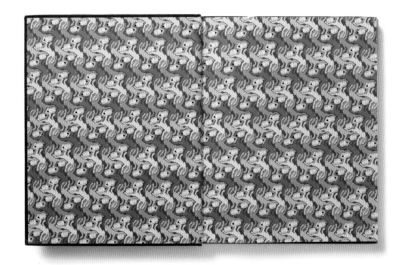

Growing Pains

成長期の苦しみ

3

3 D&AD Student Awards
Product Design *Call
for Entries*, 2005

D&ADステューデント・アワード
プロダクトデザイン 募集要項
2005

4

5

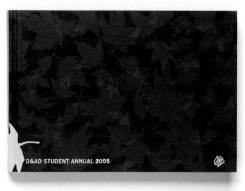

Airside by Airside

エアサイド バイ エアサイド

Growing Pains

成長期の苦しみ

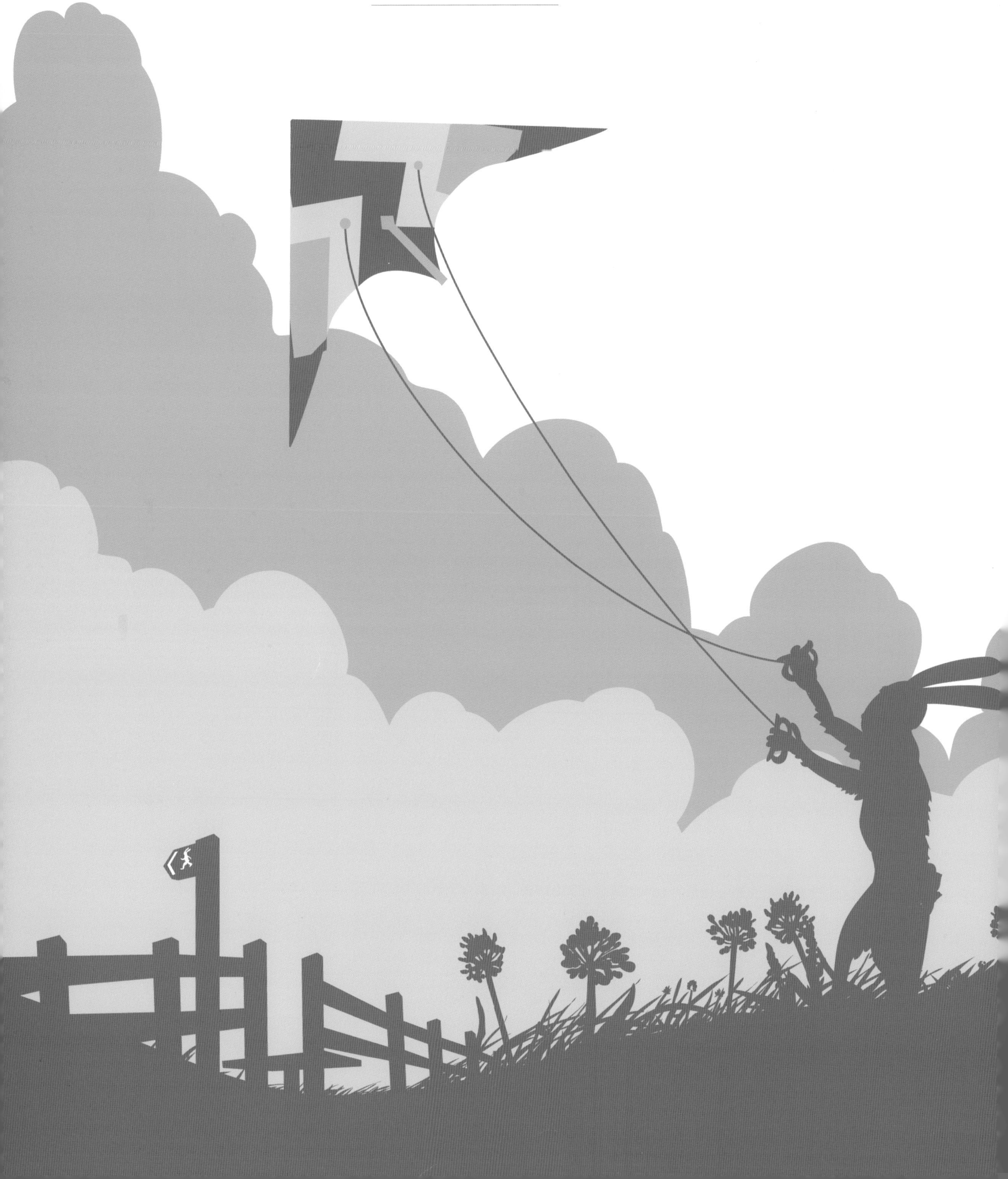

6 Illustration from
D&AD Student Awards
annual, 2004

D&ADステューデント・アワード
年鑑カタログ イラストレーション
2004

Growing Pains
成長期の苦しみ

RCA

Fred Another confirmation that we were doing something right came when the Royal College of Art asked us to make their website. We said no the first time but then they asked us again!

Alex Doing the RCA website was hilarious – imagine that your client is twelve of your ex-tutors and you have to tell them why everything about their last website was wrong.

Nat It was quite intimidating, but we rose to the challenge. We were convinced that the main issue was to create a content management system that was so simple that each department would really use it on a regular basis. At the time, there was a different microsite for each department. Getting all the tutors to agree on how the site should be structured was a major act of diplomacy. We are proud of the site because it's very simple, and it uses the students' work wherever possible; the previous site had had no pictures at all, which didn't really do the college justice.

Fred Then the dotcom crash happened in 2001. We hardly noticed at first, because we were small and didn't take the cash that our competitors did – there was so much venture capital being ploughed into web design companies, and some of them believed it was a normal state of affairs.

Alex We were offered money from investors, and the chance to build our company up to 50 people and get it floated on the stock market, and we just thought, why would we do that? We had different goals.

Fred We smelt the clouds of sulphur coming in behind their black cloaks. It was like Satan coming to see you. Every time we saw someone else take the money, it was the beginning of the end – suddenly you're working for someone else and it takes away your creative freedom. They take their money back whenever they want and then you're screwed.

Nat We were motivated to make good work, not to make money. We liked being small. It would have been a strange relationship had the White Cube or Burnham Niker gone to a big web design agency. Being a small company ourselves, it was easier to work with small clients and have a relationship where we could really understand what they needed, and they didn't feel like they were being ripped off. In the end it helped us to survive the crash unlike most of our competitors who had grown so big. For example, when Deepend went under they had 80 staff in London, and 250 worldwide. And there was a cultural difference: a lot of those glitzy dotcoms were offering their staff free haircuts, private healthcare and all the beer you could drink on a Friday night. That 'funky' working culture was a new thing and people had a lot of fun spanking their new expense account; we didn't go down that road. But some of the new graduates were quite seduced by it and were faced with a dilemma – shall I go and work for Airside in a basement in Islington with 5 people, or shall I go and work for a company with free haircuts?

Alex I had a recession mentality, and kept thinking the bubble was going to burst, that it was all nonsense. Whenever I walked into an office and saw the table football, I thought, that's it, this company is going down.

ロイヤル・カレッジ・オブ・アート

フレッド RCA(ロイヤル・カレッジ・オブ・アート)からウェブサイト制作の依頼が来たときも、自分たちの方向性に間違いはないと確信したよ。最初は断ったけど、どうしてもって言われたんだ!

アレックス RCAのウェブサイト制作は傑作だったね。考えてもみてよ、かつて僕らが教わった12人の教師がクライアントで、彼らのウェブサイトがどうして問題だらけなのか、今度は僕らが教えなければならない立場にあったようなものだからね。

ナット 相当手強かったけれど、なんとか対処したわ。一番の課題は、各学部が日々気軽に更新してくれるような、シンプルなコンテンツ管理システムを構築することだと確信していた。当時は、学部ごとにそれぞれミニサイトを立ち上げていたから、新しいサイトの理想的構造について、全教員の同意を得るのがひと苦労だった。結果として、とてもシンプルで、可能な限り学生の作品を掲載したサイトができて、満足しているわ。以前のサイトには、写真が一枚もなかったのよ、アートカレッジだっていうのに。

フレッド それから、2001年に「ドットコム・クラッシュ」が起きた。僕らは規模も小さかったし、他のライバル会社のように大金を持っていなかったから、最初はほとんど気づかなかった。ウェブデザイン会社に、信じられないくらいの莫大な金が投資されていて、中にはそれが普通だと思っている人々もいた。

アレックス 投資家たちから出資のオファーが来て、50人ほど雇って会社を大きくし、株式市場に参入しないかと。でもそこで思ったんだ。どうしてそんなことをする必要があるんだ? 僕らの目標は全然違うところにあるのにって。

フレッド 彼らの黒服の下から硫黄が臭ってくる感じで、まるでサタンが会いに来てるみたいだった。誰かがお金を受け取るのを見るたびに、あぁ終わりの始まりだって思ったものさ。突然、他人のために働く羽目になって、創作の自由なんかなくなってしまうからね。彼らは、いつでも欲しい時に金を巻き上げに来るわけで、そうなったら一巻の終わりだ。

ナット 私たちは、お金を稼ぐことより、いい仕事をすることに重きを置いていたから、小規模の方が良かった。ホワイト・キューブやバーナム・ナイカーだって、巨大ウェブデザイン会社に声をかけていたら、全然違う結果になっていたでしょうね。私たちのような小さな会社にとっては、同じく規模の小さなクライアントとの方が仕事がしやすかった。私たちは彼らが必要とするものを本当に理解できたし、クライアントとしても、ぼられていないか心配しなくてすむし。結果として、私たちはなんとかクラッシュを生き延びることができたの。巨大化したライバル会社の多くはそうはいかなかったけれどね。ロンドンに80人、世界に250人のスタッフを抱えたディープエンドがその一例。彼らとは「文化」が違ったわ。こうした華やかさが売りのウェブ会社は、スタッフのヘアカットを無料にしたり、特別なヘルスケアを施したり、金曜の夜には浴びるほどビールを振る舞ったり。そういった「ファンキーな」働き方は確かに新しくて、経費がかさんでもお構いなし。でも私たちは、そうはしなかった。新卒者の中にはその華やかさに誘惑される人たちもいて、ジレンマに陥っていたわ。イズリントンの地下室で細々と5人でやってるエアサイドで働くか、無料でヘアカットしてもらえる会社で働くかって。

アレックス 僕は、いずれ不景気が来ると思っていた。そのうちバブルがはじけるんだって。なにしろ正気の沙汰じゃなかったからね。どこかのオフィスに行って、卓上サッカーゲームを見る度に「あぁ、この会社も潰れるな」と思ったもんだよ。

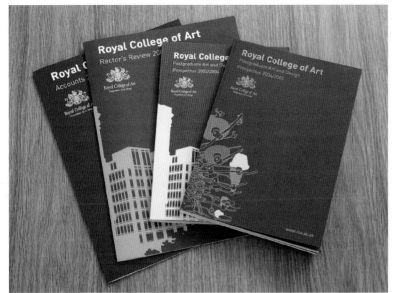

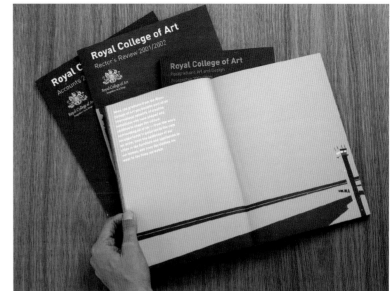

7   Royal College of Art
prospectuses and
reports, 2002–05

ロイヤル・カレッジ・オブ・アート
学校案内 2002–05

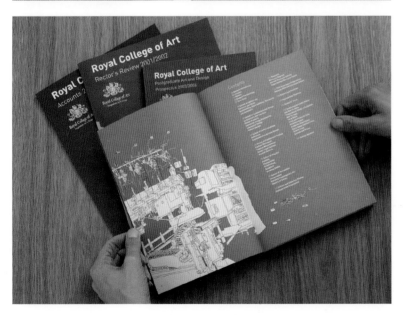

Growing Pains

成長期の苦しみ

23RD FLOOR

———— **Nat** One reason we survived the crash was that we'd just got a retainer – £10k a month from BT Cellnet for the 23rd Floor website. That was just about enough to pay our basic bills, and it saved us.

———— **Fred** This guy John Tosh from BT Cellnet had seen what was happening in Japan, how people were living through their mobiles, especially when it came to gaming. He convinced BT to set up a web portal where they could encourage kids to use their mobiles more, and publicise and distribute mobile WAP games. It had to be a place kids would go on a regular basis and check out what was new. BT was a corporate structure, and he realised that it needed a more unconventional company like us to create it. For the first and only time ever we were paid a retainer to do regular work on creating and constantly updating a site, which was fantastic. Content was king and needed to change daily, so we created this dynamic portal called 23rd Floor packed full of Flash animations, competitions, music journalism content courtesy of our friend Manish Arora who knew the scene

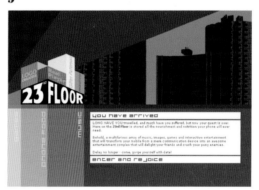

8

9

inside out, and a Habbo Hotel type avatar chatroom called the Unfair.

———— **Alex** It was a funfair where the 'f' had fallen off.

———— **Nat** The whole site was inhabited by these characters called Meanie-Maybes – like Beanie-Babies but with attitude – whose job was to explain what these games and unfamiliar functions were all about, for example forming groups with your friends via your mobiles.

———— **Alex** It was a social network – it was way ahead of its time. It was completely user-driven, and had nearly 500 kids on it at any time, which in those days was a lot. What no-one spotted, sadly, was that WAP was a crap technology – everybody thought 3G was coming, and it wasn't. So ultimately, 23rd Floor failed because the games were rubbish – the promise was everything and the end product wasn't good enough. The activity on the website was more successful than the games themselves.

———— **Nat** The project was never marketed, but it worked very well virally. BT really didn't want to make it traceable back to them, because they thought it wouldn't succeed with their name attached to it.

23階

———— **ナット** 私たちがドットコム・クラッシュを生き残れた理由のひとつは、BTセルネットから「23階」っていうウェブサイトの仕事を引き受けていて、月々10,000ポンドの定期収入があったからなの。これで基本的な支払いをカバーできたから、大助かりだったわ。

———— **フレッド** BTセルネットの担当者のジョン・トッシュが、日本で誰もが携帯電話を活用して、特にゲームに夢中になってる現状を見て来たんだ。そこで自分たちも、子供たちに携帯をもっと使ってもらえるように、BTでウェブ・ポータルを作り、携帯で遊べるWAPゲームを宣伝、配給しようと考えた。子供たちが定期的に訪れて、新作が入っているかチェックできるようなポータルが必要だったんだ。そこで彼は、BTはいわゆる堅い会社組織だから、僕らのように型にはまらない会社に制作を頼むほうがいいと思い立ち、おかげで僕らは、ウェブコンテンツを定期的に制作、更新して、月々の報酬を得ることができた。あんなに美味しい話は、あれが最初にして最後だったけどね。コンテンツこそ命だから、日々更新する必要があった。そこで制作したのが、「23階」っていうダイナミックなポータルサイト。ありとあらゆるFlashアニメーションやゲーム、音楽シーンに精通している友人マニシュ・アローラが提供してくれた音楽ジャーナリズム、それに「ハボ・ホテル（SNS）」みたいなタイプのアヴァター

を用いた「アンフェア」っていうチャットルームを盛り込んだ。

———— **アレックス** 「ファンフェア（遊園地）」のはずが「f」が剥げ落ちて「アンフェア」になったんだ。

———— **ナット** サイトの至る所に、威張った「ビーニー・ベイビーズ」もどきの「ミーニー・メイビーズ」っていうキャラクターたちが暮らしていて、ゲームや新しい機能について説明してくれるの。例えば携帯を使って友達とグループを作る方法とかね。

———— **アレックス** 当時としてはまだ珍しい、ソーシャル・ネットワークだった。完全にユーザー主導型で、常に500人近い子供たちが利用していた。当時としてはものすごい数だよ。ただ悲しいことに、WAP自体がとんでもなくお粗末なゲームだったために、見向きもされなかったんだ。とうとう3G到来かって思ってたら、そうじゃなくてね。そんなわけで、ゲームがつまらなかったために、23階は失敗に終わった。期待させるだけさせておいて、肝心の宣伝商品がお粗末じゃね。ウェブ上のアクティビティのほうが、ゲームそのものより成功してしまったんだ。

———— **ナット** このプロジェクトは大々的な宣伝をしなかったけど、口コミでかなり広がったわ。BT側は、自分たちが仕掛人だと知られたくなかったのね。社名が出てしまったら成功しないとわかっていたから。

———— **フレッド** クライアントですら、どんな結果になるかわからないまま、ネット上に遊び場を作って実験してみ

12

11

Fred It was a classic case of creating a playground and experimenting, even though the client didn't really know where it would go. It had a bit of dotcom madness to it. We decided to create toys of the Meanie-Maybe characters, so we put them into production, but by the time they'd come back from the factory, BT Cellnet had pulled the plug. We'd created these characters and made them into toys, and they were great – we couldn't just let them die. So we rebranded them as the Dot Com Refugees – the crash had come, and they were on the run, looking for survival.

10

るという典型的な事例だった。ドットコム熱の産物みたいな面もあったね。僕らは、ミーニー・メイビーズたちのキャラクターグッズを作ることにして、制作に取りかかったけど、工場から完成品が届く頃には、BTセルネットはプロジェクトを打ち切っていた。せっかくキャラクターを制作して、オモチャまで作って、それも良く出来ているのに、彼らをこのまま死なせるわけにはいかない。そこで僕らは「ドットコム・レフュジーズ」と名前を変えてキャラクターをパッケージし直した。ドットコム・クラッシュから逃れて、生き残りを賭けた難民たち、という意味でね。

8– **10**	Screens from 23rdfloor.com, 2002	**11**	Dot Com Refugee screenprint, 2002
	ウェブサイト「23階」 2002		「ドットコム・レフュジーズ」 スクリーン印刷 2002
12	3D Dot Com Refugee, 2002	**13**	Airside staff as Dot Com Refugees, 2002
	3D版「ドットコム・レフュジーズ」 2002		「ドットコム・レフュジーズ エアサイド・メンバー篇」 2002

13

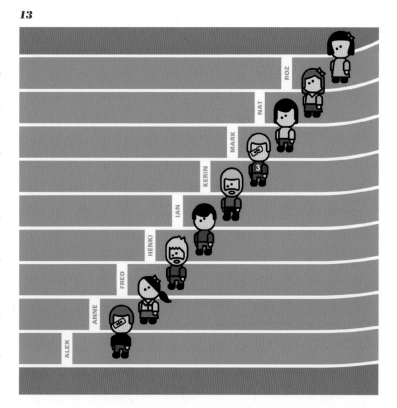

Growing Pains

成長期の苦しみ

DOT COM REFUGEES

ドットコム・レフュジーズ

Job name:	Dot Com Refugees
Client:	Airside
Media:	Product design
Summary:	Toys designed for Airside Shop and Sony Creative Products

作品名:	ドット・コム・レフュジーズ
クライアント:	エアサイド
メディア:	プロダクトデザイン
内容:	エアサイド・ショップおよびソニー・クリエイティブプロダクツ用にデザインされたオモチャ

——————— What on earth are Dot Com Refugees? In Airside's world, they are just that: refugees of an aborted dotcom design project, 23rd Floor. The Meanie-Maybes began life as archetypal Airside animated characters, created to populate the 23rd Floor website and make it an engaging, playful experience. Airside had commissioned a range of toys to extend the concept further, but the project was dropped during the dotcom industry crash of 2001, rendering the toys obsolete. With typical resourcefulness, Airside rebranded the unwanted toys as Dot Com Refugees and Sony Creative Products took them on, to be sold in Japan as toys that dangle from mobile phones. Each character has a name, a history and a setting, as well as a dotcom era job title, and their personalities are typical Airside creations – their bright, cute appearances belie some sinister character traits. The process of creating a new home for these refugees was a key inspiration for the evolution of another of Airside's self-initiated projects, the Stitches (page 182). **FS**

——————— ドットコム・レフュジーズとは一体何？ エアサイドの世界では、ドットコム・デザイン・プロジェクト「23階」の突然の打ち切りで、行き場を失った難民たちのことを指す。この元ミーニー・メイビーズたちは、本来、サイトを盛り上げ、楽しく遊べる場所にするために、「23階」の住人として、エアサイドによって生を授かったアニメーション・キャラクターたちである。その後、さらにコンセプトに広がりをもたせるために、様々なオモチャの制作を依頼されたが、2001年に起きたドットコム業界の破綻によりプロジェクトは頓挫、オモチャは行き場を失った。しかしいつものように機転をきかせたエアサイドは、見捨てられたオモチャをドットコム・レフュジーズと名付けて再ブランド化。それに目をつけたソニー・クリエイティブプロダクツが、めでたく携帯ストラップとして日本で売り出した。どのキャラクターにもドットコム時代特有の役職名と並んで、名前、経歴、生い立ちが設定されていて、その明るく愛らしい姿の奥に邪悪な性格が潜んでいるのは、エアサイドならでは。無事に難民たちの引取先を見つけ出せたことが、後の自主プロジェクト「スティッチィズ」（182ページ参照）の進化に大きなひらめきを与えた。(FS)

DOT COM REFUGEES

—————— **Alex** The Dot Com Refugees all had ridiculous boomtime job titles like director of brand strategy and that sort of thing.

—————— **Nat** They initiated our relationship with Japan. Separately, Sony Creative Products had approached us about making some toys for vending machines in Japan, so we decided that the Dot Com Refugees would be perfect. It was a nice way of rescuing the content we generated from one project and making it work in another.

—————— **Alex** So the Dot Com Refugees survived, they sold really well, and we followed them with a series of screen-prints for the Airside Shop. It encouraged us to become more entrepreneurial, and since then we've always done T-shirts, toys and prints of our own.

—————— **Fred** It also informed the evolution of the Stitches to an extent, by illustrating how we could take stuff we'd designed for the web or print and make it real. It widened our scope of media.

ドットコム・レフュジーズ

—————— **アレックス** ドットコム・レフュジーズには、「ブランド戦略ディレクター」とか、その手のドットコム・ブームに乗った、ばかげた肩書きがつけられているんだ。

—————— **ナット** このキャラクターたちが、日本との関係をスタートさせる発端になったの。その頃ちょうどソニー・クリエイティブプロダクツから、日本の自動販売機で売るオモチャを作って欲しいという依頼があってね、ドットコム・レフュジーズたちならピッタリだって即決したのよ。あるプロジェクトで作ったものを、別のプロジェクトで救済する、良い方法だったわ。

—————— **アレックス** ドットコム・レフュジーズたちは生き残り、しかもよく売れたから、その後エアサイド・ショップでも、このキャラクターたちを使ってスクリーンプリントのシリーズを出したんだ。おかげで企業家精神が養われて、それ以降も自分たちでつくったTシャツやオモチャ、ポスターなんかの販売を続けているよ。

—————— **フレッド** ウェブや印刷用にデザインしたものを、実体のあるグッズにするプロセスを体験したことは、スティッチィズの進化にも少なからず影響を与えたね。関わるメディアの領域が広がったんだ。

14 Dot Com Refugee
keychains (for Japan),
2004

「ドットコム・レフュジーズ」
キーホルダー（日本のみ）
2004

Growing Pains

成長期の苦しみ

15

RICHARD ASHCROFT

Alex As the dot com crash started to bite, we got a lucky break: Lemon Jelly's manager Marc Marot began to bring us more music industry work. Marc managed Richard Ashcroft, and so we designed a site for him with this very moody atmosphere to it, and asked Nadav Kander to do the photography. We built this dark set for Richard to sit in, and not perform, but just do really mundane things. So you're watching him, but he's not aware of it. He's just smoking or stirring a cup of tea. We turned elements of Nadav's photos into tiny little animations. The really disturbing one has him lying on his side and then suddenly he opens his eyes – it's quite creepy.

16

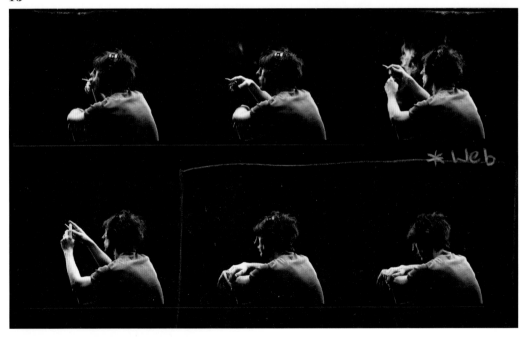

リチャード・アッシュクロフト

アレックス ドットコム・クラッシュが始まったおかげで、幸運が訪れた。例えばレモン・ジェリーのマネージャー、マーク・マローは、さらに音楽業界の仕事をくれた。マークはリチャード・アッシュクロフトのマネージメントもしていたから、僕らは、ナダブに写真を頼んで、彼のためにとてもムーディーなウェブサイトをデザインした。暗いセットの中にリチャードに座ってもらい、パフォーマンスはなしで、ごく普通の日常的な動作をしてもらった。僕らはリチャードを見ているけど、彼は僕らに気づいてないって感じで。ただタバコを吸ったり紅茶をかき混ぜたり。ナダブに撮ってもらった写真を使って、ミニアニメーションも作った。横たわるリチャードが、突然目を開けるアニメーションが、相当不穏な感じに仕上がって、かなり薄気味悪いよ。

17

18

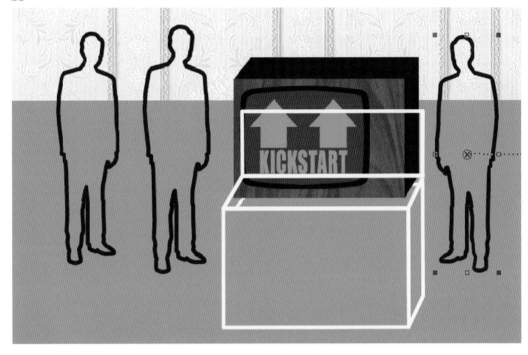

MTV STINGS

——————— **Ian** We were doing a lot of work for MTV at that time; it was the beginning of Airside's animation work. I remember making an animated ident for MTV Dance in which Michael Jackson, John Travolta and a breakdancer were dancing. We got into drawing animation from video, and it took ages – grabbing a few seconds of film, rotoscoping each frame, then smoothing out the animation. That same technique was used for the Clark's Originals website, which had illustrated landscapes based on the curves of the shoes, and silhouettes of people that you clicked on to make them jump and interact with the lines to reveal a shoe. I filmed people in the studio making individual movements, then created the animation from the footage. It was quite labour intensive.

19

20

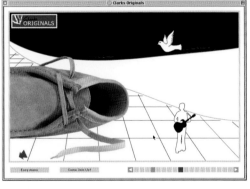

MTVスティングス

——————— **イアン** 当時は、MTVの仕事をたくさん手がけたよね。エアサイドでアニメーション制作を始めたばかりの頃だった。MTVのIDで、マイケル・ジャクソンやジョン・トラヴォルタ、それからブレイクダンサーが踊るアニメーションも作ったな。ビデオからドローイング・アニメーションを作るのにハマってて、これがえらく手間のかかる作業でね。数秒の映像を抜き出し、各フレームをロトスコープして、スムーズなアニメーションにしていく工程なんだけど。同じ手法で、クラークス・オリジナルズのウェブサイトも作った。靴の曲線をイメージした風景がイラスト化してあって、そこに描かれた人物のシルエットをクリックすると、人物がジャンプして、ラインアニメーションと絡み合って靴が現れる、という仕掛け。これは事前に人物の個々の動きをスタジオで撮影して、その素材をもとにアニメーションを作り上げたんだ。過酷な作業だったね。

21

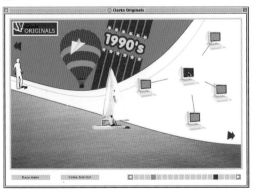

22

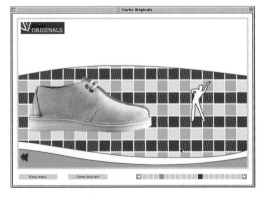

15–16	Contact sheets from Richard Ashcroft photoshoot, 2003	**17**	Screen from richardashcroft.com, 2003	**18**	Still from MTV *Kickstart* ident, 2002	**19–22**	Screens from clarksoriginals.com, 2003
	リチャード・アッシュクロフト撮影写真 2003		リチャード・アッシュクロフトウェブサイト 2003		MTV「キックスタート」ID 2002		クラークス・オリジナルウェブサイト 2003

Airside by Airside
エアサイド バイ エアサイド

Growing Pains
成長期の苦しみ

FILM T-SHIRTS

—————— **Nat** Off the back of our T-shirt Club came some work for various film companies. Craig McLean, a music journalist friend from Edinburgh recommended us to Metro Tartan, who were promoting this cult Japanese film *Battle Royale*, and we designed them a T-shirt that now sells in the Airside Shop.

—————— **Alex** We produced the identity for the London Film Festival and took it upon ourselves to create a series of prints based on the films for an exhibition at the NFT. Artificial Eye, the distributor, saw our print of the film *Zatoichi*. They loved it and

took the bold step to commission us to do all the promotional and product work including the DVD packaging. It became their most successful film in ages. That led to other work in the film industry; we made T-shirts for *Ring* and *Shaun of the Dead* – it turned into a blood and gore theme. For *Shaun of the Dead*, director Edgar Wright asked us for a load of Airside posters to decorate the student flat that appears in the film. We got a real thrill when we saw them in the final movie.

—————— **Edgar Wright** I'd become aware of Fred and Airside through our heavy use of Lemon Jelly in the second series of *Spaced*. I was a huge fan of their artwork on the albums, so when they

produced the Metro Tartan series, I had a bit of a geekgasm. Their *Battle Royale* poster was something of a classic, so much so that we put it on prominent display in Shaun's living room in my film *Shaun Of The Dead*.

—————— I'm now proud to say that two of my most FAQs by fans are Fred and Airside centric. One I always get asked is, "What's the last track on the last episode of *Spaced*?" (Answer – Lemon Jelly's *The Staunton Lick*.) The other is what is that cool *Battle Royale* poster in Shaun's flat and where can I get one?

—————— Speaking of which, I don't have one. Where can I get one? [He has one now - **Ed.**]

フィルムTシャツ

—————— **ナット** 私たちのTシャツクラブを発端に、いくつか映画会社とも仕事をしたわ。エディンバラの友人で音楽ジャーナリストのクレイグ・マクリーンが、メトロ・タータンっていう会社にエアサイドを推薦してくれて。そこが日本のカルト映画「バトル・ロワイヤル」の宣伝をしてたことから、そのTシャツを作ることになって、今もエアサイド・ショップで売っているわ。

—————— **アレックス** ロンドン映画祭のタイトル映像の制作を任されたのを機に、ナショナルフィルムシアターで開催される展示会用に、映画作品をベースにした一連のポスターを自主制作したんだ。その中の1枚「座頭市」のポスターを、配給会社アーティフィシャル・アイが気に入ってくれて、大胆に

も、DVDパッケージを含むすべての宣伝商品のデザインを、僕らに任せてくれた。結果として、彼らにとって久々のヒット作になったし、僕らも映画業界から仕事をもらうようになった。「リング」や「ショーン・オブ・ザ・デッド」のTシャツとかね。どれも血や殺人がテーマなんだけど。「ショーン〜」については、監督のエドガー・ライトに頼まれて、劇中に登場する学生の部屋に、エアサイドのポスターをめいっぱい貼ったんだ。完成した映画を見た時はすごく興奮したね。

—————— **エドガー・ライト** 僕は「スペースド」（エドガーが監督した英国のコメディー番組）の第2シーズンで、レモン・ジェリーの曲をとにかく頻繁に使用したんだ。それがフレッドとエアサイドを知るようになったキッカケだよ。アルバムのアートワークの大ファンだったから、彼らがメトロ・タータンと組

んで作った商品には、それこそオタク並みに夢中になったね。あのバトル・ロワイヤルのポスターなんか、すでに伝説だったから、僕の映画「ショーン・オブ・ザ・デッド」の中で、ショーンの居間に目立つように貼ったんだ。

—————— 嬉しいことに、ファンからよく受ける質問の上位2つがフレッドとエアサイドに関するものなんだよ。まずは「スペースドの最終回で流れる曲は？」という質問（答えはレモン・ジェリーの「ザ・ストーントン・リック」）。そしてもうひとつが、「ショーンの部屋の、あのバトル・ロワイヤルのカッコいいポスターは？ どこで手に入るの？」という質問。

—————— そういえばこのポスター、僕も持ってないんだけど。どこで手に入るんだい？（追記：今は持ってるけどね）

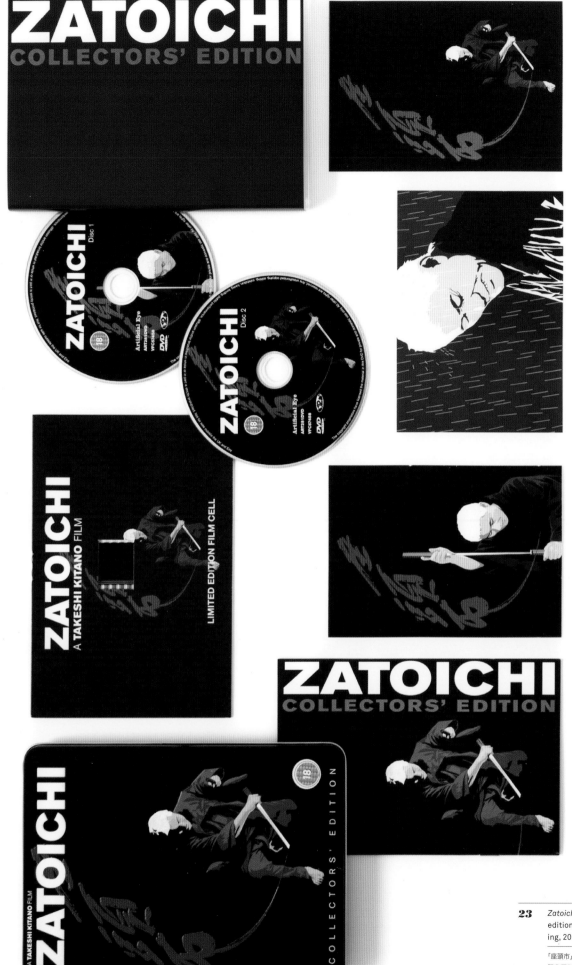

23 *Zatoichi* limited edition DVD packaging, 2004

「座頭市」
限定版DVDパッケージ
2004

Growing Pains

成長期の苦しみ

Richard When I joined Airside in early 2003 they were doing lots of nice jobs for cultural institutions – a website for London Transport's *Platform for Art* project, a website for an architect's practice: it's all good stuff, but you're not going to make money from it. They had a reputation for Lemon Jelly and other Airside work, but they'd not figured much on the radar of agencies or bigger clients.

Alex That's when things began to go wrong financially. We'd got cornered into doing low paid web jobs that led us into trouble. We'd been consistently able to deliver creative and engaging websites and we'd done it for next to nothing. But we didn't have the business knowledge to charge for our skills properly. We'd get offered something like £20k to do a site, and we'd agree, thinking that it was a substantial fee and we'd make a profit out of it. But suddenly we were taking 6-8 months to produce what were very sophisticated sites. We were filling in the rest of the time on nice little projects like prints and record covers, which didn't bring in any money even though they were very creative. We were fiddling while Rome burned.

Nat We directors were multi-tasking big time, still doing the project management ourselves as well as the creative, and these were quite big jobs. We just didn't have that project management experience to make extra changes if things overran.

Fred We had Mark, Richard, Roz, Ian, Anne and Henki working for us – it wasn't just three mates together anymore – and yet we didn't have the skills at that point to handle the business side of things. The real killer was that we had absolutely no strategy to get new work: we would just sit and wait for the phone to ring.

Nat Eventually, we realised we were about to go bust. We only had enough money to pay everyone for one more month. It was around September 2004, and we sat everyone down and explained the situation to them, saying that although we hoped it wouldn't come to actually winding things up, officially we had to give them all one month's notice.

Fred I was away making the second Lemon Jelly album, and when I got the call from Nat, my heart fell and I came back immediately. It was all hands on deck – crisis point. We told everyone we'd been looking at the books and it didn't look good. We hadn't looked up from our computers to see what was going on in the outside world. The dotcom boom was over, and Airside suddenly had a lot of competition. Everyone else had figured out the importance of user experience like we had, times were harder and budgets were lower. Clients wanted more for their money – more interactivity, more content, more everything. We were still operating mainly as a web design company, but the new climate was slowly eroding Airside.

リチャード 2003年の始めに僕が加わった頃、エアサイドは文化団体関連のいい仕事をたくさん手がけていたよ。ロンドン交通局による地下鉄構内のアートプロジェクトのウェブサイトとか、建築家のスタジオを掲載したウェブサイトとかね。すべていい仕事に違いないんだけど、そこから利益の生まれないものばかりだった。レモン・ジェリーやエアサイドの作品はそれなりに評価されていたけれど、代理店や大手クライアントのレーダーには、まだひっかかっていなかったんだ。

アレックス 資金的に苦しくなったのは、ちょうどその頃。僕らは賃金の低いウェブの仕事ばかり請け負って、窮地に立たされていた。絶えずクリエイティブで魅力的なウェブサイトを作り続けていたけれど、タダ同然で、自分たちのスキルに見合った額を請求するビジネス見識に欠けていたんだ。20,000ポンドでサイト作成のオファーがあれば、最初は結構な額だし利益が得られると思ってそれを受けるだろ。でも結局のところ、洗練されたサイトを構築するのに、6〜8ヶ月も費やしている有様でね。空いた時間にはポスターやCDジャケットのような、小さなプロジェクトを手がけていたけれど、そういった仕事はどんなにクリエイティブでも、経済的な足しにはならない。今から思えば、緊急事態だっていうのに、何の対策も講じずに相変わらず制作を続けていたってわけだ。

ナット しかも私たちディレクターは、マルチもいいところで、クリエイティブな作業だけじゃなく、依然としてプロジェクト・マネージメントもこなしていたから、大忙しだった。でもプロジェクトが予定より長引いた時に、クライアントに追加料金を催促するだけの、マネージメントの経験が欠けていたのよね。

フレッド この時はもう、マーク、リチャード、ロズ、イアン、アン、ヘンキというスタッフがいて、僕ら3人だけじゃなかったからね。にもかかわらず、ビジネス面をケアできる腕前を、まだ持ち合わせていなかったんだ。最悪だったのは、どうやって新しい仕事をとってくるかという戦略を、まったく考えていなかったこと。ただ座って電話が鳴るのを待っていたんだから。

ナット ついに、破産かってところまで行ったの。みんなに支払うお金が、あと1ヶ月分しかなかった。あれは2004年の9月頃だったわ。そこでみんなを集めて状況を説明した。こうはなりたくなかったけど、あと1ヶ月しか猶予がないのって。

フレッド あの時、僕は、レモン・ジェリーの2枚目のアルバム制作で留守にしていたんだけど、ナットから連絡をもらってびっくりして、すぐに飛んで帰った。危機的状況の緊急招集だった。そして、帳簿を見直したけど状況は芳しくないと、みんなに告げた。僕らはコンピューターの画面から顔をあげて、外の世界に目を向けることを怠り過ぎていた。ドットコム・ブームが過ぎ去り、気づけば周りにはエアサイドのライバルがたくさん出現していた。僕らが配慮してきたようなユーザー体験の重要性に、誰もが気づき始め、状況は厳しくなるし、予算はますます低くなるし。しかもクライアントの要求は高くなる一方で、よりインタラクティブに、より充実したコンテンツを、何もかも、もっともっと、という具合でね。依然として僕らは主にウェブデザイン会社として動いていたけど、それが徐々にエアサイドを蝕んでいたんだ。

Growing Pains

成長期の苦しみ

Alex Everyone was very supportive. I remember Richard saying, "Well Airside isn't going bust".

Richard I thought, I'm not going to let this happen, because this is the best job I've ever had. I'd been made redundant twice before, and I felt willing to work for less money or for free for a while if I could stay at Airside. At the same time it was a good strategy, because everyone realised they had to pull together and do something about it.

Fred It was one of the key points when Airside became a lot more than just a bunch of individuals. Everyone really stepped up to the plate.

Nat Creative Review had just come out and there was an article by Adrian Shaughnessy, talking about how broad the graphic design industry had become, which featured a picture of one of our dotcom characters. He was very complimentary about what we were doing, and I thought, we can't be getting press like this at the same time as going bust. So we took him out for lunch. He then did a day of consultancy for us, which was a turning point. He said, are the three of you doing everything? You have to split it. One of you has to be Managing Director, one Creative Director, one Executive Creative Director, you've got to have a project manager and so on. We didn't know any of this stuff at that point. We met up with Tom Roope at Tomato who was really helpful and told us that everyone was struggling a bit. We started to leave our basement and meet other people and ask them how they made it work.

Fred None of us had wanted to take responsibility for the hardcore business side of things. You didn't want to learn all that boring stuff. Famously, BT called us up once about a job and we didn't even bother calling them back. We thought they were too corporate for us. That sums up our new business policy back then.

Alex We had this bizarre notion, which I think is common amongst designers, of taking pride at being bad at business.

Adrian Shaughnessy I tried to show them that you can apply the basic logic of business without losing creative and personal integrity. When you go bust, you lose a lot more than your integrity, so it's best to avoid bankruptcy if you can help it. It was obvious to me that they were smart people so helping them was easy. I remember being nervous

27

28

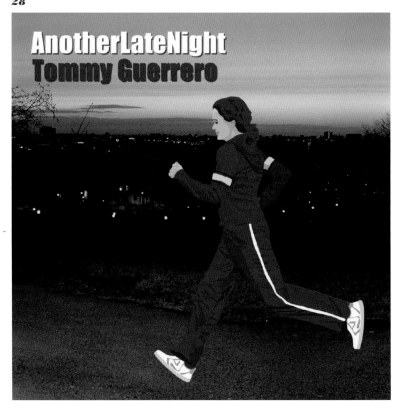

アレックス　みんなとても協力的だった。リチャードは「エアサイドは破産なんかしないさ」と言ってくれた。

リチャード　僕は破産なんかさせるもんかと思った。だって今までで最高の職場だったからね。過去に2度ほど解雇された経験があるけど、エアサイドで働けるなら、給料が減ņったって、あるいはしばらくの間お金が貰えなくたって構わないって思ってた。結果として、この事態は良かったと思う。みんなが、力を合わせて何かしなければ、と気持ちをひとつにしたからね。

フレッド　エアサイドが「個人の集まり」から、「ひとつの大きなチーム」へとステップアップを遂げた、重要な地点のひとつだった。

ナット　その頃ちょうどクリエイティブ・レビュー誌が発売されて、エイドリアン・ショーネシーの記事が載ったの。グラフィックデザインの世界がどれほど多様になっているかについて書かれた記事で、私たちのドットコム・キャラクターのひとつが写真入りで取り上げられていた。彼は私たちの活動をすごく褒めてくれていて、そこで思ったの。こんな風に取り上げてくれる人がいるのに、破産とか言ってる場合じゃないって。そこで彼をランチに連れ出して、一日かけて私たちのコンサルタントをしてもらった。あれは重要な転機だったわ。彼はこう言ったわ、「3人で全部やってるの？ だったら仕事を分けなきゃ。一人はマネージメント・ディレクター、一人はクリエイティブ・ディレクター、あとの一人はエグゼクティブ・クリエイティブ・ディレクター。それにプロジェクト・マネージャーなんかも必要だね」。こうした事を、私たちはまるで何も知らなかった。トマトのトム・

ループにも会いに行って、すごく助けてもらったわ。みんなこういう風に苦労を経験するんだって、教えてもらって。地下のスタジオにこもってないで、外の人たちと会い、彼らがどうやって仕事をやりくりしてきたのか、話を聞かせてもらったの。

フレッド　僕らは3人とも、ハードなビジネス面での責任は担いたくなかった。面倒なことがみんな苦手でね。そんな状態だったから、ある時BTが仕事の件で連絡をくれたのに、誰一人かけ直さなかったことがあった。僕らにはお堅い大手は不向きだと判断してね。これが当時の新規ビジネスポリシーを物語っているよ。

アレックス　デザイナーにはありがちだと思うけど、ビジネスに長けていないことにプライドを持つという、へんな思い込みがあったと思う。

that I might be taking them away from what they did best – freewheeling creativity and intelligent self-initiated projects. I felt it was important that they kept that side of what they did.

Fred You think you know what you're doing. When you start out, you think all you've got to do is not sell out, stick it to the bad guys and only trust the good guys and you'll be okay. When you're seventeen years old things are black and white – you won't do this, you won't do that.

Nat It was just that we were still thinking like seventeen year olds when we were in our thirties.

Fred We had always thought, "We never started this to be good at business, we want to have fun." Now came the point that we had to step up and take responsibility for running a company, and get our heads round the notion of these basic business realities.

Alex We had each gone off on a long holiday earlier in the year as we were exhausted. I was about to head off and I remember Nat saying, there won't be an Airside for you to come back to. But it was really important for us to take a breather. Nat and Fred had a three month break, then I went round the world on my credit card, and it gave us all a new perspective. We talked things over once we got back and calmed down.

Fred Dialogue was really important. We talked to everyone in the company and there was such enthusiasm and support. No one went off and looked for a new job – there was a lot of trust. We really responded to that. If there'd been a different reaction, the company wouldn't have been worth saving.

Alex Airside was definitely rescued by its component parts.

Fred Everyone enjoyed working in the space and doing what we did, so we found a way to make it work. And that way was advertising.

27–30 *Another Late Night* CD and LP covers, 2003

「アナザー・レイト・ナイト」 CD・LPジャケット 2003

29

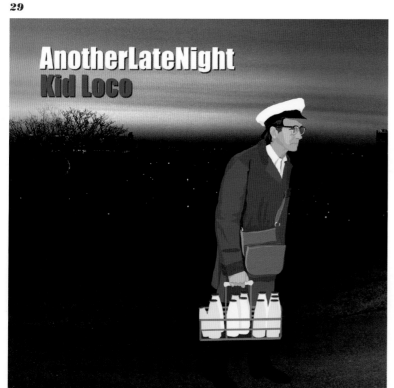

30

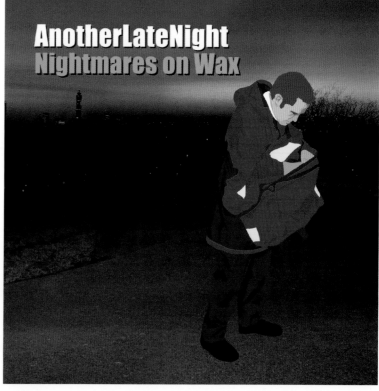

エイドリアン・ショーネシー 創造性や個人の誠意を保ちながら、ビジネスの基本的なロジックを応用することは可能だと伝えたんだ。破産となると、誠意以上のものを失うことになるから、出来ればそこは避けた方がいい。彼らは見るからに切れ者だったから、手助けするのは簡単だった。彼らが力を注いできた自由奔放な創作と知的な自主プロジェクトに、僕のアドバイスが水を差すことになるんじゃないかと不安になったのを憶えているよ。彼らの自由で知的な側面を持ち続けることは重要だと感じていたからね。

フレッド 自分たちが何をやっているのか、ちゃんと把握してるつもりだった。駆け出しの頃は、心だけは売り渡すまいと思う。悪いヤツらには文句を言って、良い人たちとだけ信用関係を築けば、OKだって。17歳の頃は、白黒はっきりしてただろう？ これはやらない、あれもやらないって。

ナット 私たちは30代だったけど、心はまだ17歳のままだったってことね。

フレッド 僕らは「ビジネスで成功するためじゃなく、楽しみたくてやっているんだ」っていつも思ってたのに、ここへ来て一歩前進して、会社経営の責任を持ち、ビジネスの現状に目を向けざるを得なくなった。

アレックス 僕らはヘトヘトだったから、その年のはじめにそれぞれ長期休暇をとっていたんだ。僕が出かける時、ナットが「戻ってきても、もうエアサイドはないかもしれないわよ」って。でもこの休暇が大いに功を奏した。まずナットとフレッドが3ヶ月休んで、それから僕はクレジットカードで世界を旅した。おかげで新たな視野が開けたよ。旅から戻って落ち着いたところで、みんなで腰を据えて話し合った。

フレッド 人と対話することは本当に大事だよ。会社のメンバーひとりひとりと話したんだけど、みんなやる気とサポート精神に満ちあふれてた。誰ひとりエアサイドを離れて職探しなんかしなかった。彼らの寄せてくれた絶大な信頼があったからこそ、僕たちはそれに報いることができたんだと思う。みんなの反応が違っていたら、この会社を救う価値がなかったかもしれないからね。

アレックス まさしく、エアサイドは担い手たちに救われたんだ。

フレッド みんなエアサイドで働くことを楽しんで、いい結果を出してきたからこそ、なんとか打開策を見つけたいと思った。そこで見えてきたのが、広告だった。

MOVING INTO ADVERTISING

広告の世界へ

Nat So we had found ourselves in the position where we didn't have any choice but to bite the bullet and move into advertising. We'd always said that we wouldn't, and we were really, really worried about making that move. Airside had been very anti-advertising until then. We had huge discussions around the table about whether or not to do it, so after much debate we gave ourselves six months to try it out and see if we could make it work without any big compromises. We had lots of advertising contacts through Alex's friends working at agencies, and we felt we could leverage the interest in Lemon Jelly to get some work out of them.

Alex We always liked that Bill Hicks quote: "By the way, if anyone here is in advertising or marketing... kill yourself." It's a valid point of view. But things weren't that simple.

Fred We'd already done idents and stings for MTV, which were practically advertising anyway; what difference would it make if you stuck a different brand on it?

Alex It was time to capitalise on all the work we had done and the reputation we had achieved over the last five years. All these potential clients knew about us: they loved Lemon Jelly and Airside, or they were members of the T-Shirt Club or had been to *Impotent Fury*.

Fred We went in to meet various agencies with the Lemon Jelly work, particularly the *Nice Weather For Ducks* video, and the recep-

tion to our stuff was very positive. We realised we had built a reputation and they wanted to work with us, rather than the other way round.

Alex The *Ducks* video was quite influential at the time: the whole aesthetic and atmosphere of that piece of animation subsequently popped up a lot in other places. We saw at least one ad which had the same storyboard as *Ducks*. We took it as a compliment!

Nat In the first three or four months after nearly going under, we restructured the company, hired a project manager, and sorted out a strategy for getting new business. We divided up our responsibilities and allocated job titles: I became Managing Director, Alex was Creative Director and

ナット つまり、グッと堪えて広告の世界に踏み入るほか、選択の余地がなかったのよ。でも、それまで広告なんて絶対にやらないと公言して、実際にやっていなかったから、この方針転換はものすごく不安だった。エアサイドは、ずっとアンチ広告の精神でやってきたから。みんなで大討論会を開いて、本当にこの方向に進むべきかどうか協議した結果、とりあえず半年間、大きな妥協を強いられることなくやっていけるかどうか試してみようってことになったの。代理店で働くアレックスの友達を通じて広告業界のツテはたくさんあったし、レモン・ジェリーに興味のある人たちからも、仕事をもらえるかもしれないと考えたわ。

アレックス 僕らはそれまで、まさにビル・ヒックスが言うところの「ところで、この中に広告かマーケティングの関係者がいたら…くたばっちまえ」って考えの持ち主だった。ある意味正論だけど、物事はそう単純ではなかったんだ。

フレッド 僕らはすでにMTVのIDや短い番組宣伝を作っていて、実際には広告に携わっていたわけだから、他社とも仕事したところで今更何が変わるんだ、という気持ちもあった。

アレックス 過去5年間に僕らが得た評価や業績を、資本に換える時が来ていたんだと思う。クライアントになりうる企業は、みんな僕らのことを知っていたからね。レモン・ジェリーとエアサイドを気に入ってくれていた人たちや、Tシャツクラブのメンバーになってくれた人、インポテント・フューリーの常連たちもいた。

フレッド レモン・ジェリーの作品を持参していろんな代理店を回ったけど、軒並み反応が良かった。「ナイス・ウェザー・フォー・ダックス（以下ダックス）」のビデオは特にね。まったく知られていないかと思ったら、僕らの評価はすでに確立していて、みんな僕らと仕事をしたがっていたんだ。

アレックス 「ダックス」のMVはすごく影響力があって、あのアニメーションの持つ美しい世界観や雰囲気を真似た作品を、後にあちこちで目にするようになった。「ダックス」と同じ絵コンテで作られた広告を、少なくともひとつは見かけたよ。まぁ、賛辞だと受け取ったけどね！

ナット 低迷期に入ってから最初の3〜4ヶ月は、会社の再編に費やしたわ。プロジェクト・マネージャーを雇い、新規ビジネス獲得の戦略を練った。責任を分け合って、互いの役割を決めた結果、私はマネージング・ディレクターに、アレックスはクリエイティブ・ディレクターに、フレッドはエグゼクティブ・クリエイティブ・ディレクターに就任したの。それから3人で広告代理店に出向いて、オイル・ファクトリーという代理店と仕事を始めることにした。過去の態度を改めて、次の局面に進む心の準備はできていたわ。

Moving Into Advertising

広告の世界へ

Fred Executive Creative Director. The three of us went out to meet the ad agencies and we got an agent, Oil Factory. We cleaned up our act and we were ready to enter the next phase.

——————— **Alex** Before, the directors were doing the IT, HR, the design work and everything else under the sun. But we started to delegate and got to a point where we could write our own very specific job descriptions which made life much more enjoyable. And the advertising work started coming through the door; pretty quickly we were directing TV commercials and creating illustrations for billboards.

——————— **Nat** And we've never looked back. Halfway through our six-month trial, we realised we'd been enjoying ourselves, and had worked with some very creative people who gave us real opportunities. We enjoyed the fact that our parents saw our work on TV and finally understood what we did.

——————— **Richard** Before that point, Airside had been a bit weird and old-fashioned about ad work, thinking it wasn't us. Then very rapidly it started happening.

——————— **Nat** The first advertising job we got was an ad for Surf, commissioned by BBH, and we realised how much creativity was involved in the work.

SURF

——————— **Richard** The Surf campaign featured these typically odd characters. There were several posters that went up on bus shelters, and Alex and I directed five TV animated ads – two for Britain and three for the US. It involved a simple idea with several basic rules, and we were very strict about sticking to those rules. When you work for clients like agencies and they have big clients like Unilever, it's hard to stick to your guns. We were really good with the Surf work at fighting for what we wanted it to be. They have an acronym in advertising, JFDI – just fucking do it. You go to a meeting with ideas, and the agency can often turn around and say, "Just make it how we want it." You see animated ads on TV which could be much stronger, and you can tell that the work has been compromised because the client has intervened and watered down the idea. With this, we were

quite ballsy. One of our rules was that in the world of Surf that we were creating, none of the animals had noses. This was really important, and when we were pitching for it we drew characters that weren't in the script just to get the point across – for example, we drew an elephant without a trunk. One of the scripts was about a bird, so we drew this bird without a beak. The agency kept asking us to give the bird a beak, just to see what it would look like, but we kept saying no. I think they thought we were going to give in, but we stuck to our rule. It's what makes the ad unique – it gives the bird a specific characteristic that people remember.

——————— **Alex** We realised that the point of difference for us when producing this animation was not to behave like a standard animation house, which would do whatever the client said. The result was this incredibly unique ad that didn't look like anyone else's. It was a great showcase for us.

——————— **Fred** Airside had become much more than the three of us – there were some other very talented people here making great work. Nat, Alex and I were able to steer it and facilitate it, but the whole company was growing together, and I saw

——————— **アレックス**　それまで、僕らディレクターは、ITから人事、デザインまで一切合切をこなしてきたけど、ここで役割を明確にして、僕らの生活がより楽しくなるような独自の役職を作ろうって結論に至った。それから広告の仕事が舞い込んでくるようになって、まもなくテレビCMの演出や、掲示板広告のイラスト制作を手がけるようになった。

——————— **ナット**　以後、後ろを振り返ることは1度もなかったわ。半年の試用期間も半ばにして、自分たちが広告の仕事を楽しんでいることに気づいたの。本当に素晴らしい機会を与えてくれる、すごくクリエイティブな人たちと仕事ができたし。それに、自分たちの仕事を、親にテレビで見てもらえたのもよかったわ。私たちが何をしているのか、ようやくわかってもらえたんだもの。

——————— **アレックス**　自分たちの作品を、掲示板やバスの車体で見かけては興奮したね。

——————— **リチャード**　それまでエアサイドは、広告に対してちょっと斜に構えた古風な考えを持っていて、僕たち向きじゃないと思っていた。でも、それから一気に広告の仕事が始まったよね。

——————— **ナット**　最初に手がけた広告は、BBHから依頼されたサーフの広告で、制作にどれほど創造性が求められるかを認識した仕事だったわ。

サーフ

——————— **リチャード**　サーフのキャンペーンには、エアサイド独特の奇妙なキャラクターを登場させた。バスの待合所に貼られるポスターを何種類か作り、アレックスと僕で5本のアニメーションCMをディレクションしたんだ。2本を英国、3本をアメリカ向けにね。アイデアはとてもシンプルで、僕らは守るべき基本ルールをいくつか設けた。代理店を相手に仕事をする時、とくに彼らのクライアントがユニリーバのような巨大企業だと、アイデアを曲げずに貫くのはかなり難しいことだろ？でもサーフの仕事に関しては、そこを守り抜くために、よく戦ったよ。広告業界にはこんな略語があるんだ。「JFDI（just fucking do it）つべこべ言わずにとにかくやれ！」って。例えばアイデアを持参してミーティングに行っても、代理店は「いいから俺たちの言う通りにやれ」って言うのさ。テレビで流れているアニメーションCMを見てると、もっとインパクトのあるものが作れたのにって思う作品があるけど、それはクライアントが介入してアイデアを薄めてしまったんだなっていうのがわかる。この点に関して、僕らはかなり根性があったんだ。僕らが創り出すサーフの世界にいる動物たちには鼻が無い、というのがルールのひとつだった。これはとても重要なポイントだったから、コンペの時に充分理解してもらえるよう、スクリプトには載っていない動物まで描

いて、見本を見せたんだ。例えば鼻の無いゾウとかね。スクリプトの中に、鳥が出てくるものがあったから、くちばしの無い鳥も描いた。代理店は、くちばしのある鳥も取りあえず見せてくれって、しつこく言ってきたけど、僕らは断固拒否した。むこうは僕らが折れると思っていたみたいだけど、こっちはルールを貫き通したんだ。こうして、ユニークな広告が出来上がった。あの独特な鳥の姿は、1度目にしたら忘れられないからね。

——————— **アレックス**　このアニメーションを作ったとき、普通のアニメーション制作会社のように、クライアントの言いなりになって何でも作るのは、エアサイドらしくないと気づいたんだ。結果的に、ユニークで他には類を見ないものができて、僕らを知ってもらうのにうってつけの作品になった。

——————— **フレッド**　エアサイドはすでに、僕ら3人の枠を超えて、素晴らしい作品を生み出す多才な仲間たちが集っていた。ナットとアレックスと僕は、舵取りや手助けはしたけど、今や会社全体が同時に成長していて、ヘンキとリチャードが自らの創造性を発揮して楽しく働き始めていた。こうして、エアサイドで働く仲間たちが、最高の仕事ができる余裕と自由を確保することが、突如として僕らの最も重要な使命になった。

——————— **ナット**　アニメーションや広告のディレクションを始めたのは、結果的に自然な流れだったと思う。以前スタジオの隣にあるタンデムという制作会社と一緒に、レモン・ジェリー

2

Henki and Richard having a lot of fun experimenting with their creativity. Suddenly the most important part of our job was making sure the people who worked for us had the head space and the freedom to create the best work they could.

——————————— **Nat** The move into directing animation and ads felt quite smooth. After we worked with Tandem, the production company next door to our studio, on the Lemon Jelly *Ducks* video, we realised the animation process wasn't rocket science. Alex in particular can draw brilliantly, and found that he had an undiscovered talent for storyboarding. He's got the kind of brain that can work out camera angles and fully visualise scenes. Once you've got a good storyboard in place everything else is easy. Realising that was the key for us.

——————————— **Richard** Nearly going bust had changed the company outlook, not in terms of the creative structure and the spirit, but in terms of being proactive about getting work, and looking at where we were going and what we really wanted.

の「ダックス」のMVを作っていたから、アニメーション制作が難解なプロセスでないこともわかっていた。特にアレックスは絵を描くのが抜群に上手くて、絵コンテづくりの才能があるってことが発覚したのよ。彼はカメラアングルを考慮して、映像を思い描くことが出来る人なの。絵コンテさえきちんと準備できれば、後は簡単。それに気づいたことが、大きかったわね。

——————————— **リチャード**　破産寸前のところまで行って、会社のものの見方が変わった。クリエイティブの構造や精神は変わらなかったけど、自主的に仕事をもらいに行くようになって、自分たちの方向性や本当に必要としているものにじっくり目を向けるようになったんだ。

Previous spread:
前頁

1 Sketches for *Nice Weather For Ducks* music promo, 2002

MV「ナイス・ウェザー・フォー・ダックス」スケッチ
2002

2 Surf *Babysick* poster, 2004

サーフ洗剤「ベイビー・シック」ポスター　2004

Moving Into Advertising

広告の世界へ

3

3 Surf posters for USA, 2003

オール洗剤 (サーフ USA)
ポスター 2003

4 Development work for Surf *Bird* animation, 2003

サーフ洗剤 CM「鳥」篇
アニメーション制作過程
2003

5 Surf posters for UK, 2003

サーフ洗剤 (UK)
ポスター 2003

4

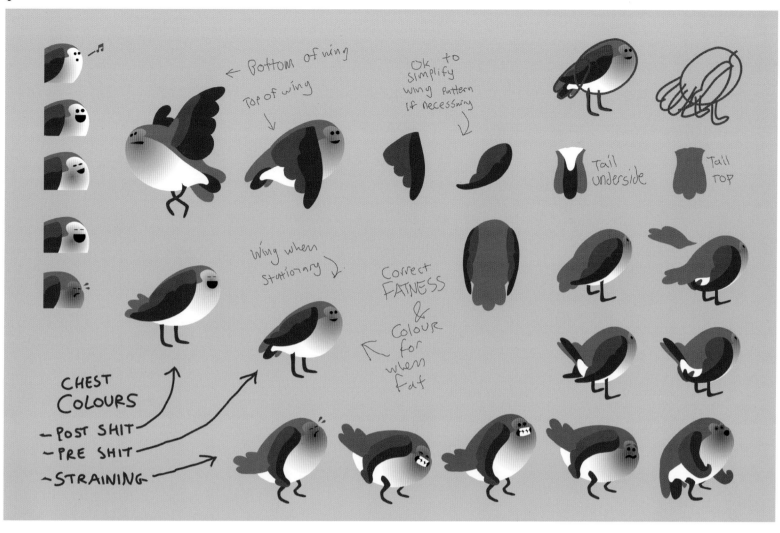

5

6

7

8

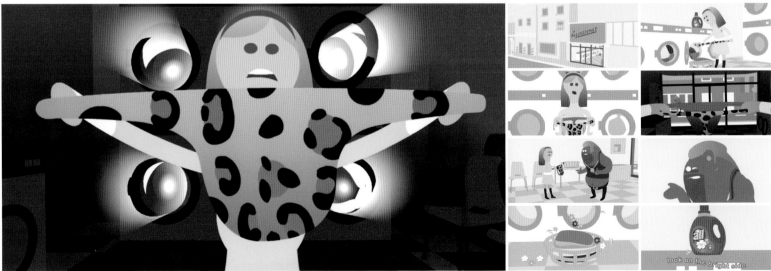

9

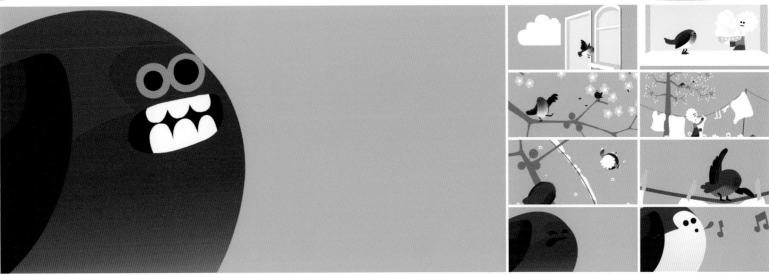

10

PANASONIC

パナソニック

Airside by Airside

エアサイド バイ エアサイド

Moving Into Advertising

広告の世界へ

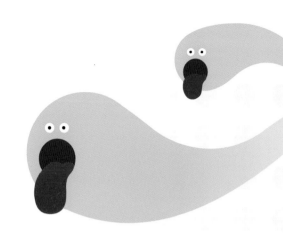

Job name: Panasonic phone launch
Client: Panasonic Japan
Agency: Xenn/Dream Ranch, Tokyo
Media: Moving image, product design

Summary: A limited edition gift set for the launch of a new Panasonic mobile handset in Japan including a specially composed animated ringtone and merchandise.

——————— In Japan, Airside projects can become even more eccentric and hedonistic than usual – if that's possible. Thanks to the shared enthusiasm between Airsiders and their Japanese contemporaries for colour-saturated pop culture and cute Manga-like characters with emotional personalities running high into the surreal stakes, this project offered Airside a chance to indulge its cute character aesthetic at fever pitch. Dream Ranch in Tokyo asked Airside to create designs for a limited edition Panasonic phone being launched in Japan only, so Airside duly came up with kaleidoscopic creatures to appear on the phone covers and as an animated ringtone, with original music composed by Fred. As the client offered complete creative freedom, the storyboards featured an angry giant Cyclops, a pooing monkey and a happy hand. Anywhere else this may seem weird, but in the world of Airside and its Japanese fans, it seems entirely logical. **FS**

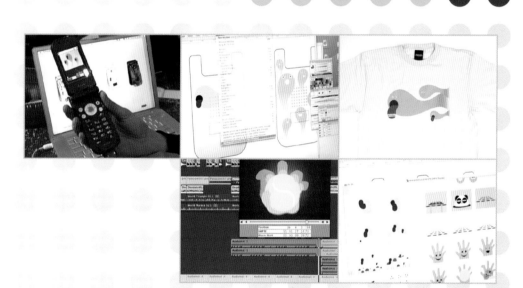

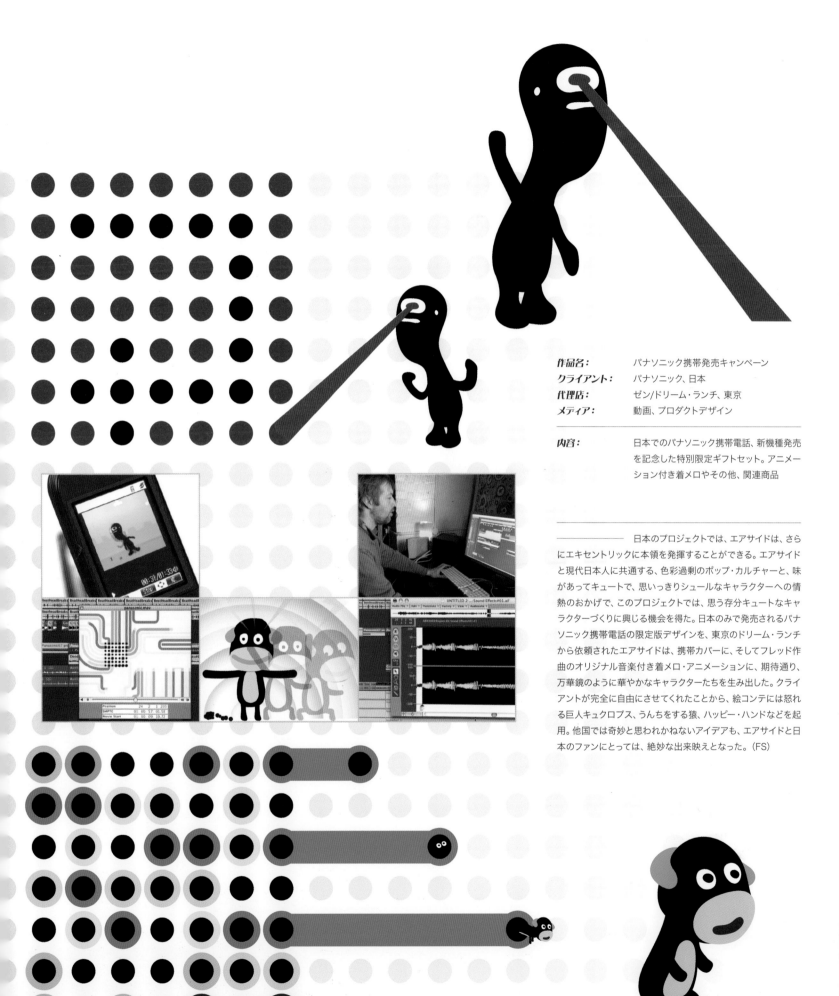

作品名： パナソニック携帯発売キャンペーン
クライアント： パナソニック、日本
代理店： ゼン/ドリーム・ランチ、東京
メディア： 動画、プロダクトデザイン

内容： 日本でのパナソニック携帯電話、新機種発売
を記念した特別限定ギフトセット。アニメー
ション付き着メロやその他、関連商品

日本のプロジェクトでは、エアサイドは、さらにエキセントリックに本領を発揮することができる。エアサイドと現代日本人に共通する、色彩過剰のポップ・カルチャーと、味があってキュートで、思いっきりシュールなキャラクターへの情熱のおかげで、このプロジェクトでは、思う存分キュートなキャラクターづくりに興じる機会を得た。日本のみで発売されるパナソニック携帯電話の限定版デザインを、東京のドリーム・ランチから依頼されたエアサイドは、携帯カバーに、そしてフレッド作曲のオリジナル音楽付き着メロ・アニメーションに、期待通り、万華鏡のように華やかなキャラクターたちを生み出した。クライアントが完全に自由にさせてくれたことから、絵コンテには怒れる巨人キュクロプス、うんちをする猿、ハッピー・ハンドなどを起用。他国では奇妙と思われかねないアイデアも、エアサイドと日本のファンにとっては、絶妙な出来映えとなった。(FS)

Moving Into Advertising
広告の世界へ

ORANGE

オレンジ

Job name:	Orange 'Playlist' bumpers	作品名：	オレンジ「プレイリスト」番組ID
Client:	Orange	クライアント：	オレンジ
Agency:	Mother London	代理店：	マザー、ロンドン
Media:	Moving image	メディア：	動画
Awards:	Design Week Awards 2006 – TV/Film/ Video Graphics and Best of Show	受賞歴：	デザイン・ウィーク 2006／テレビ／映像／ ビデオ・グラフィック部門、および総合部門 ベスト・オブ・ショー

Summary: Sponsored bumpers shown during ITV's music video show, Playlist.

内容： ITVのミュージックビデオ番組「プレイリスト」 の中で流れるスポンサーCM

———— Surreal humour regularly appears in Airside's work, and this animated sequence for Orange is a perfect demonstration of their slightly strange take on what constitutes amusing entertainment. The client, Orange, wanted a series of short commercial bumpers for Playlist, an ITV music show it was sponsoring. The aim was to connect the Orange brand to music, and the creative agency, Mother, approached Airside with a script about singing farmyard animals. In just a week, the team drew, storyboarded and animated six commercials. The singing, the characters, the animated movement, the idea itself - all combined to create an original and successful piece of work with that proven Airside deftness of making people laugh. It went on to scoop various prestigious awards. **FS**

———— シュールでユーモラスな作品が得意なエア サイド。このオレンジのアニメーションIDでは、そんな彼らの一 風変わった持ち味が、立派なエンターテイメントになり得るこ とを実証した。ITVの音楽番組「プレイリスト」のスポンサーを するクライアントのオレンジは、番組の合間に流す短いCMが 何本か欲しいと考えていた。狙いは、オレンジというブランドと 音楽を繋げること。代理店のマザーは、歌を唄う農場の動物た ちをテーマに脚本を作成し、エアサイドに制作を依頼。それか らわずか1週間で、チームはストーリーボードを作り、6本のア ニメーションCMを仕上げた。歌、キャラクター、アニメーショ ン、アイデアそのもの、すべてが合致してオリジナルな傑作が完 成し、エアサイドの笑いのセンスが証明された。この作品でエア サイドは、様々な権威ある賞を獲得している。(FS)

Moving Into Advertising

広告の世界へ

Moving Into Advertising

広告の世界へ

ORANGE

Henki We were all working on the Lemon Jelly animations for '64–'95 when we got a very last-minute call from Mother asking if we could squeeze in a project to do six animated idents for Orange, which was sponsoring a TV show called *Orange Playlist*. We had a spare week, so we thought we'd go for it. We gave our illustration portfolio to the writer, Al MacCuish, and as soon as he saw a picture of a bear in a tree, he decided that was the style he wanted. It was my drawing, so I was chosen to draw the rest of the characters. It was crazy because it was so quick; with only a week to deliver the finished product, we had a day to draw the characters, storyboard and animate them, so there was no messing around. Everyone loved the end result; people were really engaged and laughing out loud when they watched them. We submitted them for the Design Week Awards and they won the category for best TV idents and also scooped the awards' overall prize for Best of Show.

Al MacCuish It was a ridiculously short timescale and very little money in the end, so we were so delighted with what Airside produced; they really over-delivered. With those constraints you're rarely able to get everything you want, and Henki worked at breakneck speed to get all the work done. Our idea had been to do something unconventional, and we thought we'd create a world populated by farmyard animals which sang famous music. We couldn't afford the original recordings of *Ace of Spades* or *Dy-na-mi-tee*, but that might not have been as funny as housewives and navvies with strangulated voices singing them instead. As soon as we began thinking about how we would execute them, Airside popped to mind and it was clear very quickly that this sense of humour would appeal to them. I'd known Alex socially a little, but I'd also been a big fan of their work and of Lemon Jelly. It was cool that they had that music side to them, given that this was a sponsorship of a music show. I'd always liked their aesthetic. We went and talked to Alex and Henki, and straight away our conversation was just very funny. We were competing over what sounds would be coming out of a cow's mouth. Laughter is always a good sign when you're trying to create something that will be different or unusual. Many design groups can be very serious and contemplative about things, whereas there's a real energy about Airside and it always feels very positive. When you look at the work it's always got that positivity: it's upbeat, kooky and clever. Other companies fall into the trap of taking things too seriously, and I don't think these guys do. They just try to express themselves using pencils and their computers.

Alex It was exciting to throw ourselves into this new work, and fortunately most of the stuff we worked on had really good scripts. When something like Orange came along, the script was already genius. Of course, some jobs weren't and we struggled with that. We're more willing to rewrite scripts now – we're better at questioning and negotiating with the agency, which wasn't necessarily the case in the early days.

Fred Creatively, the work was good. With people like Mother and BBH advertising had improved a lot and we hadn't really noticed. Before, it was all very Eighties in a bad way – not up our street at all. If we'd gone in earlier we wouldn't have been ready for it.

オレンジ

ヘンキ みんなでレモン・ジェリーの「'64–'95」のアニメーションに取りかかっていた時、代理店マザーから土壇場で連絡があって「オレンジ・プレイリスト」というテレビショーのスポンサーをしている携帯電話会社オレンジのために、アニメーションIDを6本作ってもらえないかって言われたんだ。納品まで1週間しかなかったけど、やってみようってことになった。それで僕らのイラストレーション・ポートフォリオをライターのアル・マクイッシュに送ったところ、木に登るクマの絵を見てすぐに、これが僕の求めていたスタイルだ！って。そのイラストは僕のだったから、他のキャラクターも僕が描くことになった。速効性が勝負のクレイジーな仕事だったね。1日でキャラクターを仕上げて絵コンテを描いて、さらにアニメーションを完成させるまでたったの1週間だからね。もたもたしている暇はなかった。結果、誰もが満足のいくものが仕上がって、みんなに見せたら夢中になって大笑いしたよ。この作品は、デザイン・ウィーク・アワードに出品して、最優秀テレビID賞をはじめ、総合部門でもベスト・イン・ショーを受賞したんだ。

アル・マクイッシュ あり得ないくらい時間も予算もない中で、エアサイドが制作してくれたものには、本当に感激したよ。まったく期待以上のものを仕上げてくれた。あれだけ制約がある中で、満足いくものを得られることなど滅多にないのに、ヘンキはそれを猛スピードでやってのけた。型にはまらないものを作ろう、というのが元々のアイデアで、有名な音楽を口ずさむ家畜が暮らす世界を作ってみたいと思っていたんだ。エース・オブ・スペイズやミス・ダイナマイトのオリジナルを使えるだけの経済的余裕はなかったけど、だったら主婦や労働者たちの真似るダミ声の方が、よっぽど面白いんじゃないかと思いついた。じゃあ、このアイデアをどうやって実行しようかと考えたら、エアサイドのことが思い浮かんだ。このユーモアのセンスは、彼らなら絶対気に入るぞって。アレックスとは多少面識があったけど、彼らの作品や、レモン・ジェリーの大ファンだったんだ。音楽番組のスポンサーCMであることを考えると、エアサイドに音楽面のバックアップがあるのは強みだったし、彼らの美的センスがとにかく好きでね。そんなわけでアレックスとヘンキに会いに行ったところ、すぐに打ち解けて盛り上がったよ。牛の口からどんな音を出すかで激論を交わしてね。これまでにない、独自なものを作ろうという時に、笑いがあるっていうのは良い兆候だ。デザイナーによっては、ものすごく真面目で黙考するタイプの人たちもたくさんいるけど、エアサイドからは、いつもすごくポジティブでリアルなエネルギーが感じられる。どの作品にも、彼らのポジティブさが溢れているだろう？ 陽気で前向きで、馬鹿げていながら気が利いている。深刻になりすぎるという罠に陥る会社もあるけど、エアサイドなら大丈夫。鉛筆とコンピューターを使って、自分たちを表現することにせっせと打ち込んでいる奴らだからね。

アレックス こうやって新しい仕事の世界に飛び込んでいくのは楽しかったし、幸運にも僕らが手がけた作品のスクリプトは、本当に良いものばかりだった。オレンジのスクリプトなんか、初めから抜群だったからね。もちろん時には冴えないのもあって、なんとかしようと格闘したこともある。今なら、迷わず書き直すけどね。初期の頃と比べると、僕らも代理店に疑問を投げかけたり、交渉することに長けてきたから。

フレッド クリエイティブな意味で、あの仕事は良かったね。当時ははっきり意識していなかったけど、マザーやBBHといった代理店の人たちのおかげで、広告はかなり進化してきていたんだ。それまで広告とえば、悪い意味でモロ80年代って感じで、とてもじゃないけどお断りってものばかりだった。その頃広告の仕事を始めていたら、割り切れないままだっただろうね。

Urban music to your phone, with Orange World

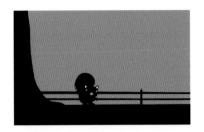   

Soul to your phone, with Orange World

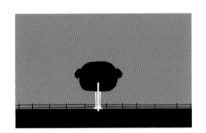  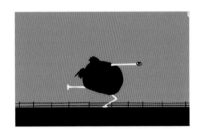 

Rock to your phone, with Orange World

 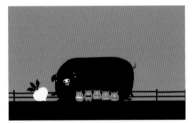  

Urban music to your phone, with Orange World

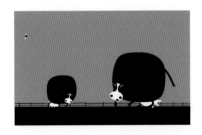  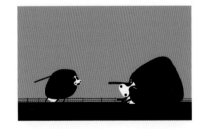 

Soul to your phone, with Orange World

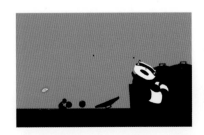   

Rock to your phone, with Orange World

COCA-COLA

コカ・コーラ

Job name:	'Love' – Outdoor print campaign	作品名：	「ラブ」屋外印刷キャンペーン
Client:	Coca-Cola	クライアント：	コカ・コーラ
Agency:	Mother London	代理店：	マザー、ロンドン
Media:	Print	メディア：	印刷物
Awards:	Epica nomination	受賞歴：	エピカ賞ノミネート

Summary:	A summertime refreshment outdoor print campaign.	内容：	夏の清涼飲料水、屋外広告キャンペーン

The classic Coke bottle and its iconic figure presented an aesthetic challenge to Airside: how to give that familiar form a fresh, summery identity to appear in a July poster campaign? Working alongside Yanny Elliott at Mother, Airside produced months of concept work; eventually they paired up two bottles, somehow convinced Coca-Cola to ditch their logo, and in its place wove the word 'Love' in a manner suggestive of a romantic clinch. The concept is completed by the psychedelic burst of rainbow pattern glowing in the background: it's as though the curvy couple are in their first flush of love and everything is rosy. The campaign shows how well their bubbly illustration style translates into large environmental graphics. Aesthetically and emotionally it's very warm, very positive, and very Airside. **FS**

昔ながらのコーラの瓶とお馴染みのロゴマークに、エアサイドがその美学に挑んだ作品。誰もが見慣れたその外観を、7月のポスターキャンペーンにむけて、いかに新鮮で夏らしくみせるか？ マザーのヤニー・エリオットと共に、エアサイドは数ヶ月を費やしコンセプトを作り上げた。2本の瓶を抱き合わせるように配置して、コカ・コーラのロゴを消すようクライアントを説得し、代わりにロマンチックな抱擁を思わせる「ラブ」の文字をあしらった。背景には、サイケデリックに輝く虹を描いて、ついに完成。まるで、曲線美の恋人たちが、たった今恋に落ちて、すべてがバラ色に見える、そんな場面を想起させる。エアサイドの陽気なイラストレーションの魅力が、屋外の大型看板でも充分に発揮されることを証明する、見た目も受ける印象も、和やかで元気な作品となった。（FS）

12

13

14

15

COCA-COLA

Alex I had showed Yanny Elliott, a creative at Mother, the *Ducks* animation at a meeting with all the directors, and from that point on I think they were trying to find a project to work with us on. Up came a brief for a poster campaign for Coca-Cola, which was to incorporate the word 'love'. They'd been working on some artwork, but Yanny thought that it didn't feel lovely enough. He approached Airside, and we went through about five months of concepts exploring how we could enhance the idea.

Yanny Elliott You can collaborate a lot in advertising with very varying results, and it was great being able to work with good people who really understood what they were doing and were totally open to collaborating. I chose them simply because I liked their work, but the fact that they weren't particularly in the advertising world was a good thing. I knew they'd come up with something different. What was really refreshing about working with Airside was their commitment to having the same level of energy at the end of the process that they had at the beginning of it. The tricky thing about the Coca-Cola project was knowing that the client would want the bottle to be as big as possible, so I had to tackle that head-on. I thought Airside's style would be perfect for it, and we ended up with this poster campaign with rainbows sitting behind the Coke bottles. It was a lovely, happy-looking thing, with 'love' written on the bottle; it really communicated that spirit. When you're thinking of doing outdoor graphics like posters and ad shells, you want something to really zing out from the clutter on the street, and I knew using Airside would give us that, because their style is very distinctive and simple and quite iconic.

Alex The end result is so simple and so Airside – it's really like the Lemon Jelly work. After all the concepts and the brainstorming and the big ideas around the table, one day Richard just sat down and drew that rainbow illustration. There was a hell of a lot of development to get there, although it's never wasted work – all the good un-used stuff goes into the calendar.

Yanny I always found Airside were open to anything. They won't necessarily have a solution there and then; they'll listen to what the problem is, then really look at that in a unique way and do what they do. They try and do something different for each job. And they're very flexible – if one route isn't working you can move them to a different area.

コカ・コーラ

アレックス ある時、僕はマザーのクリエイティブディレクターたちの会合で、ヤニー・エリオットに「ダックス」のアニメーションを見せたことがあった。それ以来、僕らと組めるプロジェクトを探してくれていたみたいなんだ。そうして連絡をもらったのが、ボトルに「love」の文字を描いた、コカ・コーラのポスター・キャンペーンの話だった。マザーはすでにアートワークを作っていたんだけど、ヤニーがいまいちラブリーじゃないと感じていて。それでエアサイドに連絡をしてきて、僕らはアイデアを改善しながら、コンセプト作りに5ヶ月を費やした。

ヤニー・エリオット 広告では、プロジェクトによってたくさんの人とコラボレーションするけど、自分たちの軸足がしっかりしていて、かつコラボレーションに乗り気な人たちと一緒に仕事をするのは最高だったね。僕が彼らを選んだのは、単純に作品が好きだったこともあるけど、彼らが広告業界以外でも仕事をしている点が気に入っていたから。何か違ったアイデアを出してくれるという確信があった。エアサイドと仕事をしていて気持ちがよかったのは、始めから終わりまで一貫して、意欲的な態度で打ち込んでくれたこと。コカ・コーラのプロジェクトで厄介だったのは、クライアントがボトルをできるだけ大きく見せると言ってくるのがわかっていたから、それに真っ向から取り組まなきゃならなかったことかな。その点エアサイドのスタイルはまさにうってつけだった。結局コーク・ボトルの背後に虹を描いたポスターが出来上がった。ボトルには「love」と描かれていて、ラブリーでハッピーな気持ちにしてくれる、まさに愛の伝わる作品になった。ポスターや看板塔のような屋外グラフィックを手がけるとき、雑踏のなかでひときわ目を引くものを作りたいと誰もが思うはずだけど、エアサイドとならそれを実現できると確信していた。彼らのスタイルは独特かつシンプルで、とてもアイコン的だからね。

アレックス 出来上がった作品は、シンプルでエアサイドらしいものになった。レモン・ジェリーのアートワークみたいにね。テーブルを囲んで、コンセプトだのアイデアだのさんざん出し合った後で、ある日リチャードがおもむろにあの虹のイラストを描いたんだ。そこに辿り着くまでにえらく時間がかかったけど、決して無駄ではなかったと思う。採用されなかったけどいい作品は、全部、僕らのカレンダーで紹介できるしね。

ヤニー エアサイドは何事にもオープンなんだよ。必ずしもその場で解決法を見つけ出すのではなく、まず問題に耳を傾けてから、独自の方法で掘り下げて、そしてやるべきことをやる。それぞれの仕事で、いつも新しいことに挑戦しているし、すごく柔軟なんだ。ある方法がダメなら、別な方法を試してみようってね。

KNIT 2 TOGETHER

Fred We were getting offered a lot of commercials, but one of the deals we made with ourselves to justify our move into advertising was to make sure we carried on with the less commercial work we'd been doing in the early days. It was something we felt we needed to be involved in.

Alex *Knit 2 Together* was an exhibition for the Crafts Council, and it was the first time we'd worked with mæ Architects; we worked together on the concept and exhibition design, identity, graphic design and signage. We knitted a poster in Illustrator, and it just took forever. It probably took longer to simulate in Illustrator than it would have taken to actually knit.

ニット・2・トゥギャザー

フレッド こうしてたくさんのコマーシャルのオファーをもらうようになったけど、広告の世界に足を踏み入れるに当たって自分たちに課した約束は、初期の頃に手がけたような非商業的な仕事もちゃんと続けていこう、ということだった。そういった仕事に関わることは、絶対に必要だと、みんなが感じていたから。

アレックス クラフツ・カウンシルの展覧会「ニット・2・トゥギャザー」で、僕らは初めてメイ・アーキテクツと仕事をしたんだ。コンセプトから、展示場のデザイン、ロゴ、グラフィックデザイン、看板まで一緒になって考えた。イラストレーターを使って編み目柄のポスターを制作したんだけど、これがもう永久に終わらない作業で。おそらく本物のニットを編むよりも時間を費やしたと思うよ。

Moving Into Advertising

広告の世界へ

16

17

18

19

GREENPEACE

Nat We were also working with Greenpeace – we respected what they did and it seemed like a natural fit. We'd designed an earlier project to raise awareness of genetically modified milk in the food chain, and later came a campaign to promote the idea of decentralised energy. This was a 72-page booklet and a film to explain the difficult concept of locally produced energy, in which communities use small power stations in a much more efficient way, rather than taking electricity from the national grid. Henki did these beautifully simple diagrams and we animated them in a very pared-down way, with a smattering of humour. We worked with a film production company, and the animations were interspersed with the live action interviews in the film. It was important for us to be able to use our growing animation and directing skills for those sorts of clients too.

グリーンピース

ナット それからグリーンピースとも仕事をしたの。彼らの活動をリスペクトしていたから、自然な流れだったと思う。初期の頃に、遺伝子組み換えの牛乳が環境に与える影響について関心を持ってもらうプロジェクトを、その後、分散型電源とは何かを広めるキャンペーンのデザインを手がけたわ。72ページに及ぶ冊子と映像資料の中では、各地域で小規模な発電所を利用すれば、全国規模の送電設備に頼るよりも、ずっと効率的に電気が使えるっていう、地域発電の難しいコンセプトをわかりやすく説明しているの。ヘンキがすっきりとしたシンプルな図表を作ってくれて、ちょっとユーモアも加えて、無駄のないアニメーションに仕上げたわ。映画制作会社と一緒に作業をして、実写のインタビュー映像の合間にアニメーションを挿入したんだけど、私たちが洗練されたアニメーションと演出技術を提供できるということが、こうしたクライアントとの仕事でも大いに役立ったわ。

20

Moving Into Advertising

広告の世界へ

John Sauven (director of Green-peace) Airside has worked with us several times, but for this campaign, if you went up to anyone in the street and said, "decentralised energy", they wouldn't know what you were talking about. We were starting off with a phrase that didn't mean anything, and talking about very difficult concepts for people to understand. People see a switch and don't give a second thought about where the power comes from, or the use of power stations and grids, so we needed a way to explain the campaign accessibly to people. Airside used very simple diagrams and animated graphics in the film, which made the idea come alive. The result was excellent, and we managed to achieve exactly what we wanted:

many people have commented on how it made the penny drop. I'm full of praise for Airside; the work they did was really spot on. It's important for us to work with people who have empathy for what we're trying to achieve in order to provide that emotive and engaging connection. Greenpeace wouldn't be able to afford a lot of design agencies, so if we're to access design with that level of professionalism, creativity and innovation, it has to be done for free or for a reduced rate, and inevitably that is only going to happen because people support you. We live in a very visual world with so many competing images, and that relentless onslaught is only going to grow, so you've really got to be able to stand out. Airside manages to pursue that really well.

Alex Advertising turned out to be a very exciting way of saving Airside, and we were all really up for it. You should be good at anything you get enthusiastic and excited about. Previously, we'd thought the way to save the company was by getting bigger and more mainstream website jobs, but they bogged us down very quickly. When this came along it was completely liberating in comparison. The way Airside evolved meant that we arrived in the advertising market at exactly the right time. If we'd tried to do it three years previously, we would have been adrift – we wouldn't have had a strong identity, or a way to apply our artwork and ideas to these briefs. When we did arrive, we already had a viewpoint.

ジョン・ソーヴェン エアサイドとグリーンピースは何度か一緒に仕事をしてきた。このキャンペーンを行ったきっかけは、そもそも街行く人に言っても、何のことか理解してもらえない「分散型電源」という難解なコンセプトを、なんとか人々に理解してもらうためだった。実際、人々はスイッチを目にしても、電力がどこからやって来るのか、あるいはどこの発電所や送電所から運ばれてくるのかなんて考えもしない。そこで僕らは、このキャンペーンをもっとわかりやすく説明する必要があると感じていた。映像の中で、エアサイドは非常にシンプルな図表とグラフィックアニメーションを用いて「分散型電源」を実にわかりやすく表現してくれた。出来上がった作品は素晴らしく、このキャンペーンでは期待していた通りの結果を得ることができた。多くの人々から、僕らの主張がやっと理解できたというコメント

をもらったよ。僕はエアサイドを賞賛してやまない。僕らがまさに求めていたものを作ってくれたからね。人々の感情に訴え、関心を引きつけるためには、僕らが目指すことに共感してくれる人と一緒に仕事をすることがとても重要なんだ。グリーンピースは、そもそもデザイン会社に仕事を頼めるほど財力がなく、これほどレベルの高い専門性、創造性、革新性を兼ね備えたデザインを頼むとなれば、ボランティアか、かなりの低予算で手がけてもらうしかない。となると必然的に、僕らを支持してくれる人々と出会った時にのみ、引き受けてもらえる事になる。今の世の中は視覚情報の占める割合が大きく、競争率も高い。次々と容赦なくイメージが氾濫する中で、しっかりと目立たないといけない。エアサイドはその点本当によくやっていると思う。

アレックス 結果的に広告の世界は、エアサイドを救う術として、とにかくエキサイティングな分野だった。興味を引かれることやワクワクすることには、素直になった方がいいからね。はじめは、会社を救うには、規模を拡大して、もっとメジャーなウェブサイト制作の仕事を増やすべきだと勘違いして、すぐに行き詰まった。それに比べて、広告の仕事は、僕らを完全に解放してくれた。エアサイドが進化できたのは、絶妙なタイミングで広告業界に参入できたからだと思う。もし3年早く始めていたら、僕らは見失っていただろうね。これという強いアイデンティティーもなく、僕らのアートワークやアイデアを企業の提示するブリーフにどう応用したらいいかもわからなかっただろう。エアサイド独自の見解を確立してから、広告を始めたのが良かったんだ。

21 *What are we waiting for?* Stills and DVD packaging, Greenpeace, 2006

グリーンピース 短編ドキュメンタリー 「何を待っているの?」 アニメーション/ DVDパッケージ 2006

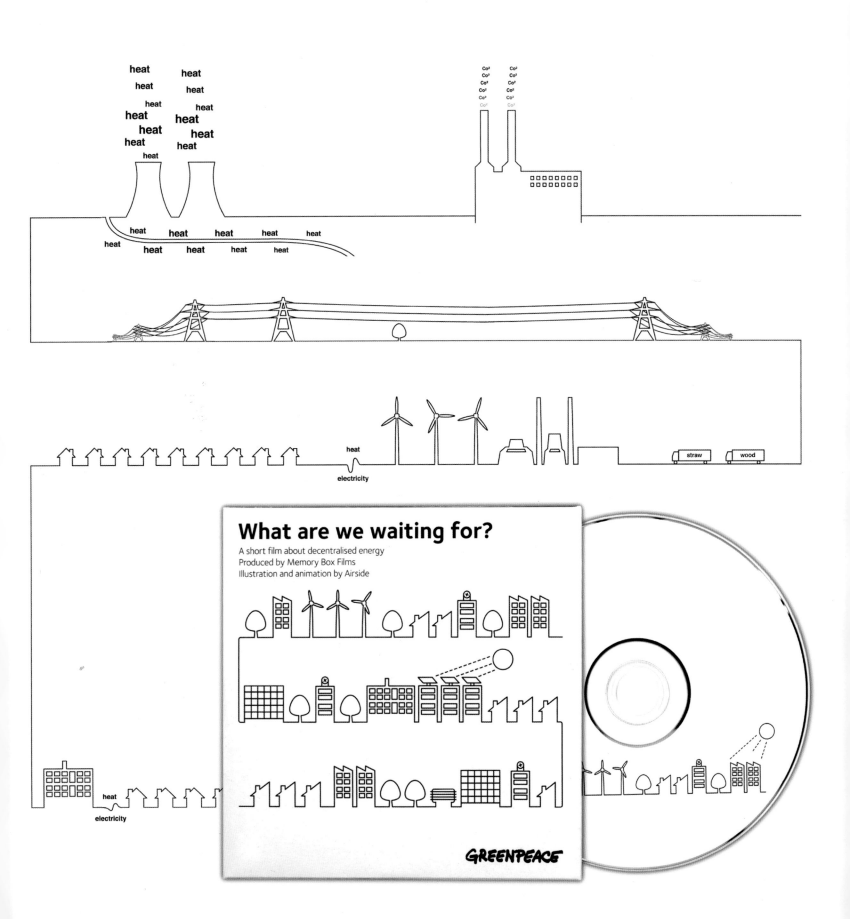

Moving Into Advertising

広告の世界へ

MASTERCARD

マスターカード

Job name:	MasterCard
	Airport Poster Campaign
Client:	MasterCard
Agency:	McCann Erickson, London
Media:	Print
Awards:	HOW 2007
	International Design Award

作品名：	マスターカード、
	空港用ポスターキャンペーン
クライアント：	マスターカード
代理店：	マッキャン・エリクソン、ロンドン
メディア：	印刷物
受賞歴：	HOW 2007
	インターナショナル・デザイン・アワード

Summary: A worldwide illustration project to demonstrate MasterCard's global acceptance.

内容： 世界で通用するマスターカードの、ワールドワイド・イラストレーション・プロジェクト

True to its globe-trotting name, Airside's work has appeared in airports across the world from Sao Paulo to Paris to Delhi, as part of a global MasterCard campaign. These large illustrated billboards, depicting warm, aspirational scenes, are an ideal corollary from the 1940's transport posters that initially triggered Fred's visual aesthetic. Using their trademark vector illustration, Airside adopted the MasterCard palette of red and yellow to create welcoming scenes of each of these iconic travel destinations: whilst aiding brand recognition. The result, rather than feeling like a corporate colour scheme, makes these places look like they are bathed in a sunlit glow. There's an other-worldliness to these pared back, simple visions of what lies beyond the terminal door. This illustrates Airside's skill in applying its classic aesthetic – uplifting, friendly and inspiring – to any commercial brief with beautiful results. This is the largest illustration work the agency McCann Erickson has ever commissioned: the project was intended to be split between artists in different countries but Airside's first submission was deemed so successful they were commissioned to carry out the whole project, which has run for three years to date. **FS**

世界を股にかける「エアサイド」という名の通り、エアサイドの作品がマスターカードのグローバル広告キャンペーンの一環として、サン・パウロ、パリ、デリー他、各国の空港にお目見えした。そもそも1940年代の交通局のポスターがきっかけでフレッドのイラストレーション・スタイルが生まれたことを考えると、この温かく、気持ちを高揚させるような巨大イラストレーション広告は、夢のようなプロジェクト。お馴染みのベクター・イラストレーションで、マスターカードの赤と黄色を基調に、各国のアイコン的な風景を、歓迎ムードで表現した。いかにもブランドカラーを用いたという印象はなく、まるで太陽に照らされて光輝くように各都市を描いている。ターミナルのドアの向こうに広がる別世界を、シンプルで無駄のないデザインで表現したこの広告は、人々の気持ちを高揚させ、フレンドリーに活気づける、エアサイドお馴染みの手法が、効果的な結果をもたらした好例といえる。本作は、代理店マッキャン・エリクソンが手がけた、最も大規模なイラストレーション・プロジェクトで、当初は各国の様々なアーティストに依頼する予定だったが、エアサイドの最初の作品に満足したマッキャンは、それ以来3年間、このプロジェクトをすべてエアサイドに任せている。(FS)

22

23

Title: The Final

football fever, priceless

24

26

25

Airside by Airside

エアサイド バイ エアサイド

Moving Into Advertising

広告の世界へ

27

28

This and next page:
本頁＆次頁

**27–
33** Finished artwork for
various MasterCard
billboards, 2005–08

マスターカード大型ポスター
完成版 2005–08

29

31

30

MASTERCARD

———————— **Alex** For over three years now we have been creating a series of over fifty giant billboards for MasterCard which have ended up in virtually every international airport. Each individual billboard illustrates a specific local landmark or activity; they are over 30 metres wide and have a hell of an impact when you see them after arriving at your destination! If you look carefully in the film *The Bourne Ultimatum* you will see one appearing in the assassination scene at Waterloo station.

———————— This project has been an ongoing partnership with the agency McCann Erickson and has won various awards; it just seems to keep on going as MasterCard discover more airports for us to create new work for.

マスターカード

———————— **アレックス** 既に3年以上になるけど、僕らは文字通り、世界中の国際空港のマスターカード用巨大広告看板を、50以上手がけている。各地のイラストには、その土地の歴史的建造物や文化を描いているんだけど、広告看板は幅30メートル以上あるから、旅行者が目的地に到着してそのポスターを目にすると、ものすごいインパクトなんだ！映画「ボーン・アルティメイタム」を注意して見ると、ウォータールー駅での暗殺のシーンに、僕らのポスターが登場しているよ。

———————— このプロジェクトはマッキャンと組んで今もなお進行中で、様々な賞を獲得している。マスターカードが、僕らのために次々と新しい空港を見つけてきてくれるから、どうやらしばらく続きそうだね。

34

35

38

36

39

37

40

SONY BRAVIA

ソニー・ブラビア

Job name:	Sony Bravia UEFA Champions League Idents	**作品名：**	ソニー・ブラビア UEFA チャンピオンズ・リーグ ID
Client:	Sony	**クライアント：**	ソニー
Agency:	Fallon, London	**代理店：**	ファロン、ロンドン
Media:	Moving image	**メディア：**	動画

| **Summary:** | TV idents for the Sony-sponsored coverage of the 2006-2007 UEFA Champions League football. | **内容：** | 2006〜7年度 UEFA チャンピオンズ・リーグ用、スポンサーCM |

————— An enormous neon globe explores a deserted football stadium accompanied by a jarring unearthly soundtrack: not the most conventional way to introduce an evening's football coverage. But with a client as bold as Sony and an agency and creative as confident as Fallon and Juan Cabral, a partnership emerged prepared to explore the path less travelled. These short glimpses of alien activity contrast strongly with more traditional advertising , creating a forceful impact that takes the brand into exciting new territory. Airside's traditional moving image style was put aside for this project; although animation techniques were used the goal was a seamless filmic feel. The end result is testament to Airside's agility when embracing other aesthetics; put this project next to the photographer Nadav Kander's website and you could be looking at the work of a completely different design company. **FS**

————— 異次元を思わせる不協和音にのって、巨大なネオンボールが、ひと気のないサッカースタジアムを漂う。深夜のサッカー番組には、あまり見慣れない出だしに違いない。しかし、ソニーという何事にも大胆なクライアントと、ファロンのフアン・カブラルという自信たっぷりの代理店クリエイティブと組んだ以上、いままでと違ったやり方にチャレンジするしかない。この異質で短いCMは、従来の広告とは対照的に、見るものに強力なインパクトを与え、ブランドをエキサイティングな未知の領域へと押し上げた。このプロジェクトで、エアサイドは、彼らの典型的な動画スタイルとは異なる手法を用い、アニメーション技術を応用したものの、あくまでシームレスな実写の質感を目指した。結果的に、この試みは見事に成功し、エアサイドの手腕を示す作品に仕上がった。本作をナダブ・カンダールのウェブサイトの隣に並べたら、まるで別のデザイン会社の作品のように見えるだろう。（FS）

Moving Into Advertising

広告の世界へ

41

41–
44

Development work for
Sony Bravia idents,
2005

ソニー・ブラビア ID 制作過程
2005

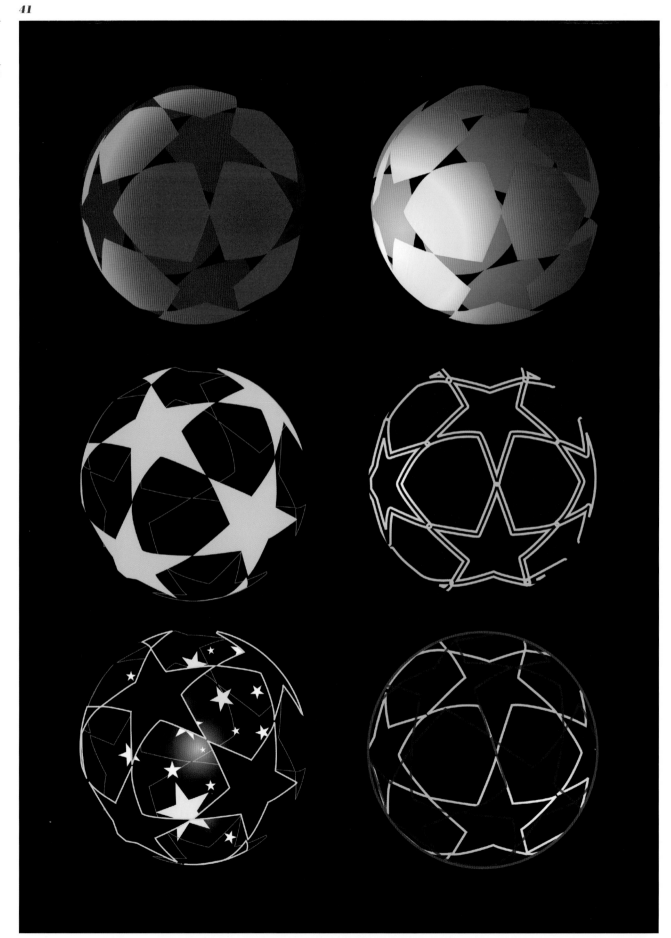

42

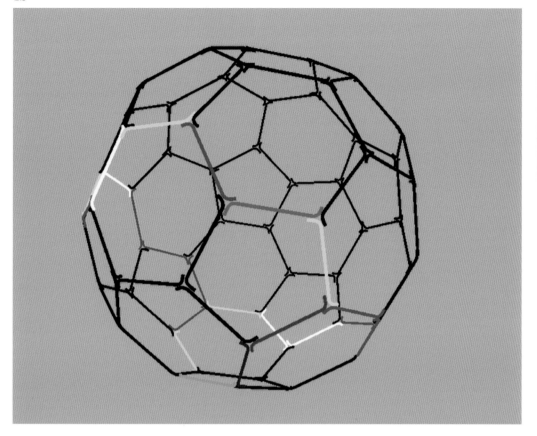

43

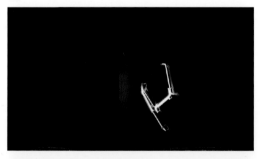
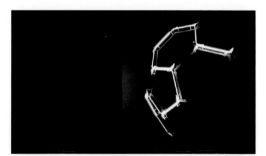
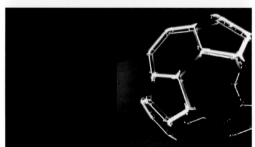

44

SONY BRAVIA

Alex The Sony Bravia idents were a really enjoyable collaboration with Juan Cabral at Fallon which ran during the TV coverage of the 2006-2007 UEFA Champions League. The idea began as an abstract discussion about colour and lights that also touched on Steven Spielberg's *Close Encounters*. We ended up doing a shoot in the middle of the night at Reading's football ground, holding a giant globe of light on the end of a fishing rod to dangle over the grass because we were forbidden from stepping on the hallowed soil of the pitch!

Our response to the brief ("What do you get when you add colour to football?") was a hovering neon football that generates a range of mysterious patterns. The football itself was computer generated, but to this day we regularly get emails asking where to buy the neon tubes we used to build it.

ソニー・ブラビア

アレックス 2006〜7年のUEFAチャンピオンズ・リーグの放映に合わせて流れたソニーのブラビア用ID は、ファロンのフアン・カブラルとのコラボレーションで、すごく楽しい仕事だった。スピルバーグの「未知との遭遇」なんかにも触れながら、色と光に関する抽象的なディスカッションをするうちに生まれたアイデアでね。結局、レディングのフットボール・スタジアムで真夜中に撮影したんだけど、グラウンドの神聖な土に足を踏み入れることを禁じられていたから、なんと釣り竿の先に巨大な光の球体をぶら下げて、芝生の上に吊したんだ！

「サッカーに色を添えたら何になる？」というブリーフへの僕らの回答は、浮遊しながら、ミステリアスなパターンを醸し出すネオンボール。ボールそのものはCGで作ったんだけど、いまだにあの球体に使ったネオン管はどこで買えるのかと、よく聞かれるよ。

SELF-INITIATED PROJECTS

自主プロジェクト

——————— **Fred** Our self-initiated work has always been central to Airside. It gets us out there, via exhibitions, festivals, parties and online activity. It's an extension of the club philosophy; we want people to enjoy our work and have a good time when they are interacting with it. We cross the line – normally a design company wouldn't be communicating directly with the public, but the self-initiated work and the Airside Shop enables us to create our own world and reach our own audience, rather than just working for clients.

——————— **Richard** Airside has a more mature approach to self-initiated projects than a lot of other design companies. Others see it as a trade-off with the commercial work, and think they'll do the shit work for the money and the self-initiated work to show that they're still sensitive, creative people. That way it becomes a vanity project, and they don't take it very seriously. Airside has always said, "How are we going to make money out of this? Are we going to sell T-shirts, is there a product there or is it just a promotional thing?" It's integrated into their practice.

——————— **フレッド** 自主プロジェクトは、エアサイドの中心的活動で、エキシビションやフェスティバル、パーティー、オンライン活動などを通して、僕らのいいプロモーションになっているよ。クラブ哲学の延長みたいなもので、人々に僕らの作品に触れて楽しんでもらい、いい時間を過ごしてもらいたい。普通のデザイン会社では、一般の人たちと直接コミュニケーションする機会がないけど、自主プロジェクトとエアサイド・ショップのおかげで、僕らは独自の世界を展開しながら、クライアントのための仕事だけでなく、その境界線を超えて、オーディエンスと触れ合うことができるんだ。

——————— **リチャード** エアサイドは、他の多くのデザイン会社に比べて、はるかに成熟した自主プロジェクトの経験とノウハウをもっている。他の会社では、自主プロジェクトを商業的な仕事の対極と捉えていて、お金のためにつまらない仕事をこなす一方、自主プロジェクトを通して、自分たちにまだ感受性と想像力が残っていることを示そうとする。だから、自己満足プロジェクトになっていて、結局はあまり真剣に取り組んでいないんだ。その点、エアサイドは常に「これでどうやって稼ごうか？Tシャツを作って商品として売る？ それとも、宣伝グッズとして使おうか？」と考えている。はるかに総合的な視野を持って実践しているよ。

AIRSIDE SHOP

エアサイド・ショップ。

Client:	Airside	クライアント：	エアサイド
Media:	T-shirts, prints, calendars	メディア：	Tシャツ、ポスター、カレンダー
Summary:	Ongoing self-initiated products	内容：	常に進行中の自主プロジェクト

———————— Familiar to any discerning design junkie, the Airside Shop is the place to buy T-Shirts, prints, calendars and products designed by members of Airside's studio. For the designers, this provides an outlet for unbridled creativity, and the darker, weirder recesses of their imaginations. It's an important balance to their client work, and keeps everybody playing and enjoying what they do, which is one of the studio's central maxims. The Shop is also a key way for Airside to interact with the public, and the friends they regard as the wider Airside family. This is summed up by the T-Shirt Club, where for an annual membership fee, people receive four unknown designs a year, created by carefully selected external and internal designers. Crucially, Airside's T-shirts are limited edition and engender a spirit of belonging to a club, as well as presenting the opportunity to own a piece of unique design. Its early forerunner was the T-shirt Olympics, where the public submitted T-shirt designs of their own for the winners to be made. This idea may be ubiquitous now, but Airside was one of the first design companies to produce and sell T-shirts, and the enthusiasm for this simple commercial venture has been contagious. Since Airside began designing calendars and T-shirts back in 1998, they've never grown tired of staying in friendly contact with those people who appreciate their work. **FS**

———————— スタジオのメンバーがデザインしたTシャツやポスター、カレンダーその他様々な商品を購入できる、目利きのデザイン・ジャンキーたちにはお馴染みのエアサイド・ショップ。デザイナーたちにとっては、制約のない創造性や、よりダークで奇妙な想像力を発揮でき、クライアントのいる仕事とのバランスを取るためにも、エアサイドの「何をするにも楽しんで、遊び心を忘れない」というポリシーを実践する上でも欠かせないプロジェクトとなっている。ショップはまた、エアサイドが一般の人々や、エアサイド・ファミリーと位置づけている友人たちとの交流の場でもある。このことは、Tシャツクラブを見ればよくわかる。年会費を払うと、エアサイドが自信を持って選んだ様々なデザイナーの手がけたTシャツが、年に4枚手元に届くという仕組み。重要なのは、ユニークなデザインのTシャツが手に入るというだけでなく、これらのTシャツが限定アイテムだということと、クラブの一員としての一体感をもたらしてくれること。このシステムの前身は、一般からデザインを募集し、優勝者のデザインをTシャツとして生産する「Tシャツ・オリンピックス」。こうしたアイデアは、今ではありふれたものかもしれないが、エアサイドはTシャツを作って販売した先駆的デザイン会社のひとつで、このシンプルなビジネスモデルは、その後一気に火が点いた。1998年にカレンダーやTシャツのデザインを始めて以来、エアサイドは彼らの作品を喜んでくれる人々との交流を、いつも楽しみにしている。（FS）

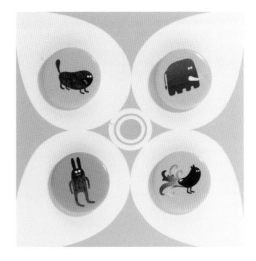

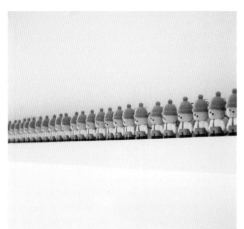

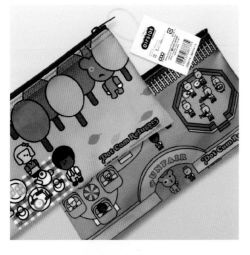
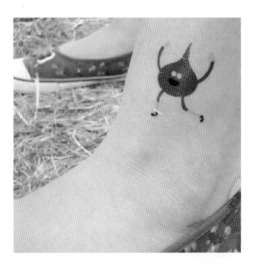

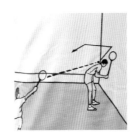

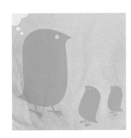

AIRSIDE SHOP

Roz Davies I joined Airside and started running the Shop because I loved the T-shirts. The designs were great and at the time nobody else was doing anything like them. We always did small runs of T-shirts so they would be highly collectible, and that was a good selling point; it got people interested in buying something a little less mainstream. Most of our customers were initially part of Fred's fan base from his clubs and Lemon Jelly, then the T-shirt Club began to grow, we got into more cult film T-shirts, and it slowly spread through word of mouth. The designers in the studio were always really excited about making T-shirts because it gave them a break from the client work. I loved interacting with the customers; it was very important to me that there was this person-to-person contact. Airside is such a friendly open company, and we felt that should be reflected in the Shop.

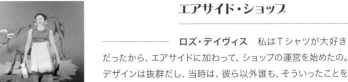

エアサイド・ショップ

ロズ・デイヴィス 私はTシャツが大好きだったから、エアサイドに加わって、ショップの運営を始めたの。デザインは抜群だし、当時は、彼ら以外誰も、そういったことをしていなかった。Tシャツの生産数はいつもそう多くないから、かなりのコレクターズアイテムなわけで、それもいいセールスポイントだったわ。メインストリームから外れたものを買ってみたい人たちの好奇心をそそったのね。はじめは、ほとんどのお客さんが、クラブやレモン・ジェリーでフレッドのファンだった人たちで、それから少しずつTシャツクラブが大きくなっていったの。私たちもカルト映画のTシャツ作りに更に入れ込んだりして、やがて口コミで広がっていった。Tシャツのデザインっていうのは、クライアントの仕事を終えた後のいい気晴らしになるから、スタジオのデザイナーたちはいつも喜々としてデザインしているわ。お客さんとのやりとりも楽しかったし、こういった直接的なコミュニケーションは大切なことなのよ。エアサイドは、すごくオープンでフレンドリーな会社だから、それをショップにも反映させないとね。

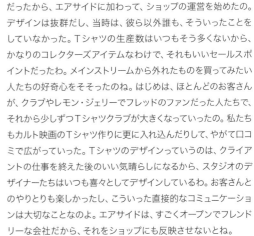

This and previous spread:
本頁 & 前頁

2 Selection of
Airside T-shirts
and merchandise,
1999–2008

エアサイドのTシャツ
その他商品
1999–2008

T-SHIRT CLUB

Tシャツクラブ

'02

'01

'99

Anthony Burrill
Jasper Goodall
Laura Lees
Fred Deakin

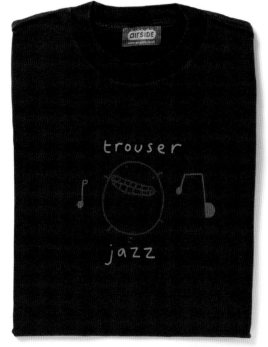

Fred Deakin
Tom Hingston
Mark Pawson
Mode 2

Fred Deakin
Swifty
Rian Hughes
Pete Fowler

'00

Mr. Scruff
Graham Rounthwaite
Fred Deakin
Subtle Ruckus

Michael Gillette
Kid Acne
Fred Deakin
Rinzen

'03

*Kozyndan
Eh?
Fred Deakin
Laurent Fetis*

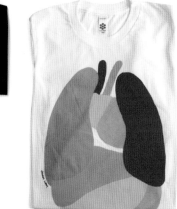

*James Joyce
Jason Munn
Shoboshobo
Fred Deakin*

*Ian Stevenson
Andy Votel
Sweden Graphics
Fred Deakin*

*Johnny Kelly
Fred Deakin
Julian House
Lucy Mclauchlan*

*Jon Burgerman
Al Murphy
Fred Deakin
Katharina Leuzinger*

Self-initiated Projects

自主プロジェクト

T-SHIRT CLUB

———— **Roz** When you join the T-Shirt Club, you pay a subscription fee upfront and then over the summer you receive four T-shirts, one every month. We announce who the designers are, but the members never know what the specific design is going to be. There is an incredible level of trust, and the idea of being part of this club, where we never reprint any designs, and you can only buy them as a group of four – it all makes the experience unique. Every year we come up with some crazy packaging idea for the initial membership pack itself and every T-shirt has a letter of authenticity with information about the designer and their design. People are interested to know the background to the design, and with a lot of T-Shirts that you get off the shelf you never find that out.

3

4

Tシャツクラブ

———— **ロズ** Tシャツクラブというのは、入会して先払いでメンバー料金を支払うと、夏の間、毎月1枚、計4枚のTシャツが届くシステム。事前にデザイナーは告知するけど、一体どんなデザインのTシャツかは、届いてからのお楽しみ。クラブに属するということ、2度と同じデザインのTシャツをプリントしないということ、4枚1組でしか購入できないことなど、信頼関係が大きくないと成り立たないけど、これらすべてがTシャツクラブの体験をユニークなものにしているの。毎年、クレイジーなパッケージをデザインして、Tシャツと一緒にデザイナーとデザインに関する解説書を同封してメンバーに届けるのよ。どうやってこのデザインが出来上がったのか、興味を持つ人は多いけど、既成のTシャツでは、そこまでわからないわよね。

Airside

T-SHIRT CLUB

2008 MEMBERSHIP + DESIGNERS

2008 Airside T-shirt Club membership introductory pack. Featuring two badges, certificate and Club House model (pictured as assembled).

Examples of previous work by 2008 Airside T-shirt Club designers.

NB: these images are for illustrative purposes only. They are not the t-shirt designs for the 2008 Airside T-shirt Club

3 Airside T-shirt Club membership pack, 2004

エアサイド・Tシャツクラブ
会員用パック 2004

4 Domino T-shirt Club membership pack, 2007

ドミノ・Tシャツクラブ
会員用パック 2007

5 Airside T-shirt Club flyer, 2008

エアサイド・Tシャツクラブ
チラシ 2008

T-SHIRT CLUB '08

CLUBHOUSE

KATERINA LEUZINGER
AL MURPHY

JAN BURGERMAN
FRED DEAKIN

Airside

Self-initiated Projects
自主プロジェクト

6

BLACK SABBATH, THE EARLY YEARS

Fred Collaborating with outside designers helps us build bridges with the rest of the creative community. For the T-shirt Club we ask our personal design heroes as well as up-and-coming people that we rate so it's always a combination of big names and emerging talent.

Pete Fowler (monsterist) I thought it was a great idea, not knowing what designs you would get. The excitement grew with the anticipation of the mystery item inside the parcel, and I was proud to be included in the first series alongside such heavyweight designers. To me, Airside and the T-shirt Club offers a mark of quality, just like buying music from a trusted record label without hearing it first. Later I was invited to join the T-shirt Olympics with my *Black Sabbath, The Early Years* design, and again I loved the concept behind the project. That's the thing with Airside; they seem to just be playing and having fun but then you realise they're clever buggers!

Nat T-Shirts are about creating work that doesn't necessarily take a long time but is fun to make and connects with people in some way.

You make a T-shirt and then go out and see people wearing them. It's almost more exciting for us than making a website because that's intangible, whereas this is visible on a human scale. In the beginning, whenever we saw people out and about wearing our designs, we'd always have to pluck up the courage to go and say hello. It's a thrill to see our work out there in the real world.

Richard When Airside started selling T-shirts on the internet it was a novel thing. The idea that you could enter a competition to design one yourself was really unusual.

Nat *Battle Royale* was the first of our film T-shirts. It started off as a commission from Metro Tartan who wanted to generate some cool press around their film, a cult Japanese ultra-violence movie. Henki drew two illustrations, of a girl and a boy getting shot, and they've continually sold well in the Shop.

Alex Quentin Tarantino wore one to a premiere, and when Jarvis Cocker saw Kerin from Airside walking down the street wearing one he told him how cool he thought it was.

フレッド 外部のデザイナーとコラボレーションすることで、クリエイティブ・コミュニティーに架け橋を築くことができる。Ｔシャツクラブでは、僕らのヒーローみたいなデザイナーに依頼することもあれば、目をつけている新進のデザイナーに頼むこともあるから、たいがい大御所と新人デザイナーのコンビネーションだね。

ピート・ファウラー どんなデザインが届くかわからないっていうのは、すごくいいアイデアだと思った。包みの中の謎のアイテムへの期待が高まるからね。ヘビー級のデザイナーたちと並んでシリーズ第１弾のデザイナーに選んでもらって光栄だよ。僕にとっては、エアサイドのＴシャツクラブっていうだけで、品質保証みたいなものさ。つまり、信頼の置けるレコード会社の出す音楽は、レーベル自体が、聴く価値があることを物語っているから試聴せずに購入する。それと同じことなんだ。後に「ブラック・サバス：ジ・アーリー・イヤーズ」のデザインで、Ｔシャツ・オリンピックスに誘ってもらったけど、このプロジェクトのコンセプトも気に入ったね。すごくエアサイドらしい。楽しく遊んでいるだけかと思ったら、それだけじゃないことに気づかされる。「チクショー、なんて利口な奴らだ！」って。

ナット Ｔシャツ作りのいいところは、必ずしも時間をかけずに、楽しみながら人と繋がることのできる点なの。Ｔシャツを作ったら、どこかで誰かが着ているのを見ることができる。使い手の反応が見えないウェブサイトに比べたら、実物が目の前を歩いているのを見ることができるんだから、はるかにエキサイティングだと言ってもいいわね。はじめの頃、

自分たちがデザインしたＴシャツを着ている人を見かける度に、勇気を奮い起こして声をかけずにはいられなかった。現実の世界で、自分たちの作品に出会うのは、ほんとうにスリリングなことなのよ。

リチャード エアサイドがインターネットでＴシャツを売り始めた頃、それはまったく新しいことだった。自分でＴシャツをデザインしてコンペに加わることができるというのは、本当に画期的な発想だったね。

ナット 「バトル・ロワイヤル」は、私たちが初めて映画を題材に作ったＴシャツなの。日本の超カルト・バイオレンス映画を売り込むのに、クールなプロモーションをしたがっていたメトロ・タータンから依頼を受けて始まった企画で、少年と少女が撃たれるシーンのイラストレーションをヘンキが制作したんだけど、このＴシャツは、ショップでコンスタントに売れ続けているわね。

アレックス クエンティン・タランティーノがプレミアの席で着ていたり、ケリンがこのＴシャツを着て街中を歩いていたら、通りかかったジャーヴィス・コッカーに「なんてクールなんだ」と声をかけられたって。

ロズ エアサイドのデザインする作品に関心がある人たちにとって、クライアントにならずとも、エアサイドと接触できる手段がショップなの。このショップの人気には感染力があったから、みんなとコミュニケーションを図るためのブログを始めて、アンと私がエアサイド流のコミカルなスタイルでよく書き込むわ。エアサイドで働くのがどんな感じなのかを知

りたがる人たちからのＥメールにも、よく返事を書いた。クリスマスには、スタジオを開放して、みんなを招いて遊びにきてもらったこともあったわね。ファンたちはスタジオを見て回って、フレッドがＣＤや他の商品にサインしたりなんかして。個人レベルでお客さんたちと繋がることができるのは、なかなかいいものね。和気あいあいとした家族みたいな、リアルなつきあいができたわ。

フレッド 何年か前のクリスマスシーズン、コベントガーデンに本物のショップをオープンしたんだけど、すごく楽しかったよ。僕たちの作った商品がカウンターに並んで売られているのを見るのは新鮮で、ショップを切り盛りすること自体、本当に楽しかった。２人の才能ある若手クリエイター、ルーシー・バーバーとピーター・ハウエルを店員として雇って、いくつかのパーティーを企画して、口コミでショップ情報を広めたんだ。すごく雰囲気のいいお店だったから、僕らも何とはなしに、よく顔を出したよ。あれは最高の経験で、フルタイムで店を経営しようとは思わないけど、間違いなくその楽しさは味わえたね。

ナット エアサイドのファンには、かなり強烈な人もいてね。エデン・プロジェクトでフレッドがギグをやっている最中に、私のところへやって来て、奇妙な目つきでこう言うの。「君らのやった事はわかってる。バトル・ロワイヤルＴシャツの襟元のネームタグを『Airside』から『Airside Shop』に変えたよね。僕の目はごまかせないぞ。新しいのも買ったから！」って。完全にマニアよね。

Roz People respect Airside's corporate design work and the Shop is a way of accessing that without being a huge client. The enthusiasm for it became infectious. We started a blog to communicate with everyone, which Anne and I would write in this funny Airside style. I'd be answering emails from people who would just want to know what it was like to work at Airside. At Christmas we'd open up the studio and invite everyone to come down. The fans got to look round the studio, and Fred would be signing CDs and anything else we were selling. It was just nice to connect with our customers on that individual level. There is this real community, a family environment.

Fred A couple of years ago in the run up to Christmas we opened a real shop for a few months in Covent Garden which was great fun. It was a revelation to see our products on sale over the counter and we had a ball running it. We employed Lucy Barber and Peter Howell, two talented young creatives, to be our shopkeepers and threw a series of parties to spread the word. Some of us used to just go down regularly to hang out

because the atmosphere was so good! It was a great experiment and although I don't think we'll be moving into retail full-time it definitely gave us a taste for it.

Nat Some of Airside's fans can be pretty intense. Someone came up to me during one of Fred's gigs at the Eden Project and said with a strange look in their eye, "I've seen what you did: you changed the branding on the label inside the *Battle Royale* T-shirt from 'Airside' to 'Airside Shop.' You didn't fool me – I bought the new one as well!" That's the collector mentality.

6 Black Sabbath, The *Early Years* T-shirt by Pete Fowler, 2002

「ブラック・サバス：ジ・アーリー・イヤーズ」Tシャツ
ピート・フォウラー 2002

7–8 Two Airside T-shirt labels, 2003/05

エアサイド・Tシャツネームタグ
2種 2003/05

9 *Battle Royale* Boy T-shirt by Henki Leung, 2006

「バトル・ロワイヤルー少年」Tシャツ
ヘンキ・レウン 2006

9

7

8

Self-initiated Projects
自主プロジェクト

PRINTS

プリント

10

11

12

13

14

15

Self-initiated Projects

自主プロジェクト

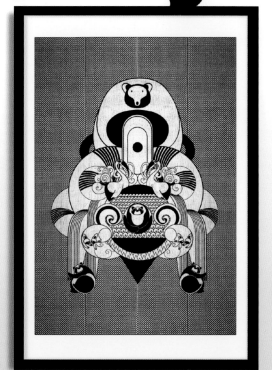

22

PRINTS

——————— **Fred** Prints were an obvious step forward. We sell them online through the Shop and via occasional exhibitions. The first was at the Merz Gallery in Edinburgh and since then we've held exhibitions at Magma in London and Speak-For in Tokyo. Screen-prints are really dear to me – I love that original limited edition feel, half way between one-offs and mass production. We screen printed these great promotional posters in UV ink for the first Lemon Jelly album and then used the leftovers to paper the walls in the back room of the London club Fabric for our first gig there.

——————— **Richard** There were several quite incredible projects that we pulled off. Airside has these Monday morning meetings where everyone sits round the table and talks about ideas. A lot of it sounds quite unrealistic, but soon I realised that a high proportion of that stuff actually happens.

プリント

——————— **フレッド** プリント制作を始めたのは、大きな前進だった。ショップを通してオンラインで販売したり、時にはエキビジョンでも販売している。初めてのエキビジョンは、エディンバラのメルツ・ギャラリーで、それからロンドンのマグマや東京のスピーク・フォーでも開催した。スクリーンプリントは僕にとって、とても大切なものなんだ。一点ものと大量生産の間の、あのオリジナル限定版ってところがミソでね。レモン・ジェリーの初アルバムの宣伝用に、スクリーンプリントでUVインクを使って最高のポスターを作った。残った分は、初のギグをやったファブリックのブラックルームの壁一面に貼付けたよ。

——————— **リチャード** 僕らが成し遂げてきたプロジェクトには、驚くべきものがいくつかある。エアサイドでは、月曜の朝、みんなで机を囲んでアイデアを出し合うミーティングを行うんだ。そこで出るアイデアの多くは非現実的に聞こえるんだけど、実はかなりの確率で実現するってことに、すぐに気づいたよ。

23

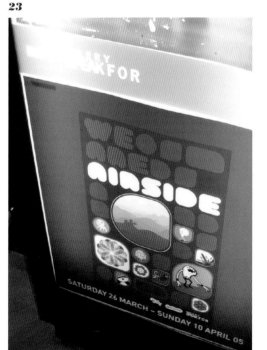

24

SPEAK FOR (TOKYO)

Fred For the Airside exhibition at Gallery Speak-For in Tokyo, as well as a bunch of new printed work and projections, we created a couple of interactive installations. It was the first time we'd done that outside of clubland.

Mark The first installation was two touch pads hooked up to the characters from *The Shouty Track* video; hitting each pad made your on-screen character hit your friend's character. That tapped into quite a simple emotional pleasure, and people were really having a good time with it. The second piece was more complex; the audience interacted with a series of sensors placed in lines on the floor that triggered ever more complex visuals and audio, culminating in a full Lemon Jelly video. We learned a lot of lessons from these installations that flowed into our later work. When you're doing self-initiated projects, they can function as live tests and help you to see how people behave.

25

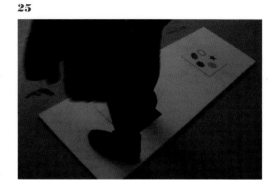

26

27

スピーク・フォー（東京）

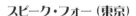

フレッド　東京のギャラリー・スピーク・フォーでのエキシビションでは、プリント作品や映像上映だけでなく、インタラクティブ・インスタレーションもいくつか制作した。そういうことをクラブ以外の場所でやったのは、初めてだったんだ。

マーク　1つ目は、2つのタッチパッドを「ザ・シャウティー・トラック」のMVのキャラクターに連結させて、観客がそれぞれのパッドを叩くと、スクリーン上のキャラクターが相棒を叩く仕組みになっている。それがかなりシンプルな快感を生み出すから、みんなものすごく楽しんでいたね。2つ目の作品は、もっと複雑で、観客が床の上に一列に並んだセンサーに触れると、映像とオーディオが連動するようになっていて、これらの素材は、後にレモン・ジェリーのビデオにもなった。この時のインスタレーションを通して学んだ多くのことが、後の作品に活かされているよ。自主プロジェクトをやることは、ライブ実験をしているようなもので、人々がどんな反応をするのかが手に取るようにわかるんだ。

28

Airside by Airside

エアサイド バイ エアサイド

Self-initiated Projects

自主プロジェクト

MEEGHOTEPH

ミーゴテフ

Job name:	Meeghoteph, Ancient Alien God
Client:	Airside
Media:	Moving image, digital
Summary:	An interactive piece originally created for the Big Chill music festival.

———————— Airside enjoys encouraging adults and children to play. Meegoteph was a famous example of this: a self-initiated interactive experiment based on a crazy idea that Richard had for an installation at the Big Chill festival, which was later recreated at the V&A Museum. It updated one of the oldest forms of entertainment – a puppet show – as a hi-tech, animated on-screen character. People entered a booth and met the alien god Meeghoteph, who engaged them in conversation. Thinking the character on the screen was controlled by a pre-programmed computer, people would try to trick it by asking unusual questions, but Meegoteph always had the right response. Eventually they realised that the character was simply operated by one of the Airside folk behind a screen with a voice modulator. That moment of understanding always prompted laughter, and a desire to interact with Meeghoteph further. FS

作品名:	古代宇宙神ミーゴテフ
クライアント:	エアサイド
メディア:	動画、インスタレーション
内容:	ビッグチル音楽祭向けに制作されたオリジナル・インタラクティブ作品

———————— 大人も子供も遊ぶことを応援するのがエアサイド。ミーゴテフは、正にその好例。ビッグチル音楽祭のインスタレーション用に、リチャードが思いついたクレイジーなアイデアをもとに作られた自主インタラクティブ作品で、後にV&A美術館用に再制作された。古典的エンターテイメントの元祖とも言える人形劇を、よりハイテクに、アニメ化したキャラクターを画面に登場させる手法で蘇らせた。ブースに入ると、宇宙神ミーゴテフが現れ、話し始める。人々は、ミーゴテフがあらかじめコンピューター入力されたプログラムだと思い込んで、きまって変な質問をしてミーゴテフを試そうとするが、彼の返事はいつも的を射ている。というのも実は、エアサイドのメンバーが、スクリーンの裏で音声モジュレーターを使い、ミーゴテフに成りすましているのだ。これに気づいた客たちは大笑いし、ますますミーゴテフと話したくなるのだった。（FS）

Airside by Airside

エアサイド バイ エアサイド

Self-initiated Projects

自主プロジェクト

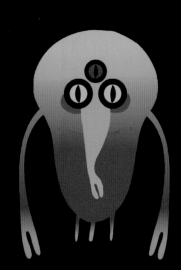

29

30

31

MEEGHOTEPH

———— **Nat** We all go to the summer music festivals and one year we decided to run a T-shirt stall at *The Big Chill*. For the second year, Richard came up with the Meegoteph concept.

———— **Richard** We were trying to come up with something that would be interactive and fun. I presented this crazy idea, and everyone said, "What the hell is that? Go on then, why not." The concept was very old fashioned: it's just a puppet show, but because it uses a combination of low and high technology, people don't realise how simple it is. They see Meeghoteph, this animated character on a screen, and automatically assume it is computerised, not realising there's a person sitting behind the screen operating it. The first thing people do is to try and fool it by asking tricky questions, but when Meeghoteph responds correctly they are surprised. When the penny drops

32

ミーゴテフ

———— **ナット**　私たちは毎年、夏になるとミュージック・フェスティバルに行くんだけど、ある年、ビッグ・チルでTシャツの屋台を出すことにしたの。次の年はリチャードが「ミーゴテフ」のコンセプトを思いついたわ。

———— **リチャード**　インタラクティブで楽しいことをやりたかったんだ。僕がこのクレイジーなアイデアを出したら、みんなが「何それ? いいね、やろうよ」って。コンセプトはすごく旧式で、要は人形劇なんだけど、ローテクとハイテクを組み合わせて使うと、それがどんなに単純な仕掛けなのか、みんな気づかないんだ。スクリーン上に、アニメーションでキャラクター化されたミーゴテフが現れる。すると当然みんなプログラミングされていると思い込む。スクリーンの後ろに人間が座ってミーゴテフを操作しているとは夢にも思わない。だから決まって、難しい質問を投げかけてミーゴテフをからかおうとするんだけど、ミーゴテフが正確に答えるから、みんな驚くんだ。そのうち人間がスクリーンの裏に座っているという仕掛けに気づくわけだけど、がっかりするどころか、みんな最高の笑顔になる。それから、壁を叩いたり、裏に回ってきたり。せっかくオズの魔法使いに出会えたのに実は普通の人間だった、みたいな感じで、すごく愉快な経験だったね。僕はそういう、びっくりさせるようなインタラクティブっていうのが好きなんだ。コンピューターを用いて、ボタンを押すだけのインタラクティブ・デザインやインタラクティブ・

33

ATTENTION PUNY BIPEDS
ANCIENT ALIEN GOD
MEEGHOTEPH
WOULD LIKE TO MAKE YOUR ACQUAINTANCE
(MEEGHOTEPH RESERVES THE RIGHT TO SNAP YOUR HEAD OFF AND SUCK OUT YOUR TINY BRAIN)

it's not a moment of disappointment – when they realise it's just a person behind the screen, that's when people smile the most. Then they bang on the wall or come round the back – that moment is like meeting the Wizard of Oz and realising he's just a man. It's a delightful experience. That's what I like about it – it's interactive in a very surprising way. So much interactive design and art just uses a computer and involves pushing a button. This was interactive in the old-fashioned sense of meeting somebody in an unusual way.

———————— **Nat** It was typical of a lot of our work in that we like to find a way to let adults play. Meegoteph's just a bit of fun, but for some reason people started confiding him. One little boy told Meeghoteph he was being bullied at school and Meeghoteph's advice was to tell his mum and dad. He came back the next day to say it had really helped. I love that real human connection.

アートがあまりにも多いけど、この企画は意外な方法で人と出会うという、旧式のインタラクティブだったんだ。

————————**ナット**　あれは、大人を遊ばせる方法を見つけるのが大好きな、エアサイドのプロジェクトの典型とも言えるわね。ミーゴテフはちょっとしたおふざけのつもりだったけど、どういう訳か、ブースに入った人がミーゴテフに告白を始めてね。ある少年はミーゴテフに、学校でいじめられていると告白したの。そこでミーゴテフが、おうちでお母さんやお父さんにも話すんだよ、とアドバイスしたら、その子が翌日戻ってきて「ほんとに助かった」って。私はそういった人とのリアルな繋がりが大好きなの。

34

STITCHES

スティッチィズ

Job name:	Stitches	作品名：	スティッチィズ
Client:	Anne Brassier / Airside	クライアント：	アン・ブラーシエィ／エアサイド
Media:	Product design	メディア：	プロダクトデザイン

Summary: A self-initiated project to find new homes for woolly creatures.

内容： ニットの生き物たちの里親を探す、自主プロジェクト

——————— Airside's Anne finds the Stitches behind her toolshed, and brings these bruised, knitted creatures into Airside to be adopted into responsible new homes. So goes the legend of the Stitches, a growing international family with proud parents who love a spot of fantasy nurture. Each and every Stitch is an individual, with its own name and defining characteristics, but they all share the recurring tropes that Airside bestows on most of its characters: they draw people in with their cuteness only to reveal a slightly sinister side. Airside HQ now receives regular updates from doting parents, elaborating in huge detail on the latest adventures of their adopted Stitch, accompanied with 'Where's Wally' style snaps from across the globe. Stitches are currently enjoying their new lives as record collection minders, sushi chefs and Alpine chalet guests. There are only a few hundred Stitches in the world, making them a rare but growing species, and they're only available from Airside. **FS**

——————— ある日、エアサイドのアン・ブラーシエィが、物置小屋の裏でスティッチィズを見つけた。このニットの生き物たちは傷を負っていたため、エアサイドに引き取り、責任を持って里親を探すことにした。このスティッチィズの伝説は、いつの間にやら広がって、里親ごっこに楽しみを見いだす人々が、世界各地に増え続けている。スティッチィズはすべてが1点もので、それぞれ名前も顔つきも異なるが、性格は、お馴染みのエアサイドのキャラクターと同様、愛くるしい容姿で人々を惹きつけるが、ちょっと邪悪な面を隠し持っているのだ。エアサイド里親本部には、毎日のように世界中の里親たちから、それぞれのスティッチの詳細な近況報告と「ウォーリーを探せ」並みのスナップが届いている。我が子を溺愛する里親たちによれば、レコードコレクションの見張り番を務めている者もいれば、寿司職人になっている者、アルプスの別荘に滞在している者もいるようだ。現在、世界に存在するスティッチィズはわずか数百匹。エアサイドを介してのみ養子に迎えることができる。（FS）

Adoption Certificate

JOHN STITCH

is hereby given in adoption

28 AUGUST 2005

Date of birth: 30th January 2005
Place of birth: London, England
Sex: Stitch

The above-mentioned has been adopted by

JOHN DOE

Resident of

LONDON

Authorised by Adrakk Sheep Limited, of 28 Cross Street,
London N1 2BG, England, and by the Adopted Stitch Register

Self-initiated Projects

自主プロジェクト

35

36

37

スティッチィズ

—————— **ナット** スティッチィズもそのいい例ね。事の始まりは、ちょっとしたバカ話なんだけど、おかげで大人が遊べるようになったわ。

—————— **アン・ブラーシェイ** 表向きの話はこうなの。ある日私が、物置小屋の裏にスティッチィズがいるのを見つけてね。彼らは皆、肉体的にも、心理的にも少し傷を負っていたので、エアサイドで引き取って面倒をみながら、彼らに新しい家を提供してくれる里親を探し始めたの。彼らはひとりひとり個性的で、大きさもニットも形も、私が世話を焼いた日数もまちまちだけど、共通しているのは、目がうつろで、必ずどこかに傷を負っているということ。エアサイドは可愛いキャラクター作りをするけど、どこかに必ず、ひとひねり入っているでしょ。お砂糖みたいにただ甘いわけじゃなく、常に暗い部分が潜んでいるのよ。

—————— 養子縁組を斡旋するというアイデアは、エディンバラでのエキシビションの時に始まったの。人々がスティッチィズのことを知りたがるから、聞かれるたびに「この子たちを連れて行くなら、ちゃんと世話をしてもらわないと困るんだけど、あなたたちいい人？ 素敵な家に住んでいる？」と答えるようになって。あっという間に彼らが捨てられた生き物だという物語ができあがったわけ。

—————— **ナット** 初めて日本に行った時、スティッチィズのひとりを、日本のレモン・ジェリーのA&Rの女性、田端花子さんにプレゼントしたのね。そうしたら、初めてのシリアスなビジネスミーティングで、スーツ姿の男性が並ぶ中、ハナがスティッチのビュールを取り出して、皆さんにご挨拶させたの。2回目のミーティングでは、ビュールがハナの耳元で囁くと、ハナはみんなに、ビュールが日本語をしゃべれるようになったと告げて、終いには、このスティッチが新しいビジネス戦略の提案までする始末。私たちが帰国するや否や、さらにハナがビュールに着物を仕立てたこと、ビュールは寿司職人を目指して修行中であること、ビュールのために旅の手配をしたことを知らせるメールを受け取ったわ。

—————— **アン** リアクションがほんとにおかしいし、スティッチィズを通して、いろんな人たちと、ものすごくバカげた出来事に関わることができる。現実の世界を離れて、とても人間らしい方法で物事を話し合うことができるのよ。子供もペットも欲しくないというような人が、ひょっとしたらスティッチなら欲し

STITCHES

Nat The Stitches are another example of Airside's methodology – the whole thing starts with a silly little story which allows people to play and enjoy themselves.

Anne Brassier The official story is that I find the Stitches behind my tool shed. They're a bit scarred, physically and emotionally, and I bring them into Airside to be looked after and adopted by people who can give them a new home. They're all individually made and vary depending on size, wool, shape and my attention span, but they've all got these certain traits in common that make them quite sinister. Their eyes are a bit wonky and they all have scars somewhere. Airside can be perceived as the people who do cute characters, but there's always a bit of a twist. It's not all saccharine sweetness – there's usually an underbelly of darkness.

The idea of handing them over for adoption started at our exhibition in Edinburgh. As people enquired about them I just developed a habit of saying that if they were going to take

them they'd have to look after them, so were they good people and did they have a nice house? It was easy to go into this fantasy story that they were abandoned creatures.

Nat We gave a Stitch as a present to Hana Tabata, Lemon Jelly's A&R woman in Japan, when we first went out there. So, at the first serious business meeting that we had with her, full of Japanese men in suits, she brought out Bulle Stitch and he bowed to everyone in the room. At the second meeting, he whispered in Hana's ear, and she announced to the room that he could speak Japanese now. By the end of the day Bulle is making suggestions for new business strategies. As soon as we got home we were getting emails telling us she's making kimonos for him, that he's training to be a sushi chef, and she's arranging trips for him.

Anne The reaction is really odd. It allows you to engage with people over something incredibly stupid, to leave the real world and talk about these things in a really human way. You imagine the sort of people who don't want a child and don't want a pet, but might want a Stitch. It defi-

nitely brought out the nurturing side of some adults. There's something really funny about talking to strangers about how they're going to act as parents to a knitted toy.

Lynda Relph-Knight (editor of Design Week) The first hint I had that Bill Moggridge, founder of IDEO, was serious about the Stitches was spotting him at dinner in Cape Town after Airside's presentation at the Design Indaba conference. He had Griffin Stitch tucked into his shirt pocket and said they were getting to know each other. And so it continued overnight, with Griffin, a greyish creature with a rubbery nose, joining us for breakfast, still in Bill's pocket (though it was a different shirt). Bill said he was a bit concerned about Griffin's nose, but a relationship was clearly forming. We discussed adoption, but Bill was non-committal. The next day, Bill came bouncing up, with Griffin still in his shirt pocket, to show me the adoption papers, duly signed. Griffin had found a new home in San Francisco, where I'm sure he'll be truly loved.

38

がるかもしれない。大人の中には、明らかにスティッチに子育て本能をくすぐられている人たちがいるのよ。ニットのオモチャの親としてどう振るまっているかを、赤の他人相手に話すっていうのは、なにかすごく滑稽なものがあるわね。

リンダ・ラルフ＝ナイト（「デザインウィーク」編集長） アイデオの共同創設者ビル・モグリッジがスティッチィズに惚れかけてると初めて気づいたのは、デザイン・インダバ・コンファレンスでエアサイドがプレゼンテーションを行った後、ケープタウンで夕食を取っている彼を見つけた時だったわ。彼は、ゴムの鼻をつけた灰色の生き物グリフィンを、胸ポケットに差し込んでいて「僕たち、仲良くなろうとしているんだ」と始めたかと思うと、一晩中その調子。翌朝も、ビルはまたポケットに（シャツは着替えていたけど）グリフィンを連れて朝食に現れた。ビルは、グリフィンの鼻がちょっと気になるけど、関係は確実に深まっていると言うから、養子縁組の話を持ちかけたの。でもまだ心が決まらない様子だった。翌日、またビルはグリフィンを胸ポケットに入れて弾むようにやってきて、正式に署名をした養子縁組の書類を見せてくれた。グリフィンは、新しく見つけたサンフランシスコの家で、間違いなく愛されているでしょうね。

39

Page 188

Airside by Airside

エアサイド バイ エアサイド

Self-initiated Projects

自主プロジェクト

McKenzie Stitch, adopted by Rob Manley "Dear Mummy, you will be pleased to know I had a great time hanging out with Pete and Rob in Hong Kong. I DJed, watched fireworks from the roof of a skyscraper, and hung out with some pretty girls. I hope to go back soon and meet all my new friends. I am so happy you allowed Rob to adopt me. There wasn't much attention to start with but he really loves me now!"

Parents of Angelo Stitch When travelling with Angelo, there is no special preparation required except for one thing: our 'Angelo Stand', this is made of aluminum wire, primarily used for shaping Bonsai plants to grow in beautiful form. Wherever we may be, whether it is a restaurant table or on a sandy beach, Angelo can easily pose. Angelo enables us to record various memorable scenes on camera. Especially tasty dishes, dainty flowers and cute items – these things are not best taken with Gulliver-size human beings. Only Angelo can be the all-round model to do them justice. While we spend our lives with Angelo, we do face occasional moments of regret when we unexpectedly come across rare objects or breath-taking scenery and Angelo is not with us. If we had expected what we would see, we would have definitely taken Angelo along.

Nat The strange thing is that people feel it's perfectly acceptable to write a load of nonsense about their Stitch. They really enter into the spirit of this tongue-in-cheek fantasy world. The demographic of Stitches adopters has been mostly twenty-something British men and thirty-something Japanese women, which is a bizarre twist. Our latest idea is to start a dating agency that will bring these two groups together, which has the potential to really take off!

40

41

マッケンジー・スティッチ（里親：ロブ・マンレイ） お母さん、僕が香港のピートとロブのところで、楽しく暮らしていることを、きっと喜んでくれるよね。僕はDJをやったり、高層ビルの屋上で花火をみたり、可愛い女の子たちと出かけたりしてる。また近いうちにそっちに顔を出して、新しい仲間たちにも会いたいな。ロブを里親に選んでくれて、本当に幸せだよ。始めはあまり世話を焼いてくれなかったけど、今はとても愛されてるよ！

アンジェロ・スティッチの里親 アンジェロと旅をするとき、準備するものはひとつだけ。それは「アンジェロ・スタンド」で、盆栽の枝を美しく整える時に用いる、アルミニウムの針金を使って作られたもの。これがあると、レストランのテーブルでも砂浜でも、アンジェロに簡単にポーズを取らせることができるのね。アンジェロのおかげで、思い出に残る様々な風景をデジカメで記録するようになったわ。特に美味しい食事や、優美な花、可愛らしいアイテムなどは、ガリバーサイズの人間と写真に納まったのでは、様にならなくて、アンジェロだけが、それらの美しさを引き出すオールラウンドモデルなの。アンジェロを連れていないときに、思いがけなく珍しいものを見つけたり、息を飲むような光景を目にしたりすると、最初から分かっていたらアンジェロを連れてきたのにって思うことがあるわ。

ナット 不思議なことに、みんな自分たちのスティッチの話になると、延々とナンセンスなことを書けるのよね。みんな、このふざけた空想の世界に浸ってしまうの。スティッチズのファンの平均構成層は、25歳のイギリス人男性と35歳の日本人女性だってことがわかったんだけど、まったく予想もしていなかったわ。最近考えているのは、スティッチィズをこの2つのグループ間の結婚相談所の主要ツールとして使えば、大繁盛するんじゃないかってこと！

40	McKenzie Stitch DJing with Pete Fowler, 2007		41	Angelo Stitch with Catdog, 2006
	ピート・フォウラーとDJを楽しむマッケンジー・スティッチ 2007			アンジェロ・スティッチとキャットドッグ 2006
			42	Stitch family portrait, 2008
				スティッチ・ファミリー・ポートレート 2008

Alan

Angelo

Bruce II

Bulle

Cassius

Charlotte

Clayton III

Denzel

Dulce

Duncan

Edna

Elvis

Ern

Geraint

Giles St. Laurent

Godrun

Griffin

Hamish

Jean-Claude

Juno

Lady Nutley

Maude

McKenzie

Nelson

Nudd

Paco Primo

Patrick

Philip

Reuben

Rita

River

Silas

Stitch Armstrong

Tina

Tito

Waldo

43

INSYDE

———————— **Fred** We were asked to create an exhibit for the Liverpool Triennial by Ann Bukantas, director of the Walker Gallery. She wanted something visually exciting that would connect with a younger audience, and gave us an open brief which was very generous of her. So we created a large interactive booth containing a world called *Insyde*, filled with little creatures that you could play with by stepping into various light beams. Stepping into these beams made different things happen, so you could jump around the booth and the creatures would follow you. We worked with our mate, interactive whizz-kid Matt Brown who boldly embraced the hardcore coding side of things, I wrote a new piece of music as the soundtrack and all the Liverpool Jellyheads came out in force to party on the opening night.

———————— **Alex** It was our first fully integrated exhibition installation, bringing together sound design, music, architecture and visuals. It was designed to look like an enormous packaging crate that had just dropped into this traditional Victo-

rian stone gallery. We followed that up at London's Designersblock in 2007 with another installation, an interactive billboard featuring an Airside world populated with characters and buildings. Behind lots of spyholes were video iPods playing various animated loops that you could Bluetooth to your mobile to use as a ringtone.

———————— **Fred** All the self-initiated projects that we do are a lot of fun, but they're also a great way of communicating with our clients. They see us doing these crazy projects and it keeps things buzzing. At the same time we get to reach out to a whole bunch of people and invite them to become part of the wider Airside family.

44

インサイド

———————— **フレッド** リバプール・トリエンナーレに際して、僕らは、ウォーカー・ギャラリーのディレクター、アン・ブカンタスからの依頼で、エキシビションを行った。彼女は、若い観客層にアピールするような、視覚的にエキサイティングなものをやりたがっていて、すごく寛大なことに、僕らの好きなようにやらせてくれた。そこで僕らは、大きなインタラクティブ・ブースを作って、「インサイド」と名付けたんだ。その中には、一緒に遊ぶことの出来る、小さな生き物たちがたくさん住んでいて、様々な光線を踏むと、色んな出来事が起こる仕掛けになっている。観客が跳ね回れば、生き物たちも一緒になって跳ね回るんだ。この複雑なプログラミングを、友人でインタラクティブの鬼才マット・ブラウンが快諾してくれて、僕がサウンドトラックに新しい曲を書いた。オープニング・パーティーには、リバプール中のレモン・ジェリーファンが大挙してやって来たよ。

———————— **アレックス** あれは僕らが、効果音、音楽、建築、映像など、いろいろな要素を融合させた、初めてのインスタレーション・エキシビションで、伝統的なビクトリア朝の石造りのギャラリーの中に、突如として巨大な木箱が不時着したみたいなデザインだった。それから、ロンドンの2007年デザイナーズブロックでも様々なキャラクターと建物を描いたインスタレーションを制作したよ。エアサイドの世界をフィーチャーしたインタラクティブな壁を作り、そこにiPodビデオをはめ込ん

だいくつものののぞき穴を開けた。穴をのぞくといろいろなアニメーションが見える仕組みで、そのアニメーションをブルートゥースで携帯にダウンロードすれば、着メロとして使えるんだ。

———————— **フレッド** 僕たちが手がけてきた自主プロジェクトは、ただ楽しいだけじゃなく、クライアントとのコミュニケーションにも大いに役立った。クライアントは僕らのクレイジーなプロジェクトを見てくれて、それで関係が続いていく。同時に、僕らはたくさんの人たちと触れ合うことで、より大きなエアサイド・ファミリーを築いているんだ。

45

46

47

48

THE AIRSIDE PROCESS

エアサイドの働き方

Nat We had conceived Airside as a place where you could fulfil all of your creative dreams; where you would not get frustrated or feel there was a lid on you. We are all naturally curious people, so we imagined a place where you could creatively explore without being pigeonholed. We never saw ourselves as directors and employees.

Fred It was a reaction to the experience we had all had as freelancers. Work was being compromised, money was wasted and creativity was squashed. Our mission statement ended up being: "Have fun, blow people's minds, and make money." The idea is that you have fun in the studio, and by having fun your creative work benefits. We believed that people would give their best and appreciate the opportunities available if they were enjoying themselves and feeling supported.

Nat Our original intention was to exist as a collective. Organisationally the London design group Tomato was our initial role model; they were very successful at the time and seemed to have found a new and better way to run a design studio that was more democratic than the traditional model. Airside did not quite become a collective, but we did find a way of working where the three of us would do our best to treat our staff as equals and keep their interests at heart.

Alex It's always been our philosophy to break down barriers: we believed that in the studio you have to share knowledge. Some of the industry had a macho competitive spirit, and we didn't relate to that; we wanted to be fun, generous and good to work for. It's abundance theory vs scarcity theory. Scarcity theory says: "Tiny little cake – I'll try to get as much as possible for myself". Abundance theory says: "There is an unlimited amount of cake and let us help each other get as much of it as we like".

Nat Very early on we realised we had to take the ego out of our creative process. If you've got a creative director in the office and everyone follows their style then that is an ego-driven office. At Airside, an intern's idea is as valid as a creative director's idea, so if that is the best idea then we are happy to run with it. Every job that comes into the studio starts with a process that has become known as the 'group brain'. It can take on a very different form depending on who is present, but it usually involves at least four or five people.

ナット 私たちはエアサイドを、クリエイティブに関する夢を、すべて実現できる場所にしたかったの。みんなすでに博学で、固定観念にとらわれず、創造的な探求をすることが出来るんだもの、自分の力を発揮できずにフラストレーションを感じる必要なんてないでしょ。自分たちがディレクターか社員かなんて考えたこと、1度もないわね。

フレッド 僕らがかつてフリーランスで働いていた時の反動なんだ。仕事は妥協だらけ、お金は無駄遣いされ、クリエイティブ精神はないがしろにされていた。だからこそ「楽しみながら、人々を驚かし、お金を稼ごう」というのが僕らの目標になったんだ。作業場が楽しいと、結果的に良い作品が生まれると思う。楽しい上に、周囲にも支えられていると感じると、最高の力を発揮できると信じているからね。

ナット もともとはディレクターの共同体のようなものを作りたいと思っていたの。つまり、トマトのような組織形態を考えていた。当時彼らはとても成功していて、従来の会社組織よりもっと民主的なデザインスタジオを運営するのに相応しい、新しい方法を見出していると感じたわ。エアサイドは共同体にはならなかったけど、私たち3人がスタッフをできる限り同等に扱って、彼らのモチベーションを保つ方法を見つけたのよ。

アレックス 垣根をなくすことが、僕らの哲学なんだ。スタジオでは皆、知識を共有すべきだと思っている。業界にはマッチョな競争精神が広くはびこっているけど、僕らには縁がない。楽しみたいし、気前よくありたいし、一緒に働いて気持ちのいい存在でありたい。豊富か不足かの理論だよね。「全員で分けたら、ケーキは足りないから、先に取れるだけ取っておか

ないと」というのが不足の理論。「ケーキはいくらでもあるから、みんなで助け合って取れるだけ取ろう」というのが豊富の理論。

ナット かなり初期の頃に、創造の過程では、エゴを捨てるべきだと気づいたの。社内のクリエイティブディレクターのスタイルを、みんなが真似するようじゃ、エゴに仕切られた会社になってしまう。エアサイドでは、インターンのアイデアもクリエイティブディレクターのアイデアと同じ価値があるわ。だからインターンのアイデアが一番良かったら、私たちは喜んでそれを実行するわけ。スタジオに来る仕事はすべて、まず「グループ・ブレイン」と呼ばれるプロセスから始まるの。誰が参加するかによって形式は様々だけど、少なくとも4〜5人は関わっているわね。

Airside by Airside

エアサイド バイ エアサイド

The Airside Process

エアサイドの働き方

Fred We knew we didn't want to have one person doing all the design work in isolation, because it limits the scale and breadth of the creative work – it's only ever going to be about one individual aesthetic and can be done with one set of skills. We were looking for something broader than that: collaboration. So at Airside, whenever a job comes into the studio, the first thing we do is to get everyone around the table and really try to understand the brief; then we all come up with as many ideas as we can. Everyone yacks away and we all jam; this is the group brain coming together. Inevitably you get two or three strong ideas emerging out of the pot, and although it's a collaborative process, people still have some ownership of their ideas. Those ideas go off to the client, and if the client picks the junior's idea then they get to run the job. We always believed that whoever had the best idea should then be empowered to deliver it, whether they were junior or senior.

Alex The end result is that for every single piece of creative output from the studio, several people will have had a chance to conceive it, argue for or against it, develop it and reassess it. So nothing leaves the studio that we are ashamed of and we all share responsibility for that.

フレッド　はじめからひとつのプロジェクトを1人が手がけるようなスタジオにはしたくなかった。創作の規模も幅も制限されてしまうからね。そのやり方だと、1人の好みしか反映されないし、その人の技術で完結するものしか仕上がらない。僕らはもっと幅のある何か、つまりコラボレーションを求めていたんだ。仕事が舞い込む度に、僕らはみんなでテーブルを囲んで、全力でブリーフを理解しようと努める。それから出せるだけアイデアを出すんだ。みんな好きなだけしゃべりまくるから、これぞ「グループ・ブレイン」って感じだよ。その中から、やがて2〜3個、強力なアイデアが出てくる。コラボレーションといっても、アイデアは個人のものだからね。最終候補に残ったアイデアの中から、クライアントが後輩のアイデアを選べば、彼らが中心になってその仕事を進めていく。先輩であろうと後輩であろうと、僕らは常に、一番良いアイデアを思いついた者が、そのプロジェクトを手がける権限を持つべきだと信じているからね。

アレックス　結果的に、僕らのスタジオから世に飛び出す作品はどれも、何人もの人間が知恵を絞り、賛否両論議論を交わして、何度も練り直して出来上がるものだから、恥じるものなどひとつもないし、全員が責任を共有していることになるんだ。

Sibylle Preuss When I first started at Airside, I was very impressed by their creative brainstorming process. The entire team (including non-designers) have several meetings until two or three really good ideas have been found which everyone is happy with. These ideas are then developed by the designers and again presented to the whole team for feedback. This creates a very high level of quality control in all the creative work that goes out of the door.

Fred If you've had an idea on your own, nine times out of ten you can find a way to deliver it and it will be pretty good. But if you let it go to the group brain, then you will get something you were not expecting, and that is much more exciting. That cumulative effect enables us to be a great deal more exploratory.

Alex It's the best part of the job. If you skip that part, the outcome is totally different. The group brain works very well, on the whole, because there are only twelve of us – if the team was any bigger it wouldn't be possible.

Fred We throw a lot of ideas out there, and it's like user testing. Until everyone gets really excited about it, the idea is just not good enough. The idea definitely has to have the spark, and that is when everyone can invest in it emotionally.

Henki I don't fight hard in meetings; I'll take a back seat most of the time, but if an idea is good I'll champion it. You get a warm fuzzy feeling when that happens, and you know it's the idea to get behind.

Guy Creative meetings are open to anyone who wants to throw in their twopence worth. Everyone's individual talents are valued and we are all always encouraged to bring our own viewpoint to the table. But the feedback is ruthless! I will always remember Nat saying, "This is no place for wallflowers."

Richard In terms of ideas it is very democratic – work experience people are often surprised that within a few days they are taking part in creative meetings and are being encouraged to contribute ideas. It's not just a big love in; it is always argumentative and boisterous. A lot of design companies aren't like that – if someone comes out with an idea, no one dare criticise it, especially if that someone is the boss. Airside has a healthy atmosphere of people challenging you, and telling you if they don't like your idea, so you learn how to justify yourself.

シビラ・プルース エアサイドで働きはじめた頃、クリエイティブ・ブレインストーミングのやり方にすごく感動したわ。チーム全員（デザイナー以外も含め）で何度も話し合いを重ね、納得できるアイデアをいくつか見つけるの。デザイナーがそれらのアイデアを更に展開させて、全員の前で再度発表し意見を聞く。それが、ここから発信されるすべての作品のクオリティーを高める秘訣ね。

フレッド 自分のアイデアがひとつあれば、十中八九、制作方法は見つけられるだろうし、出来も悪くはないと思う。でもグループ・ブレインにかけると、思いもよらなかったアイデアが出てきて、断然面白いんだ。知恵を集めることで、もっと冒険することが可能になる。

アレックス 実はこのプロセスが一番楽しいんだ。このプロセスを抜かすと、結果はまったく変わってしまう。僕らは全員で12人だから、グループ・ブレインは概ね効果的だよ。チームがこれ以上大きいと、難しいだろうけどね。

フレッド とにかくたくさんのアイデアを出すから、まるでユーザーテストみたいだ。みんなが心から沸きたつアイデアが出てこないかぎり、まだまだ不充分。アイデアに光るものがあってこそ、みんな本気で動き出すからね。

ヘンキ 僕はミーティングで激しく議論を交わすほうじゃないから、大抵後ろの席に座るけど、いいアイデアが出たら支持するよ。そういう時は、なんとなくしっくりきて、これは支持すべきアイデアだと確信するんだ。

ガイ クリエイティブ会議には、意見を出したい人は誰でも参加できる。個人の才能が尊重されていて、みんなが自分の見解を述べることが期待されているからね。その代わり、容赦ない意見が飛び交うよ！「黙っていちゃ参加してる意味がない」ってナットが言うのをいつも思い出すんだ。

リチャード アイデアに関して、僕らは極めて民主的だと思う。インターンに来た人々は、入って数日後のクリエイティブ会議で自分のアイデアを発表する場があることに驚くんだ。それに、そこで出た新人のアイデアが採用されることも少なくない。愛があるだけじゃなく、散々議論するし、大荒れになることもある。でもこういったことは、多くのデザイン会社では起こらないだろ。誰かがアイデアを出しても、面と向って批判したりしないからね、特に上司には。エアサイドには、人のアイデアに反論したり、気に入らないと言える、健全な空気がある。自分の意見をわかってもらう術も、だんだん身についてくるんだよ。

Fred Those meetings are tough, because when you have come up with an idea you are naturally very attached to it. It may not be the best idea at the table but it's hard to be as objective as you should be because it's your baby and you want it to be the idea that's chosen for the final job. People are encouraged to be objective about their own work and let go of it when there is a consensus that it is not really the best idea on the table. That is a struggle, but we have become very good at it. The alternative is that you battle it out for your idea regardless, which is the standard model – the person who wins is whoever can shout the loudest or has the most power internally, and their idea gets implemented regardless of merit. That kind of creative culture rules out many of the more exciting possibilities and quickly becomes very macho.

Nat We constantly acknowledge that we have to remove our egos to get the best work. We encourage a culture where you say what you think – if you do not like an idea you say so, and the person who did the work has to be able to accept criticism. For this to be successful, you have to respect each others' work and value each others' opinion.

Fred I remember showing everyone one of the videos I'd directed for the '64–'95 DVD, and everybody was saying nice things and I was feeling great, and then Richard said he thought it was really amateurish and told me exactly why. He was brave enough to say what he thought, and I listened to him, took his criticisms on board and went back and re-edited the video completely. It hurt my ego to realise that he was right, but the end product was much better as a result of his input. However, that kind of dialogue has to happen in a really safe container with people you trust, otherwise it's just not possible.

Mark There's an openness to being critical about each others' work at Airside, which means that people are not protected in the way they are at some companies where people just do their own thing and don't like people telling them what to do, but do not really feel accepted either. The design process happens very openly, and that is great because just by one person suggesting a really small change, a good project can easily become a really great project. It is essential to have that open discussion, and people are never afraid to voice their opinions. Everything is a collaborative process and that definitely adds more value because there's a lot of thought processes going into the job before anyone puts pen to paper.

フレッド ミーティングは試練だよ。だって自分が思いついたアイデアには、当然思い入れがあるだろ？ ベストとは限らないけど、自分が生んだアイデアである以上、最終的に選ばれてほしいし、客観的になることは難しい。自分のアイデアが選ばれず、客観的になって、諦めるよう諭される時は、そりゃ、ほんとに辛いよ。今じゃ、へっちゃらだけどね。一方では、何がなんでも自分のアイデアに固執するという態度もあって、これが世間では一般的なんだと思う。一番声高に主張しまくるか、社内で一番権力を握っている奴が勝って、良し悪しに関係なくそのアイデアが採用される。このルールでいくと、ワクワクするような可能性の芽は摘まれて、すごくマッチョな世界になってしまう。

ナット 最高の作品を生み出すには、エゴを捨てることが大切だと、いつも肝に銘じているの。みんなが言いたいことを言える環境を作ろうと努力している。アイデアが気に入らなければ、そう言うべきだし、その作品を手がけた人は、その批評を受け止めなくてはならない。互いの作品に敬意を払い、互いの意見を尊重してはじめて、こういった関係が築けるのね。

フレッド '64–'95のDVD用に、僕が監督した作品をみんなに見てもらった時のことは忘れられないよ。評判は上々で、僕もいい気分だったのに、リチャードがすごく素人くさいと言うんだ。そしてその理由も的を射ていた。彼は勇敢にも思ったことを口にしてくれたから、僕はその批判を謙虚に受け止めて、ビデオを完全に編集し直した。彼が正しいとわかって自負心が傷ついたけど、でもあの助言のおかげで完成した作品はずっといいものになった。こうしたやりとりは、真に信頼する者同士の間でなければ、起こり得ないと思う。

マーク エアサイドには、同僚の作品を批評できる開放的な空気がある。つまり、みんな保護されているわけではないということ。会社によっては、自分の仕事だけに専念して、周囲に口出しされることを嫌がるけど、かといって受け入れられているという実感もない。デザインのプロセスが極めてオープンなエアサイドでは、誰かが少し違った提案をするだけで、良いプロジェクトが、一気に傑作プロジェクトになったりする。オープンに話し合い、みんなが恐れずに自分の意見を言えることが不可欠だね。すべてがコラボレーションの積み重ねなんだ。実際の作業を始める前に、みんなで何度も知恵を交換することで、間違いなく作品の質は高められているよ。

The Airside Process

エアサイドの働き方

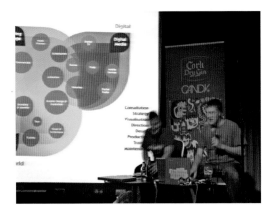

Nat It's always rewarded us to sit down and bash out the idea. The idea is the most important thing and that's what the group brain refines. We have been through phases where we didn't bother with the group brain and it's always caused problems further down the line.

Malika Favre It is so much more effective when designers work together and come up with something better. Even if you are a good designer, mixing different people's ideas together is a way of coming up with something really creative. We would not end up with the results we get by working on our own, and I'm always proud of our collaborative output.

Chris Rain Maybe two people will have the strongest ideas – whoever it is, they go off and do the work and put it all together. Once they've worked on it individually, they'll come back in and we will have another meeting about it and everyone can offer their opinions. It is a great process, and because of it I've been able to work on different projects that I probably would not get involved in had people's particular specialisms been more clearly defined in the company.

Nat We also decided early on that we could not have individual credits on projects because it is never as simple as that. The group brain equals group authorship. Airside is always the credit, and we are very careful to name every member of the studio on our website, so that it is clear who the team includes. The exception is the Shop, which is the one place where people can have an idea and then make it into a T-shirt or print and put their name to it.

Fred Airside is the entity that is creating all the work so everyone has to feel part of Airside. Our staff have to know that they have creative ownership of the company or the whole thing falls apart.

Alex The group brain is all about getting everybody to buy into that idea, and you have got to move that idea on all the way to the finish line. You have to stick to the idea, and constantly check: are we delivering what we said we were going to achieve? Since we first all sat down and agreed on this great idea, are we still pursuing it, or do we need to sit down again and re-examine it? The most important thing of all is that we are all very proud of the work that comes out of the office. It is not one individual's responsibility.

ナット みんなで腰を据えてアイデアに磨きをかけるだけの価値は、必ずあるの。アイデアは一番の根幹だし、グループ・ブレインでこそ洗練される。このプロセスを抜きにすると、後になって必ず問題が起きるのよ。

マリカ・ファーブ デザイナーが集まって作業する方が、ずっと効率的だし、より良いアイデアが出せるわ。どんなに優れたデザイナーでも、複数の人たちのアイデアを合わせることで、よりクリエイティブなアイデアを得ることができる。1人で取り組んでいては得られない結果が出るから、コラボレーションすることを常に誇りに思っているわ。

クリス・レイン たとえば2人が強力なアイデアを出したとすると、それが誰であろうと、アイデアを具体的にまとめる作業に入る。それぞれが作業を終えたら再びミーティングを設けて、みんなで意見を交わすんだ。とても良いプロセスだと思うね。おかげで、仕事内容が明確に細分化された会社では携われないような様々なプロジェクトに、僕も関わっているよ。

ナット シンプルに誰の作品と言えないから、クレジットに個人名を記載しないことも、初期の頃に決めたの。グループで話し合いをするってことは、みんなの作品。だからクレジットは常にエアサイド。その代わり、ウェブサイトにはスタジオのメンバー全員の名前をきちんと記しているわ。例外はショップね。ショップでは、アイデアを思いついた人がTシャツやポスターをデザインして、個人の名前を載せているのよ。

フレッド エアサイドこそ、すべての作品を創り出している実体だから、全員がその一端を担っていることを自覚する必要があるんだ。スタッフはひとりひとり、この会社の創造的所有権を有していることを頭に入れておいてほしい。でなきゃ、すべてが崩れてしまうからね。

アレックス グループ・ブレインとは、メンバー全員が支持できるようなアイデアを出して、そのアイデアが最終的な形になるまで見届けること。決定したアイデアには忠実であるべきだし、「達成すると言ったことを実行できているか」とか「この素晴らしいアイデアで行こうと意見が一致したけど、このまま進めるべきか、あるいはもう1度話し合った方がよいか?」など、常にチェックする必要がある。一番重要なのは、完成して外に出て行く作品に、全員が満足していること。個人の責任ではないんだ。

フレッド ここまで来るのは簡単なことではなかったよ。苦い経験をしながらも、よりクリエイティブなものを創りたい、よりよい制作環境を作りたいという純粋な思いで、発展させてきたものなんだ。苦労して勝ち取った結果なんだよ。

ガイ エアサイドには、階級制のようなものがないからうまくいくんだ。もちろん最終判断を下すのはディレクターだけど、彼らは、自分たちの意見を検証したり、間違いを指摘されたりすることに、とにかくオープンなんだ。クリエイティブ

Fred Our process was not easily achieved. It was evolved as a result of bitter experience, and through a genuine desire to have both highly creative work and a really positive environment to produce it in. It was hard fought for.

Guy The process works because Airside does not have a hierarchical structure as such. Of course the directors have ultimate say, but they are incredibly open to testing their own opinions and being proven wrong. I find this a much more confident approach than the classic scenario of the creative director dictating how people should do their job and the best way to go about it.

Alex It takes a while to get used to working at Airside. Art school is bad training for working here; it convinces you not to show anything until it is finished. It is really tough to make the change and open up but when people realise the whole atmosphere is supportive, it is a relief that you do not have to do everything on your own.

Fred You have to say "I am thinking about this, here is a rough sketch, is it a good idea? Or should I be pursuing something else?" And almost certainly that idea will get mercilessly mauled and thrown around.

Nat What you hope is that someone else will say yes, it is a good idea, but if you added something here or did that a bit differently, it'd be even better. You resolve things together.

Alex It's a shocking place to come and do a work placement if you are not used to responsibility. We tend to employ people who want that responsibility. Some people don't like it and prefer the more traditional design company model with the creative director issuing the ideas.

Richard A lot of people would not be very happy working within Airside's structure because they don't have compatible personalities. The directors have always been careful to recruit the right people. Whenever new people come into the company, as interns for example, it is very much about seeing whether they are the right sort of person to slot into that framework. You might be really talented but prefer to work alone and come up with something that is really amazing; Airside is not that sort of place. You have got to be willing to share your ideas.

ディレクターが一方的に仕事の進め方を指示したり、一番良いと思うやり方を命令する古典的なやり方に比べると、僕らのアプローチの方がずっと自信に満ちていると思う。

アレックス エアサイドの働き方に慣れるには、多少時間がかかるよ。アートスクールで受ける従来の教育が、ここではかえって邪魔になることがあるからね。学校では作品が完成するまで人に見せないように教わるから、途中で修正を入れたり、オープンに話し合うことに、相当抵抗を感じるかもしれない。でも周囲が皆協力的であるとわかれば、全てをひとりで抱え込む必要はないと気づき、返って安心するんだ。

フレッド 何か思いついたら「今こんなアイデアがあって、これがラフスケッチなんだけど、どうかな。この方向でいいかな?」とみんなに尋ねる。すると、アイデアはスタジオを駆け巡って、容赦ない評価に晒される。

ナット 「ああ、いいアイデアだね、だけどどこに何か足したら、もしくは、ここをちょっと変えれば、もっとよくなるかもよ」というような意見を期待しているのよね。ここでは一緒に物事を解決していくから。

アレックス 責任を持つことに慣れていないと、インターンに来るにはショッキングな場所かもしれないね。僕らは責任を持つことを厭わない人を雇うけど、中にはそれを嫌がって、クリエイティブディレクターがアイデアを出してくれる、従来のデザイン会社のやり方のほうが性に合ってるという人もいる。

リチャード 多くの人たちが、自分の性格に適さない組織構造のなかで働いて不幸になっている。エアサイドは、人選にはとても気を遣っているよ。たとえば新しい人がインターンとして入って来る時も、まずはここのやり方に溶け込めるかどうかを見るんだ。中には、とても才能があるけどひとりで作業するのが好きで、そのほうが素晴らしいアイデアが浮かぶ人もいる。でもエアサイドはそういう場所ではなく、アイデアをシェアすることを楽しむための場所なんだ。

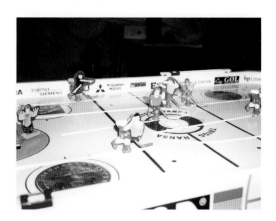

The Airside Process

エアサイドの働き方

Chris You wouldn't get the job or come to work here if your personality wasn't right. Because the people in the studio are well matched, the humour is the same and it's easy to fit in.

Malika They have always cared about employing staff that get along well together as well as how talented they are. That is good, because when you work on projects it is with people you respect as designers as well as individuals. Once you work at Airside you can't work anywhere else. It's like a family; it's a really great thing. I've worked at other agencies and it was more divided into designers and producers – at Airside it's much more open, friendly and relaxed which means that everyone works really well together.

Fred We have a very good relationship with our freelance staff too, and like to get them very involved in projects. Hopefully we treat them differently from how we were treated as freelancers.

Alex We've always found freelancers through friends' recommendations rather than using an agency, and that's maintained the family feel at Airside.

クリス 性格的に合っていなければ、ここでは採用されないし、そもそもここに働きに来ようと思わないだろうね。スタジオのみんなの相性はバッチリだから、ユーモアのセンスも合うし、仲良くやるのは簡単だよ。

マリカ 新しい人を雇う時は、その人がどれだけ才能があるかということだけじゃなく、どれだけみんなと仲良くなれそうかということを考慮しているわね。プロジェクトを始めたら、デザイナーとしてだけじゃなく、人としても尊敬する仲間たちと働くわけだから、これはとても良いことだと思う。1度エアサイドで働き始めたら、もう他では働けないわね。家族みたい。ほんとに素晴らしいことだと思う。他の代理店でも仕事をしたことがあるけど、デザイナーとプロデューサーにはっきりと分けられていたわ。エアサイドは、もっとオープンでフレンドリーでリラックスしているから、楽しく仕事がはかどるのよ。

フレッド 僕らはフリーランスのスタッフたちともすごく上手くやっているし、彼らにもプロジェクトに深く関わってもらっている。僕らがフリーランスだった頃に受けたような扱いとは、違った関わり方ができていると思うよ。

アレックス フリーランスのスタッフを探すときに、エージェンシーを通さずに、必ず友人の紹介で見つけていることも、エアサイドのアットホームな空気を保つのに役立っているかもしれない。

アン エアサイドは大きく変わってきたけれ

Anne Airside has changed a lot but it is still a creative, free place. The fact that I am in an administrative role has not prevented me from participating creatively. If I want to sit in on a creative meeting I can, and I've been able to get involved with the Stitches and pursue photographic projects. I've produced film shoots for MTV idents and a dance video for Lemon Jelly. There's a freedom here to wear lots of hats.

Henki I came from quite a straight-forward design background, but the work is so diverse that you can try your hand at illustration, online content or animation.

Guy Essentially, there is always the feeling that if we, as a workforce, are happy as people, then we will want to do the best we can and go the extra mile in our work. It's an idealistic theory and fortunately it's one that's true.

Alex Despite what people might think, the process we have developed is a commercially viable one. The core of any new creative business model is the creativity itself, and so you have to do everything you can to nurture it; it is a valuable resource. It's almost a new way of doing business, because the other way is the factory way, which is fine for making tins of beans but no use if you want people to create decent work. Companies like IDEO have proved it; they have a similar ethos but on a much bigger scale. Over the last five years, the business world has been waking up to the fact that it needs to understand and respect creativity more, and vice versa; the creative industries have realised that they need to understand and embrace business practice to get beyond the starving artist situation. Together they are much greater than the sum of their parts. So in hindsight it's been a very astute business move to evolve this kind of process. That in essence is the core of Airside's value, that methodology for generating the creative spark.

ど、常にクリエイティブで自由な場所なの。ここでは管理の仕事を担当しているからといって、創作に関われないなんてことはないのよ。私がブレインストーミングに参加したいと思えばそれは可能だし、実際スティッチィズや写真のプロジェクトに携わっているわ。MTVのID制作の撮影や、レモン・ジェリーのダンスビデオの撮影も私が準備したのよ。ここでは色んな役割を演じる自由があるの。

ヘンキ 僕はデザイン畑の出身なんだけど、エアサイドのプロジェクトは多種多様だから、イラストレーションからオンラインコンテンツ、アニメーションまで、いろいろ自分を試すことができるんだ。

ガイ 基本的に、働き手である僕らが、人として幸せであれば、当然仕事でもベストを尽くしたいと思うし、さらにその先にも挑戦したいと感じると思うんだ。理想論だけど、嬉しいことに、ここでは現実なんだよ。

アレックス 他人の意見はどうであれ、僕らが培ってきたプロセスは、商業的にも実行可能なんだ。これからのクリエイティブ・ビジネス戦略の核は、やはり創造力そのものなわけで、それを育てることに全力を注がなくてはならない。創造力は、価値のある資産なんだ。これはほとんど新しいビジネスのやり方だと言ってもいい。なぜなら、従来の工場生産的なビジネスは、豆の缶詰を作るのには適していても、クリエイターにまともな作品を創造させるには、まったく相応しくないからね。アイデオのような企業がそれを証明したよね。規模はずっと大きいけど、僕らと似た気風の持ち主だ。ここ5年ほどで、ビジネスの世界では、創造力をもっとよく理解して尊重することが重要だと気づき始めたし、また逆も然り。クリエイティブ産業では、ビジネスへの理解をより深めることで、アーティストがあえぐ状況を克服しなければならないと気づき始めた。個々の業界の総計よりも、ビジネスと創造の世界が一緒になれば、さらに大きな効果が期待できる。だから後から考えてみると、僕らが辿ってきたプロセスは、なかなか先見の明のあるビジネス展開だったと思うよ。つまるところ、創造力を生み出していく方法論こそ、エアサイドが最も価値を置いている核心部なんだ。

THE WAY WE ARE NOW

エアサイドの今

Fred Recently we have been exploring how we can expand our self-initiated projects into a larger part of our activities. We've built the confidence to initiate our own commercial projects, to go out and find the funding needed to take them all the way to completion. We're also happy partnering with clients and coming up with new content together. It feels like we have a lot more options as a result, which is really important.

Nat We're still enjoying client work, but we've broadened our scope from advertising to include content generation, and we do that for ourselves as well as for our clients.

Alex Now we're creating the concepts, making them happen ourselves and keeping ownership of them as a result. We're more interested in taking the project all the way through and having a share of the final profits than being at the bottom of the food chain. Everyone fantasises about becoming a film director; the question is how you're going to actually make it happen. In the last two years, we've been focusing much more on using our animation and directing skills on self-initiated projects such as our two short films for Live Earth.

フレッド　最近僕らは、自主プロジェクトをより大きなスケールで展開していく可能性を探っている。コマーシャルなプロジェクトに着手して、完成にこぎつけるまでの資金を調達する自信もついたし、クライアントと組んで、一緒にコンテンツを創り出すことも楽しんでいる。結果として、選択肢が色々あることに気づいたんだ。すごく重要なことだよね。

ナット　クライアントのいる仕事も楽しみながら、広告に留まらず、自らコンテンツを生み出すことに活動の領域を広げているわ。自主制作だけでなく、クライアントのためにもコンテンツを創っているの。

アレックス　今では、自分たちでコンセプトを生み出し、自主的に作業を進め、結果的に作品の権利を保有している。食物連鎖の底辺にいるよりも、作品の一部始終に携わって、最終売り上げをシェアすることに関心を持っているんだ。みんな映画監督になる夢を抱くよね。問題は、どうやったらなれるのかということ。この2年間、僕らは、アニメーションやディレクションの技術を、主にライブアース用に制作した2本の短編のような自主プロジェクトにつぎ込んできた。

LIVE EARTH
THE BEGINNER'S GUIDE
TO GIVING A DAMN

ライブアース

ビギナーのための温暖化防止ガイド

「小さいことは...気にしよう」

Unnecessarily flows from the other side of the world!

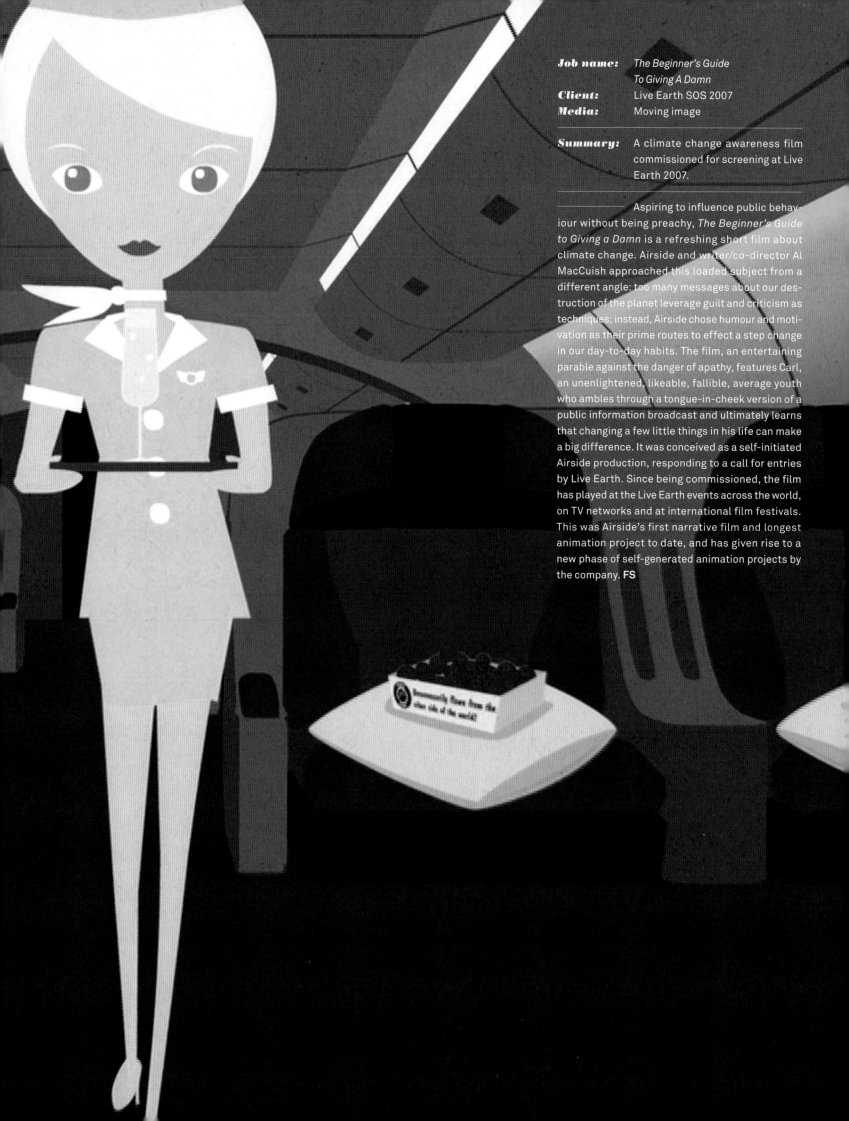

Job name:	*The Beginner's Guide*
	To Giving A Damn
Client:	Live Earth SOS 2007
Media:	Moving image

Summary: A climate change awareness film commissioned for screening at Live Earth 2007.

Aspiring to influence public behaviour without being preachy, *The Beginner's Guide to Giving a Damn* is a refreshing short film about climate change. Airside and writer/co-director Al MacCuish approached this loaded subject from a different angle: too many messages about our destruction of the planet leverage guilt and criticism as techniques; instead, Airside chose humour and motivation as their prime routes to effect a step change in our day-to-day habits. The film, an entertaining parable against the danger of apathy, features Carl, an unenlightened, likeable, fallible, average youth who ambles through a tongue-in-cheek version of a public information broadcast and ultimately learns that changing a few little things in his life can make a big difference. It was conceived as a self-initiated Airside production, responding to a call for entries by Live Earth. Since being commissioned, the film has played at the Live Earth events across the world, on TV networks and at international film festivals. This was Airside's first narrative film and longest animation project to date, and has given rise to a new phase of self-generated animation projects by the company. **FS**

作品名： ビギナーのための温暖化防止ガイド
「小さいことは…気にしよう」

クライアント： ライブアース SOS 2007

メディア： 動画

内容： ライブアース2007年用に制作された、気候
変動への関心を促す短編映像

　　　　　　　「ビギナーのための温暖化防止ガイド『小さ
いことは…気にしよう』」は、気候変動について、説教臭くならず
に人々に影響を与えようと試みた、さわやかな短編映画。エアサ
イドと、ライター兼共同ディレクターのアル・マクイッシュは、こ
の込み入った題材に、まったく異なった切り口で取り組んだ。と
いうのも、環境破壊を警告するメッセージといえば、人々の罪悪
感をあおる批判的なものばかり。そこで彼らは、日常生活を少し
変えるだけで、誰もが段階的に良い変化をもたらすことができる
という、やる気のでるメッセージをユーモラスに伝える方法を選
択した。物語の主人公のカールは、どこにでもいそうな無知な若
者。お茶目に、愚かに間違いを犯しながらも、大きな変化をもた
らすために、日々の生活の小さな事柄を変えていく様子と、無関
心であることの危機をコメディータッチで描いたエンターテイメ
ント作品。ライブアースの応募呼びかけに応える形で、エアサイ
ドの自主プロジェクトとして始まった本作は、世界各地のライブ
アースで上映されたほか、テレビや国際映画祭でも多数紹介され
ている。エアサイドにとって初の物語仕立てで、目下最長のアニ
メーション作品の制作は、自主アニメーション・プロジェクトとい
う、新たな事業を展開する契機となった。(FS)

LIVE EARTH PENGUIN IN A PICKLE

ライブアース
―――――――
窮地のペンギン

Job name:	*Penguin in a Pickle*
Client:	Live Earth SOS 2007
Media:	Moving image

Summary:	A climate change awareness film commissioned for screening at Live Earth 2007.

作品名：	窮地のペンギン
クライアント：	ライブアース SOS 2007
メディア：	動画

内容：	ライブアース2007の依頼で制作、上映した地球温暖化警告映像

――――――― *Penguin in a Pickle* is an animated short, based on a children's book written by Alex's wife Clare, for their son Oliver. Alex decided to develop the story into a film pitch, and it was commissioned as one of a series of films shown at the global Live Earth climate change awareness concerts in 2007. The film and book set out to explain the threat of climate change to young children, for whom this would present a theoretically and emotionally difficult concept. The story follows the fate of a young penguin, stranded on an ice floe that becomes detached from the South Pole. He begins a perplexing journey around the world's oceans, amid increasingly erratic weather. Eventually the shrinking iceberg melts entirely, plunging the penguin into a sub-aquatic world where he finds himself swimming amongst the submerged ruins of human civilisations, overcome by rising sea levels. Its vision of a dystopian future is carefully handled with a gently elegiac tone, a stirring soundtrack and a simple morality that makes the film easily accessible for its young audience. This was one of two films produced by Airside for Live Earth, alongside *The Beginner's Guide to Giving a Damn.* **FS**

――――――― 「窮地のペンギン」は、アレックスの妻クレアが、息子オリバーのために書いた物語をもとに制作された短編アニメーション。アレックスがストーリーに手を加え、短編映画として提案し、世界規模の地球温暖化防止コンサート、ライブアース2007で上映される作品の一環として、制作を依頼された。幼い子供たちには、理論的にも感情的にも理解することの難しい温暖化の脅威を、この原作と映画は、易しく伝えようと試みている。物語は、南極から切り離された氷の上に、ひとり取り残された幼いペンギンの運命を描く。荒れ狂う天候の中、ペンギンは、戸惑いながら広い海を漂流する。やがて、ペンギンをのせた氷塊は跡形もなく溶けて、否応なく海に放り出される。そこでペンギンが目にしたものは、過去の温暖化にともなう海面の上昇によって、その昔、海底深く沈んだ人類の文明都市であった。やさしく哀愁を帯びた色彩、胸を打つ音楽、明快な倫理性で、陰鬱な未来の展望を描き出したこの作品は、幼い子供たちにも理解しやすい内容に仕上がっている。エアサイドは、ライブアース用に、本作と「ビギナーのための温暖化防止ガイド『小さいことは…気にしよう』」の2本を制作した。(FS)

LIVE EARTH

——— **Nat** We were commissioned to make a short film for Al Gore's 2007 benefit concert, which at seven minutes ended up being the longest and most complicated animation we'd ever made.

——— **Alex** Live Earth's aim was to get its message out into lots of different media streams, and one of its strategies to do this was to commission various filmmakers to produce a series of inspirational films. We got a call from Astrid Edwards, a video commissioner we'd worked with previously on The Beatles' video (page 236) and came up with pitches for two different films, *The Beginner's Guide to Giving a Damn*, and *Penguin in a Pickle*, a script based on a children's story by my wife. To our surprise they commissioned both, and so we suddenly had to produce an enormous amount of animation very quickly in time for the worldwide concert series in July 2007.

——— **Al MacCuish (writer)** I was on a train to Scotland to see my mum when Alex phoned and said, "Is there any way you could write a short film for Monday morning?" If it had been anyone else I would probably have said no, but it was Airside

and Alex; it was an incredibly good cause and a great opportunity. We have a tradition at Mother about public service announcements, which is that they don't work if they highlight a negative. Human behaviour is a very strange thing to alter, so anti-smoking ads can have a huge impact, but soon after real life kicks back in. So our approach was to try to positively affect people's behaviour around saving energy, which led to *The Beginner's Guide to Giving a Damn*. The Live Earth people had recognised this themselves, and wanted to do something that was not about making people feel bad, or telling people that simply putting your hand in your pocket is going to change things. We picked five positive acts – the easiest things you could do to make a difference – and focussed on getting those messages across. As a kid I watched reruns of cartoons from the 1940s and 1950s which all contained short Walt Disney infomercials; they were basically educational cartoons, and when I heard the Live Earth brief I thought this had to be the approach. The script used various members of the animal kingdom to show the main character Carl what he was doing wrong, and what he could do about it. The film got a great response when it

2

4

ライブアース

——— **ナット**　アル・ゴアによる2007年慈善コンサート用に、ショートフィルムの制作を依頼されたの。結果的に、この7分の作品は、それまで制作した中でも最も長く複雑なものになったわ。

——— **アレックス**　ライブアースの狙いは、複数のメディアを介してメッセージを伝えることで、その戦略のひとつとして、様々なフィルムメーカーたちにメッセージ性のある映像の制作を依頼したんだ。僕らは以前ビートルズのMV（237ページ参照）で一緒に仕事をしたことのあるビデオ・コミッショナー、アストリッド・エドワーズから連絡をもらって、2作品をコンペに提出した。「ビギナーのための温暖化防止ガイド『小さいことは…気にしよう』」と、僕の奥さんが子供向けに書いた「窮地のペンギン」。驚いたことに、両方の案が通ったものだから、2007年7月に世界各都市で開催されるコンサートに間に合うように、膨大な量のアニメーションを短期間で仕上げることになった。

——— **アル・マクイッシュ**　アレックスから電話をもらったのは、ちょうど母に会いにスコットランドに向かう電車の中だった。「月曜の朝までに、なんとか短編の脚本を書いてくれないか」ってね。これが他の人だったら、僕はきっとノーと答え

3

appeared in the Live Earth show, and has since been taken to about 70 festivals worldwide.

——————— **Fred** *The Beginner's Guide* was a big step up for us from music videos, commercials and idents: it was our first experience of creating and sustaining a narrative.

——————— **Alex** After making the initial film, none of us wanted to leave the project behind – it got a great reception, and we were all interested in campaigning for environmental issues. Henki had created these very strong characters, so we decided to develop them further and that's evolved into an ongoing project that we're all very excited about. Watch this space!

——————— **Al** All Airside's work has got originality and heart – it's cheeky. They're good people with good business tactics, and creativity always comes first. All their decisions are based on making their work brilliant – that's what they're always striving for. In every conversation with Airside they're always excited about that spirit. It's a powerful tool to show people the positive rather than the negative; why frown when you can smile?

ただろうけど、エアサイドとアレックスの頼みだからね。それだけで充分やる価値があったし、素晴らしいチャンスだと思った。僕の務める代理店マザーでは、公共広告に取り組む際、「否定事項を強調したものには関わらない」という暗黙の了解がある。人間というのは実に不思議な反応をするもので、たとえば喫煙に反対する広告は確かに大きなインパクトがあるけど、実社会では直ぐにその反動が起きるんだ。だから僕らはエネルギーの節約に関してポジティブな影響を人々に与えようと考えて、そこで生まれたのが「ビギナーのための温暖化防止ガイド『小さいことは…気にしよう』」だった。ライブアース側も同じことを感じていたようで、人々に後ろめたい思いをさせたり、物事を変えるのにただ募金を促すのが目的ではなかった。僕らは、環境改善に効果的で、誰もが簡単にできる5つの行動を選び、いかにこれをうまく伝えるかに焦点をあてた。子供の頃に、ウォルト・ディズニーの短いインフォマーシャルが挿入されている1940、50年代のアニメの再放送を見ていたんだけど、基本的に教育アニメでね、ライブアースのブリーフを聞いた時に、あの手法でいこうと、ピンときた。仕上げた脚本には、動物王国に暮らす色々な動物が登場して、主人公のカールの愚行を指摘し、どうすべきかを教えるんだ。ライブアースの本番で大きな反響を得て、それから世界中のおよそ70の映画祭で上映されているよ。

——————— **フレッド** 「ビギナーのための〜」は、僕らにとって、ミュージックビデオやCM、IDの先へ進む、大きな一歩だったと思う。物語をゼロから作って完成させるというのは初めての経験だったからね。

——————— **アレックス** こうして最初の映画を作り終えた僕らは、このプロジェクトをここで終わりにしたくなかった。周囲の反応もすこぶる良かったし、みんな環境問題のキャンペーンに取り組むことに関心があったしね。ヘンキがこれほど説得力のあるキャラクターを作ってくれたこともあって、ここからさらに展開しようという話になった。今まさに進行中のプロジェクトで、みんなやる気満々だから、どうぞお楽しみに！

——————— **アル** エアサイドの作品には、どれも独創性とハートがあるだろ。ホントに欲張りだよ。いいビジネス戦略をもった、いい奴らで、何より創造性を重視する。すべては作品を一層素晴らしいものにするためで、そのためには決して努力を惜しまない。エアサイドと話していると、いつもそんな熱意が伝わってくるんだ。ネガティブよりもポジティブな面を見せることの方が、はるかに効力がある。笑ってもいい時に、わざわざしかめ面をする必要なんかないだろ？

STORYMAN

ストーリーマン

The Way We Are Now

エアサイドの今

Job name: *Storyman*
Client: Brown Eyed Boy / Lupus Films
Media: Moving image

Summary: A pilot for a proposed TV series featuring the character of Story-man interviewing celebrities.

——————— *Storyman*: originally a BBC Radio 4 comedy/drama in which actor and writer Andrew Clover guides an interviewee through a process of telling stories, in order to reveal a mixture of truth and fantasy from their inner psyche. After Fred Deakin was featured on the programme, Airside began working with the production company Brown Eyed Boy to create a pilot for a Storyman TV series. In this episode, actor/comedian David Walliams

reveals a dark, twisted tale, that was adapted visually by Airside into a folkloric animation. The plot dives into different fantasy landscapes filled with unusual characters, all imagined by Walliams and then visualised by Airside. It's an ideal brief on which to practise the classic Airside trope of creating warped characters and imaginative worlds. Without filmed footage of the interview, the challenge also lay in creating an animated sketch of Walliams, and incorporating some stills of his face into the animation to represent the surreal mix of reality and fiction taking place in the work. *Storyman* is one of Airside's most recent self-initiated projects, and marks a move towards producing animated series for television. The pilot has attracted interest from broadcasters in the UK and the US. **FS**

作品名:	ストーリーマン
クライアント:	ブラウン・アイド・ボーイ／ルーパス・フィルムズ
メディア:	動画
内容:	ストーリーマンというキャラクターが、有名人にインタビューするテレビシリーズのパイロット版

——————「ストーリーマン」は、もともとBBCラジオ4のコメディー／ドラマ番組で、俳優兼ライターのアンドリュー・クローバーが毎回ゲストにインタビューを行い、相手の内面に潜む真実とファンタジーを引き出しながら、一緒に物語を構築していくという内容。フレッド・ディーキンがゲストに招かれたのを縁に、エアサイドは制作会社ブラウン・アイド・ボーイとともに、「ストーリーマン」のテレビシリーズのパイロット版を制作。このエピソードでは、俳優兼コメディアンのデヴィッド・ウォリアムス

が語るダークでひねりの効いたストーリーを、民話調のアニメーションで映像化した。ウォリアムスのイマジネーションと、エアサイドによる視覚解釈から生まれた、不思議なキャラクターが多数登場し、幻想的な世界が次々と展開する。一筋縄ではいかないキャラクターやイマジネーションの世界といった、もとよりエアサイドが得意とする内容を求められた、まさに理想的なプロジェクトだった。とはいえ、インタビューの実写素材がなかったので、ウォリアムスのアニメーションスケッチを描いて顔写真と合成することで、物語の中で展開する虚像と現実がシュールに混ざり合った世界を表現する作業は、かなりのチャレンジだった。本作は、エアサイドの最新自主プロジェクトのひとつで、テレビ用アニメーション・シリーズ制作へと進むきっかけとなった。パイロット版は、英国およびアメリカのテレビ局関係者にいずれも好評を得ている。（FS）

The Way We Are Now

エアサイドの今

STORYMAN

——————— **Nat** *Storyman* is another example of our new strategy of content generation. This was a radio format that the writer and author Andrew Clover invented for BBC Radio 4. It's psychotherapy meets fiction. Andrew interviews a celebrity and gets them to make up a story on the spot with him, so the dialogue inevitably goes into the subconscious. Fred was one of the people interviewed in the original radio series, so when they wanted to make a TV pilot they thought of us and asked us to direct the animation based on David Walliams' interview. We had to figure out what he would look like as an animated character and then create animation to illustrate the bizarre story that he improvised with Andrew.

——————— **Alex** Making content like this is a whole new side of our business now. Advertising agencies come to us because they recognise we're capable of producing our own ideas – in the past

ストーリーマン

——————— **ナット** 「ストーリーマン」も、コンテンツを生み出す新しい戦略の一例ね。もともとは作家のアンドリュー・クローバーが、ラジオ4のために作ったラジオ放送用のアイデアで、心理療法とフィクションを掛け合わせたものだった。アンドリューが毎回セレブと会って、彼らと即興で架空の話を作り上げるから、対話が必然的に潜在意識を反映したものになる。フレッドもそのラジオシリーズでインタビューされたひとりだったの。その縁で、デヴィッド・ウォリアムスのインタビューをベースに、テレビ用のパイロット版を制作するから、アニメーションを監督してもらえないかって、私たちに声をかけてくれたわけ。まずはデヴィッドをアニメ・キャラクターにしたらどうなるかを見てから、彼がアンドリューと即興でこしらえた奇妙なストーリーのアニメーションを制作したわ。

——————— **アレックス** 僕らが今開拓している新しいビジネスは、こうしたコンテンツ制作なんだ。広告代理店も、僕らが自前のアイデアをプロデュースできるとわかって、声をかけて

6

7

8

5-8 Development work for
Storyman, 2007

「ストーリーマン」制作過程
2007

that was usually work for Lemon Jelly, and now we are producing other self-generated and collaborative projects like *Live Earth* and *Storyman* that are exciting projects in their own right and also show potential clients what we can do.

————— **Nat** We're being much more businesslike about our self-initiated work these days. It's good for Airside to invest in these projects, to make a space where we can experiment and create content that has real value. Some of them are one-offs while others take off: like the Live Earth film, it might begin as a one-off project but become something bigger down the line.

————— **Alex** We had always done lots of fun, interesting little projects in the past and then it was a case of minimising how much money we would lose on them. Now we're putting a lot of effort and momentum behind the creative projects that we feel can become commercially viable in the future. Part of the growing up process is understanding where you fit into the bigger marketplace and thus where your work has value.

————— **Nat** We're consciously dividing our time now. We still work with smaller companies and they're the bedrock of our client base; we love doing those collaborative projects and we're aiming to keep them at around 50 per cent of our output. Then we spend about a quarter of our time working with advertising agencies, which is mostly animation, moving image and illustration. The last quarter is the self-initiated work which fuels our wilder side: it's a playground and lets us do our blue-sky thinking. But we don't want it to take over the business because we enjoy working directly with clients too much.

————— **Fred** We're interested in having that variety on a daily basis. Our advertising clients don't just look at their agency competitors for inspiration, they also look to the worlds of music and culture. That's where we sit most happily, on the cusp of these activities.

くれる。そういった仕事は、以前はレモン・ジェリー関連のものに限られていたけど、今ではライブアースや「ストーリーマン」といった、自主プロジェクトやコラボレーションをプロデュースすることで、僕らに何ができるかをクライアントに知ってもらえるようになった。

————— **ナット** 最近では、自主制作の作品にかなりビジネスライクに取り組んでいるわ。いろいろ試しながら、本当に価値のあるコンテンツを創造する場を作るために、こうしたプロジェクトに投資することはエアサイドにとって良いことだと思う。1回限りのものもあれば、継続していくものもある。たとえばライブアースの映像は、1話完結の短編として始まったけれど、結局大きな作品に発展していくことになったわ。

————— **アレックス** 過去には楽しくて魅力的な小規模のプロジェクトに、たくさん関わってきたけど、それは損失も最小限に抑えようと考えてのことだった。でも今では、先々商業的にも成り立ちうると感じているクリエイティブ・プロジェクトには惜しみなく力を注いでいるよ。より大きな市場で、僕らの作品が評価される場所を見出すことも、成長に必要な過程だと思う。

————— **ナット** 今では意識的に時間配分をしているわ。小規模な企業との仕事も続けていて、彼らこそ私たちの基盤となるクライアントなの。彼らとのコラボレーション的なプロジェクトが大好きだから、全体の50%くらいはこういった仕事を手がけるようにしてる。それから25%は広告代理店との仕事。ほとんどがアニメーション、ムービングイメージ、イラストレーションね。あとの25%が、私たちの冒険心を満たしてくれる自主プロジェクト。これは、突拍子もない発想のできる遊び場のようなもの。でも、直接クライアントと働くことを楽しんでいるから、自主プロジェクトが主要業務になることは、望んでいないわ。

————— **フレッド** 毎日、多様な仕事に取り組めるってことが楽しいんだ。広告クライアントたちは、インスピレーションを得るのに、ライバル代理店の動きだけでなく、常に音楽やアートの世界に目を向けている。その最先端で、僕らが一番楽しそうに活動してるっていうのが理想だね。

The Way We Are Now

エアサイドの今

PET SHOP BOYS

ペット・ショップ・ボーイズ

Latest

PIXELAWARDS

Job name: Pet Shop Boys, official website

Client: Pet Shop Boys / Dorrell Management

Media: Website

Awards: Pixel Award, Webby, Interactive Media Award, Design Week Awards 2007 – Interactive Media

Summary: The official website for the Pet Shop Boys which includes their entire back catalogue and a moblogging facility.

——————— The Pet Shop Boys, one of Britain's top-selling bands, possess a fanatical global fanbase called the 'Petheads'. Whatever Neil and Chris are doing, they're eager to know about it. Airside created a website to serve this special relationship, building a system that was as easy to update as a blog but with Flash design and functionality – two things that then rarely existed together. The website looks like a newspaper, very simple on the graphics, and as stark as a newspaper front page, which it's meant to resemble. Behind this there's an enormous amount of content documenting PSB's prolific body of work – downloads, albums, lyrics, photography, video and tour information, plus a steady stream of personal news and chat. Yet the user is never overwhelmed – the modules on the home page can be moved around daily, plucking out different information as the band desires, just like a newspaper. The icing on the cake is that if the band goes on holiday, or are constantly touring and don't have time to update the site, they can text news to the website using their mobile phones. Many bands use the internet to communicate directly with their fans, but few do so through such a neat interface, and this is a site that works really hard for its owners and its users. **FS**

Read more ▲▼

New Release

On August 7, 1995 an album of Pet Shop Boys B-sides was released. It is called "Alternative".

Navigation ▲

Jukebox

Headlines

作品名：	ペット・ショップ・ボーイズ、オフィシャル・ウェブサイト
クライアント：	ペット・ショップ・ボーイズ／ドレル・マネージメント
メディア：	ウェブサイト
受賞歴：	ピクセル・アワード、ウェビーズ、インタラクティブ・メディア・アワード、デザイン・ウィーク賞2007／インタラクティブ・メディア部門
内容：	過去の全ディスコグラフィー、携帯ブログ機能も含めた、ペット・ショップ・ボーイズのオフィシャル・ウェブサイト

———————— 英国でトップセールスを誇るバンドのひとつ、ペット・ショップ・ボーイズ（PSB）には、ニールとクリスがどこで何をしているのか、逐一情報を知りたがる、ペットヘッズと呼ばれる熱狂的な国際ファンクラブが存在する。そこでエアサイドは、このPSBとファンの特別な関係に応えるべく、デザインと機能性という、めったに共存し得ない両面を備えつつ、容易にアップデートできるFlashベースのブログシステムを作り上げた。ウェブサイトは、意図的に新聞の一面のように、シンプルで無駄のない、グラフィカルな作りになっているが、そのコンテンツには、ダウンロード、アルバム、歌詞、写真、ビデオ、ツアー情報、時々配信される個人的なニュースやチャットなど、これまでの歴史を語る膨大な量のPSB情報がドキュメント化されている。ここで驚くのはまだ早い。ホームページのモジュールは、日々新たに配置換えされ、バンドが配信したい様々な情報を、まさに新聞のようにピックアップして掲載する仕組みになっている。おまけに、バンドの休暇やツアー中、サイトをアップデートする時間がなくても、携帯からニュースが配信可能。ネットを通じて、ファンと直接交流するバンドは多く存在するが、ここまで美しく整理されたインターフェースでやりとりするバンドは数えるほど。管理人とユーザーのために、日夜せっせと稼働する働き者のサイトである。(FS)

Read more　▲▼

On This Day

2000: The Boys perform the first of two consecutive nights' concerts in Tokyo.

2002: Chris and Neil bring their Release tour to Milan, Italy.

Read more　▲▼

Pet Texts

19 Jan 2008

We were in Berlin this week for a few days. Great city. Neil x

10 Jan 2008

Went to "The Masque Of The Red Death" at Battersea Arts Centre last night. Extraordinary. Each member of the audience wears a mask and you wander through a

Read more　▲▼

Lyric Of The Day

They call this a community
I like to think of it as home
Arriving at the airport
I am going it alone

Read more　▲▼

Break 4 Love (UK radio edit) ; Home and dry　 ■ ▶ ▶▶

Sign Up
▲

9

10

PET SHOP BOYS

——— **Neil Tennant** We first approached Airside because we were impressed by the elegance of their design for the White Cube Gallery website. Our brief to them was that we wanted a design that functioned as a news site (BBC News, Guardian Unlimited, New York Times were comparisons), an archive of music, photographs, lyrics and past projects, and a link between us and people interested in us. We wanted the design to reflect the comparatively minimal approach which we established with our first album. The site also had to be easy to operate for Pet Shop Boys and our management. Airside achieved all of the above so that when you look at the front page of the site you can immediately see the different activities of Pet Shop Boys, past and present, and click on the one that interests you. They also came up with a unique feature, Pet Texts, which enables Chris and I to text messages and photographs to our site from our mobile phones, a feature that has proved very popular. We look forward to working with Airside to extend and improve the site to coincide with the release of our next album.

——— **Nat** Neil and Chris's brief was for something that was rich in information but with understated presentation. There's an enormous amount of content on the site, but you wouldn't know it and you don't feel overwhelmed. The content is all cross-linked in a really useful way that the user doesn't even notice. It's quiet and dignified.

——— **Mark** The modules are very flexible, so that the home page changes every day like a newspaper's front page. The site pulls out the latest updated content from its database, so although visually not a lot seems to have changed, the content and structure is always fresh – it might feature an album, or it might just tell you that Chris and Neil have been on holiday. For a Flash site to be that adaptable is quite unusual.

——— **Chris** Like our work for the photographer Nadav Kander, it doesn't look like a typical Airside website. I treated the design like a piece of print work, and drew a good grid and kept it minimal and clean so that the information was the star.

11

ペット・ショップ・ボーイズ

——— **ニール・テナント** エアサイドが制作したホワイト・キューブのウェブサイトの上品さに惹かれて、初めて声をかけたんだ。僕らが頼んだのは、ニュースサイト（BBCニュース、ガーディアン・アンリミテッド、NYタイムズなどに匹敵するもの）、音楽アーカイヴ、写真、歌詞、過去のプロジェクト、僕らに興味のある人と僕らを繋げるリンクの機能を兼ね備えたデザイン。最初のアルバムで確立した、比較的ミニマルな世界観を反映したデザインで、尚かつペット・ショップ・ボーイズとマネージメントが運営しやすいものにしたかったんだ。以上のことを、エアサイドは完璧に叶えてくれたから、トップページにアクセスするだけで、ペット・ショップ・ボーイズの過去から現在までの様々な活動が一目でわかるし、気になるものをクリックすれば、さらに詳しい情報が得られるようになっている。さらに、ペット・テキストというユニークな機能も作ってくれてね。クリスと僕が携帯からメッセージや写真をアップすることができる機能なんだけど、これがなかなかの人気なんだ。次のアルバムのリリースにあわせて、またエアサイドとサイトをリニューアルするのが待ち遠しいよ。

——— **ナット** 情報は満載だけど、見た目はシンプルなものを作ってほしい、というのがニールとクリスの依頼だった。だから膨大な量のコンテンツが含まれているけど、見ている人にはわからないし、情報に圧倒されることのないように仕上げたの。ユーザーは気づかなくても、すべてのコンテンツが、ものすごく便利に繋がり合っていて、派手さはないけど内容のあるサイトよ。

——— **マーク** モジュールがとても柔軟に作ってあるから、このホームページは、新聞の見出しのように日々変わる。サイトはデータベースから一番最近更新されたコンテンツをトップに持ってくるから、あまり変化がないように見えても、コンテンツとその構造は常に新鮮なんだ。アルバムについて取り上げている日もあれば、「クリスとニールは休暇中」とだけ伝えている日もあったりね。フラッシュのサイトで、ここまで融通が利くものは、かなりめずらしいよ。

——— **クリス** ナダブ・カンダールのサイト同様、これもエアサイドの作る典型的なウェブサイトとは、ひと味違う。1枚のポスターをデザインするような気持ちで作ったね。情報が主役になるように、適切なグリッドを使って、すっきりとミニマルに仕上げたんだ。

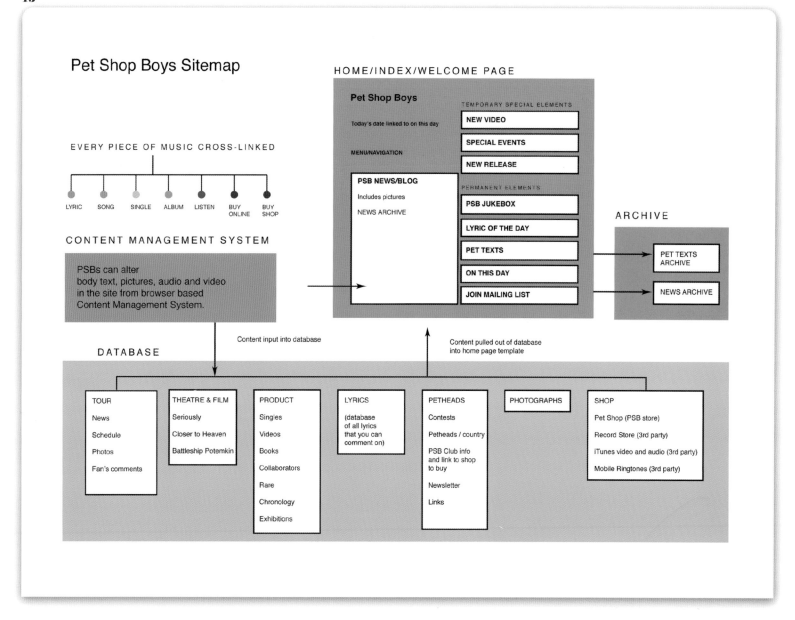

Pet Shop Boys Sitemap

EVERY PIECE OF MUSIC CROSS-LINKED

LYRIC SONG SINGLE ALBUM LISTEN BUY ONLINE BUY SHOP

CONTENT MANAGEMENT SYSTEM

PSBs can alter body text, pictures, audio and video in the site from browser based Content Management System.

HOME/INDEX/WELCOME PAGE

Pet Shop Boys

Today's date linked to on this day

MENU/NAVIGATION

PSB NEWS/BLOG
Includes pictures
NEWS ARCHIVE

TEMPORARY SPECIAL ELEMENTS
NEW VIDEO
SPECIAL EVENTS
NEW RELEASE

PERMANENT ELEMENTS
PSB JUKEBOX
LYRIC OF THE DAY
PET TEXTS
ON THIS DAY
JOIN MAILING LIST

ARCHIVE
PET TEXTS ARCHIVE
NEWS ARCHIVE

Content input into database

Content pulled out of database into home page template

DATABASE

TOUR
News
Schedule
Photos
Fan's comments

THEATRE & FILM
Seriously
Closer to Heaven
Battleship Potemkin

PRODUCT
Singles
Videos
Books
Collaborators
Rare
Chronology
Exhibitions

LYRICS
(database of all lyrics that you can comment on)

PETHEADS
Contests
Petheads / country
PSB Club info and link to shop to buy
Newsletter
Links

PHOTOGRAPHS

SHOP
Pet Shop (PSB store)
Record Store (3rd party)
iTunes video and audio (3rd party)
Mobile Ringtones (3rd party)

Pet Shop Boys : the official site

petshopboys.co.uk
the official site

12 January 2007

Latest

11 January 2007
Neil at the National Portrait Gallery tonight
Neil Tennant will be talking at the National Portrait Gallery tonight.
At 7 pm tonight, Neil will be talking about the Pet Shop Boys' approach to image and design at a special event at the National Portrait Gallery in London. He will be joined onstage by Philip Hoare and Chris Heath.
Read more

Headlines

11 January 2007
2007 tour plans
Pet Shop Boys will soon be announcing new tour dates for 2007.

01 January 2007
Bad weather hits Hogmanay show
Pet Shop Boys' New Year's Eve show in Edinburgh had to be cancelled last night because of appalling weather.

19 December 2006
Award nomination for this website
The designers of this site have been nominated for an award.
Read more

Pet Texts

05 January 2007
Nathan,Nick and Sylvia join us for a coffee after soundcheck delayed.

05 January 2007
Neil in madrid with a cold remedy.
Read more

New Release

The full Radio 2 concert with the BBC Concert Orchestra. Released October 23rd.

On This Day

1963: 'Please Please Me'?one of the few songs with the distinction of being mentioned in a PSB lyric ('Nothing Has Been Proved')?is released in the U.K. as the Beatles' second single.
Read more

Lyric Of The Day

They call this a community
I like to think of it as home
Arriving at the airport
I am going it alone

Navigation   ▲   **Jukebox**   Please click play to start the jukebox   ▪ ▶ ▶▶   **Sign Up**   ▲

MIKA

ミカ

Job name:
Client: MIKA
Casablanca / Universal /
Island Records

Media: Moving image, print

Summary: A collaborative project to develop a
visual language and produce music
packaging and promos for MIKA.

Mika's vibrant identity extends bey-
ond his songs and their boldly illustrated record
sleeves into a distinctive, fully-formed visual brand.
Airside helped to establish the Mika look, which
crossed over into posters, promo videos and YouTube
teasers featuring characters from Mika's world, like
Lollipop Girl and the Purple Popstars: in all, an array
of visual content that allows his music to reach its
audience through a variety of media, and like Lemon
Jelly, to exist as an artistic counterpoint to the
music. Airside, Mika and his sister Yasmine devised
a uniquely collaborative method to create this body
of multimedia artwork. The three-way process used
Mika's music as its starting point, took in Yasmine's
distinctive painting style, and combined them with
Airside's skill at creating fantastical worlds using
animated landscapes and characters. With Airside
acting as art directors to this pair of talented
siblings, the resulting aesthetic belongs strongly
to Yasmine and Mika. In building a visual fantasy
universe around his music, Mika has been able to
extend his fans' enjoyment of his music, providing
another window into his world. Meanwhile in an
age of downloading, it celebrates and keeps alive
the spirit of creating music and visuals that exist
symbiotically. **FS**

Airside by Airside
エアサイド バイ エアサイド

The Way We Are Now
エアサイドの今

作品名：

クライアント：　ミカ

メディア：　カサブランカ/ユニバーサル/
アイランド・レコーズ
動画、印刷物

内容：

ミカの宣伝用に、ビジュアル言語を創り出し、その楽曲や大胆
パッケージとミュージックビデオを制作した
コラボレーション・プロジェクト

ミカの元気なイメージは、その楽曲や大胆
なビジュアルブランドとしてものみならず、際立った個性を持
つビジュアルのレコードジャケットのみならず、際立った個性を持
なミカのイメージ構築に協力し、ロリポップ。エアサイドはそん
ポップスターといった、ミカの世界に登場するキャラクターを用
いたYouTube用の予告映像やポスター、ミュージックビデオを

制作した。これらの多くのビジュアルイメージが、彼らの音楽が、
様々なメディアを通じてオーディエンスに届くことを可能にし、ま
際立たせている。このマルチメディア・アーティスティックな面を
めに、エアサイド。このマルチメディア・アートワークのアーティスティックな面を
ション作業を繰り広げた。この3者のユニークなコラボレー
を拠り所に、ヤスミンが、ミカの音楽のアーティスティックな面を
それらをエアサイドの独特の技術を使ったペインティングスタイルを
やキャラクターが独特の技術を使ったペインティングスタイルで合体させて、まずミカの曲
ド、この才気あふれる姉弟のアートディレクターを務めたミ
いえ、仕上がりには、ヤスミンとミカのアートディレクターを務めたミ
れている。楽曲にふさわしい幻想的な世界観に仕上げた。エアサイ
カは、新たな引き出しを開拓して、ますます映像世界が色濃く反映さ
いる。このダウンロード時代において、ますますファンを楽しませて
うとする精神を支持し、祝福した作品だと言える。(FS)

MIKA

————— Richard Airside's involvement in the Mika campaign was very unusual. Mika and Yasmine do a lot of drawing, and decided they wanted to design their own record covers, but they were shrewd enough to realise they didn't have the necessary art direction and design skills to make them look professional enough. They knew there was something about Yasmine's drawing style which fitted with Mika's music, so they asked Airside to take all the individual elements and make them in to a coherent campaign. In the end, it was a weird collaboration. I drew sketches and then Yasmine based her paintings on them almost exactly, adding in her characters but keeping most of my objects and landscapes. We suggested they could be changed into objects that purported to the song lyrics, but she liked what I'd done and recreated them pretty faithfully. The final album cover looks a lot like the pictures I drew, but at the same time the way it's been painted makes it look completely

ミカ

————— リチャード　ミカのキャンペーンには、かなり変わった形で携わった。もともとミカとヤスミンがたくさん絵を描いていて、レコードジャケットも自分達でデザインしたがっていたんだ。でも、自分たちにはプロフェッショナルに見せるアートディレクションやデザインの腕がないとわかっていた。それでも、ヤスミンのドローイング・スタイルには、どこかミカの音楽とマッチするものがある、と２人は感じていたから、個々の要素を合わせて、首尾一貫したキャンペーンに仕上げてほしいと、エアサイドに依頼してきたんだ。結果的に、かなり独特なコラボレーションになったね。僕がまずスケッチを描き、それにかなり忠実に、ヤスミンがペインティングをしていった。彼女がそこにキャラクターを加えたんだけど、僕が描いたものや風景も、ほぼそのまま活かしてくれた。歌詞に沿った内容に描き直すことも提案したんだけど、彼女は僕の絵を気に入ってくれて、ほぼ忠実に再現してくれた。こうして出来上がったアルバムジャケットは、僕が描いたスケッチ通りなんだけど、ヤスミンのペインティングによって、まったく違うものに見える。面白いコラボレーションの仕方だっ

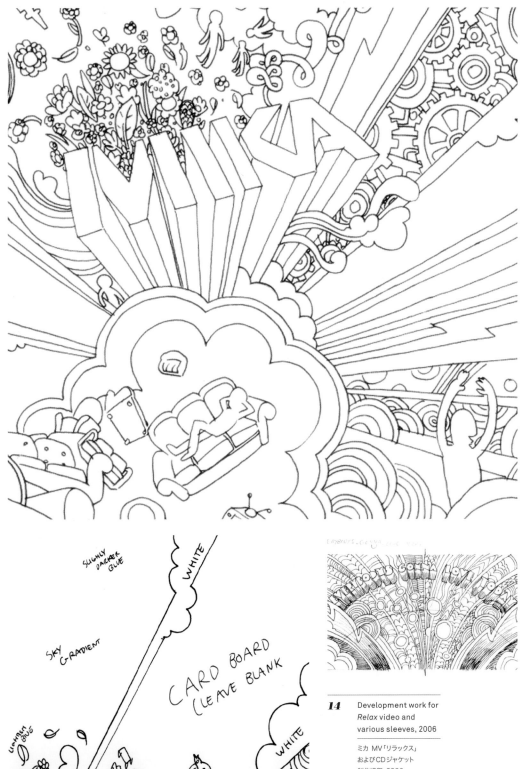

different. It was an interesting way of collaborating, and it worked because we shared similar tastes in art. The concept for drawing landscapes for the single covers was inspired by Mika being a fan of the illustrator Jim Woodring. I used that as a starting point for the cover for *Love Today* – a landscape with a slightly oriental, bright cartoony vibe. We created all the artwork, packaging and animation, including some weird teasers for YouTube, and a video for the single, *Relax*. The covers are bright and daytime, while the video is slightly darker – the imagery is coming out of black which is more about nightlife.

——————— **Nat** It was a lovely job to work on but it ended up being a huge task, not least as we drew all the text by hand and scanned it in, so if there was a last minute change, we had to write it all out again. What was refreshing was Mika and Universal being up for different formats to encourage people to buy the real world products; the singles were all interesting formats involving cut outs and inner sleeves.

たね。お互い同じようなアートを好んでいたから、うまくいったんだと思う。シングルのジャケットに風景を描くというコンセプトは、ミカがジム・ウッドリングというイラストレーターのファンだということからインスピレーションを得たんだ。それを出発点に、ちょっとオリエンタルで、明るくて漫画っぽい風景をテーマに「ラブ・トゥデイ」のジャケットを作りはじめた。それから、YouTubeで流した一風変わった予告映像や、シングル「リラックス」のビデオを含め、パッケージからアニメーションまで、すべてのアートワークを手がけたんだ。アルバムジャケットは明るく昼間の印象だけど、ビデオはやや暗め。ナイトライフを思わせる暗闇の中から、次々といろんなイメージが登場するんだ。

——————— **ナット**　すごく楽しかったけど、膨大な仕事量だった。すべての文字を手書きで描いたから、いちいちスキャンして、それでまた最後の最後で修正が入ると、初めから描き直すんだもの。嬉しかったのは、ミカとユニバーサルが、より多くの人たちに商品を買ってもらうために、特殊なフォーマットを採用するのに乗り気だったこと。こうしてシングル版のジャケットはすべて、切り抜きや内ジャケットを使った面白いものになったわ。

14　Development work for *Relax* video and various sleeves, 2006

ミカ　MV「リラックス」およびCDジャケット制作過程　2006

BEATLES

—————————— **Fred** The Beatles' record company Apple Corps asked us to collaborate with the production company Maguffin on an animated music video for a track from The Beatles' *Love* album. That was a good day! Obviously we dropped everything. Maguffin's Simon Hilton, their resident Beatles expert and hot shot director / editor moved into our studio along with their producer Astrid Edwards and we all got stuck in. We started out working on *Strawberry Fields Forever* which I think was EMI's choice, but then Apple's Neil Aspinall (the legendary personal assistant to the Beatles and chief executive of Apple) pointed out that they already had a perfectly good video for that track which was made back in the sixties when it was first released. So then we switched to *Tomorrow Never Knows* which was actually a much better choice for us, given that it is probably the first electronica / trip-hop track in music history. The day that Neil came in the studio was a bit special: he was a proper gent and gave us his honest feedback without stepping on anybody's toes. The end result is ultra trippy and we're very proud of it. Apple said that we had exceeded their expectations and I like to think that all of the Fab Four would have approved.

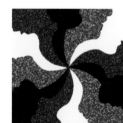

15 Stills from *Tomorrow
Never Knows / Within
You Without You* music
promo, 2006

ビートルズ MV「トゥモロー・
ネバー・ノウズ」／「ウィズイン・
ユー・ウィズアウト・ユー」
2006

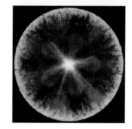

ビートルズ

——————————— **フレッド**　ビートルズのレコード会社、アッ
プル・コアから、アルバム「ラブ」に収録するアニメーションMV
を1本、マグフィンというプロダクションと一緒に制作してほしい
と連絡があった。あれは忘れ難い日だったね！もちろん、みんな
やっていた仕事をすぐさま中断したよ。マグフィンからは、ビート
ルズのことを熟知している敏腕ディレクター／エディターのサイ
モン・ヒルトンが、プロデューサーのアストリッド・エドワーズを
連れ立って僕らのスタジオにやってきて、みんなですぐに作業を
始めた。早速、EMIが選んだと思われる「ストロベリー・フィール
ズ・フォーエヴァー」のビデオ制作に取りかかったわけだけど、し
ばらくしてアップルのニール・アスピナル（ビートルズの伝説的
な専属アシスタントで、アップルの最高責任者）から、この曲は、
最初にリリースした60年代に、すでに曲に完璧にマッチするビ
デオを作っていると指摘された。そこで「トゥモロー・ネバー・
ノウズ」に変更になったんだけど、この曲が、おそらくポピュ
ラー音楽史上初のエレクトロニカ／トリップ・ホップだというこ
とを考えると、僕らにとってはむしろ好都合だったね。ニールが
スタジオに来た日は、ちょっと特別な感じだった。彼は本物の紳
士で、みんなの感情を損ねることなく率直な意見を述べてくれ
た。最終的に思いっきりトリッピーなものが出来上がって、みん
な誇りに思っているよ。アップルは、この作品が彼らの期待をは
るかに上回るものだと言ってくれた。ビートルズも、このビデオ
を気に入ってくれたと思いたいな。

POP ART GALLERY

Nat The work that we did creating Wolverhampton's Pop Art Gallery has been our most serious foray into exhibition design. We won a pitch to design the branding, interior design and interactives for a new building to house Wolverhampton's permanent collection of pop art, which is the largest in the UK outside of London. They specifically wanted a young audience to really enjoy being in the gallery, and to return on a frequent basis. The exhibition design revolves around a large white sofa and display installation in the middle of the room, with coloured lighting positioned at the base of the furniture which gives a soft, almost bar-like feel to the room, and encourages the visitor to really hang out in the space. Once you're on the sofa, you can use one of several interactives, which educate and inform the audience about pop art. You can get under the skin of James Rosenquist's *F-111* (1964–65) or take a photo of yourself and 'Warholise' it. The gallery puts a big emphasis on interpretation, so we filmed an actor dressed up as Andy Warhol, and he appears every 15 minutes projected onto the back of the sofa, telling the story of how and why he produced the particular pieces of his work that are in the exhibition.

Alex The gallery structure itself had not been built when we won the brief, so we had a unique opportunity to create something from the ground up. We immediately thought of our friends at mæ Architects and invited them to collaborate with us on the project. The final design is the solution to a paradox – all the research dictated that young people would not go in to a white gallery space. On the other hand pop art was conceived to hang in a conventional white walled gallery so that the mundane everyday objects depicted would appear in an unexpected context. Our task was to balance these two requirements and I think we pulled it off: the attendance figures certainly seem to suggest so. The finished space has a transient nature, changing in mood throughout the day and dependent upon the specific gallery event.

Michael Howe (founding partner of mæ Architects) Airside make sure they understand people's areas of competence and expertise, so the process is like playing American football: everyone goes into a huddle, then it splits up and each goes off to do what they're good at.

It's quite liberating, and on the whole it's a joy working with them. Airside appears to be a very democratic organisation – they have this working method where all projects are discussed with the team and ideas can come from anywhere within it. As long as they're good they survive, which is a refreshing approach to design. They also pursue their design without being intellectually hamstrung – their work is fantastic but it's really legible. They employ humour and other bits and pieces that make the work very approachable even though it's high quality. It's something people understand, and as an office we admire the idea that design isn't something for other designers, it's something that everyone can engage with on all sorts of levels.

16

17

ポップアート・ギャラリー

ナット ウルヴァーハンプトンのポップアート・ギャラリーの仕事では、今までで一番真剣に展示デザインという領域に踏み込んだわ。ここは、ロンドンを除く英国で最大級のポップアート・コレクションを所蔵しているんだけど、その常設展示のために設けた新館の、ブランディング/インテリアデザイン/インタラクティブのデザイン・コンペに勝ったの。ギャラリー側は、とりわけ若い人たちに楽しんでもらって、何度も足しげく通ってもらいたいと思っていた。展示デザインは、部屋の中央に設置された大きな白いソファーとインスタレーションを囲むようにディスプレイされていて、訪れた人たちが、くつろげるように、ソファーの足下に設置されたカラーライトが、部屋全体をバーのような雰囲気に演出しているの。ソファーに座ると、いくつもあるインタラクティブ画面を使って、ポップアートについて学ぶことができるようになっている。ジェイムス・ローゼンクイストの「F-111」(1964–65)について知ることも、自分の写真を「ウォーホル風」にアレンジすることもできるの。展示してあるアンディー・ウォーホルの作品を解説するのに、ウォーホルに扮した役者を撮影したわ。彼がソファーの背後にあるプロジェクターに15分おきに登場して、展示してあるウォーホルの作品のいく

18

かについて、なぜ、どのように制作したのかを語るのよ。

アレックス この仕事のオファーを得た時は、まだギャラリー本体が建てられていなかったから、ゼロから何かを創るというユニークな機会を与えてもらった。僕らは即座にメイ・アーキテクツにいる友達のことを思い出して、一緒にコラボレーションしようと誘ったんだ。最後の難関は、パラドックスの解消だった。どのリサーチでも、若者は白いギャラリースペースには結局は足を運ばなくなるという統計が出ていたけど、一方、ポップアートというものは従来、ごくありふれた日常の物が、思いもよらぬ文脈で現れてくるように、平凡な白壁のギャラリーに設置されるものと相場が決まっている。この２つの相反する条件を満たすことが僕らの仕事で、結果的にうまくいったと思う。来場者数を見れば明らかだね。完成したスペースの雰囲気は、１日のうちでも刻々と変わるし、開催されるイベントによってもガラっと変わるんだ。

マイケル・ハウ（メイ・アーキテクツ創立者の１人） 彼らはみんなの能力や専門分野をよく理解していたから、作業はアメリカン・フットボールみたいなものでね、みんなで作戦会議を行った後は、それぞれ持ち場に移って各自の得意とする作業に移ったよ。かなり自由だったし、プロジェクトを通して彼らと働くことは喜びだったね。エアサイドは、とても民主的な組織で、どのプロジェクトもチームで話し合って、誰でもアイデアを出せるような働き方をしている。アイデアは、良ければ勝ち残る。胸のすくようなデザインアプローチだよね。しかも、頭でっかちにならずにデザインを追求し続けている。彼らの作品は素晴らしいけど、とてもわかりやすいだろ。どの作品にもユーモアやちょっとした隠し味があって、クオリティーが高いのに、とても親しみやすい。誰もが理解できるものだし、「デザインは、他のデザイナーのためのものではなく、あらゆるレベルで、みんなが楽しめるもの」という彼らのポリシーを、建築家として尊敬しているよ。

19

20

21

MTV MOBILE

MTV モバイル

Job name:	*MTV Snax* and *MTV Trax*
Client:	MTV Networks Europe
Media:	Moving image, graphic design
Summary:	Channel branding and idents plus style guide for two new mobile phone channels.

作品名:	MTV スナックス & MTV トラックス
クライアント:	MTV ネットワークス、ヨーロッパ
メディア:	動画、グラフィックデザイン
内容:	チャンネル・ブランディング、ステーションID および新携帯チャンネル用マニュアル

If you were so busy watching TV on your mobile wherever you walked, would you never see your feet again? That was the humorous premise that Airside worked from when MTV came to them to produce a visual identity for two new mobile phone channels it was launching: *MTV Shorts* and *MTV Music* (known in the UK as *MTV Snax* and *MTV Trax*). In line with MTV's quirky identity, Airside evolved a series of parallel worlds visible through the phone screen 'window' where the user's feet were besieged by various animated characters as they walked along, engrossed obliviously in their phone. Airside created a full branding kit to be used in each of the European countries where the channels would be broadcast. The idents were created with a combination of live action and animation; the aesthetic was friendly and lo-fi, as a counterpoint to the style of the mobile device itself. **FS**

携帯でテレビを見ることに気をとられて歩いていると、足元を見ないのでは？ MTVが開局した2つの携帯チャンネル「MTVショーツ」「MTVミュージック」（英国では「MTVスナックス」「MTVトラックス」）用ID制作の依頼を受けて、エアサイドはそんなユーモラスな仮説を思いついた。常にひとひねりあるMTVのID向けに、携帯画面を「窓」に見立て、画面に夢中になりながら歩くユーザーの足元に様々なアニメーション・キャラクターが群がる様子を描いたパラレルワールドのシリーズを制作した。このプロジェクトでは、新チャンネルが開局するヨーロッパ各国ごとのブランディング・キットを、すべてエアサイドが作成した。IDは実写とアニメーションの合成で、携帯電話という機器とは対照的に、フレンドリーでローファイな作品に仕上がっている。（FS）

MTV
MUSIC TELEVISION ®

Airside by Airside

エアサイド バイ エアサイド

The Way We Are Now

エアサイドの今

Airside by Airside

エアサイド バイ エアサイド

The Way We Are Now

エアサイドの今

MTV

Fred The *MTV Snax / MTV Trax* job was a really interesting one. MTV were launching a mobile phone version of their channel and needed an identity for it; typically they were after something edgy. Our big idea was that when you are watching MTV on your phone it becomes a window into a parallel world. We imagined MTV's target audience, music loving teenagers, walking around town while looking at their mobile screens, so we created a series of idents that featured feet striding forward with various bizarre activities occurring around them as they walked the streets. We also had to produce a complete style guide and resource kit for all of MTV's European territories, so despite the anarchic nature of the content, the deliverables had to be highly detailed.

MTV

フレッド　MTVの「スナックス＆トラックス」は、かなり面白かったよ。MTVが携帯用チャンネルを開局するのに、IDが必要になってね。MTVといえば、いつもエッジが効いたものを求めているだろ。そこで、携帯でMTVを見ていると、それがパラレルワールドへの入り口になるというアイデアを思いついた。MTVがターゲットとする音楽好きのティーンたちが、携帯画面を見ながら街を歩く姿をイメージして、大股で街中を闊歩する足と、その周りで起こる奇妙な出来事に焦点を当てたIDシリーズを制作した。ヨーロッパ圏の全MTVで流したから、地域ごとの完全マニュアルと素材一式を制作する羽目になって、作品がアナーキーだったわりには、納品内容はやたら細かかったよな。

22 Stills from *MTV Snax / MTV Trax* idents, 2006

MTV「スナックス＆トラックス」ID 2006

SAGAWA

佐川急便

Airside by Airside

エアサイド バイ エアサイド

The Way We Are Now

エアサイドの今

Job name:	Sagawa TV commercials
Client:	Sagawa Couriers, Japan
Agency:	Robot / Hybrid, Tokyo
Media:	Moving image

Summary: TV commercials for Sagawa Couriers to contemporise a traditional family company.

Producing a series of animated TV commercials for Sagawa, a Japanese courier company, granted Airside another opportunity to indulge its admiration for Japan, and create an animated landscape that depicts the country's hi-tech urban face. In each commercial, a character based on Sagawa's new logo dodges obstacles that impede his journey to carry his cargo carefully and safely, spreading the message that although the company is modern and forward-looking, it is still diligently committed to its long-standing core business mission of delivering packages from one place to another. The aesthetic of the commercials translate the values of a company that cares for its customers and has tough business acumen, a valuable combination in the modern business world. **FS**

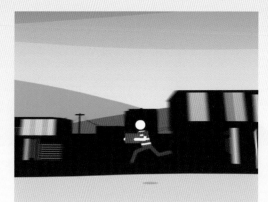

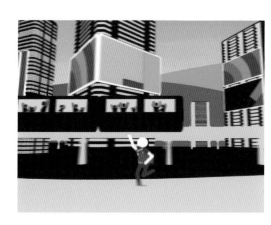

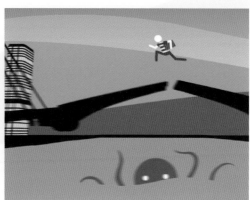

Airside by Airside

エアサイド バイ エアサイド

The Way We Are Now

エアサイドの今

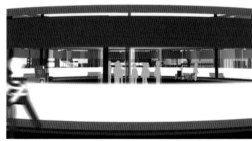

エアサイド バイ エアサイド

作品名： 佐川急便テレビ・コマーシャル
クライアント： 佐川急便、日本
代理店： ロボット／ハイブリッド、東京
メディア： 動画

内容： 伝統ある佐川急便の企業イメージを、現代的に一新するテレビ・コマーシャル

―――― 日本の運送会社、佐川急便のテレビCMシリーズの制作を通じ、エアサイドは、またも日本賛美に浸る機会を得て、そのハイテクな都市部をアニメーションで描いた。どの作品も、佐川急便の新しいロゴに基づいて作られたキャラクターが、様々な障害物を注意深くかわしながら安全に荷物を運ぶ様子を描いており、どんなにモダンで先進性のある企業に生まれ変わっても、お客様に荷物をお届けするという長年培ってきたビジネスの基本は今も変わらず、誠意を持って取り組んでいるというメッセージが込められている。結果として、顧客への配慮と優れた事業展開という、現代のビジネス界において価値のあるコンビネーションを備えた企業であることを表現したコマーシャルに仕上がった。(FS)

26

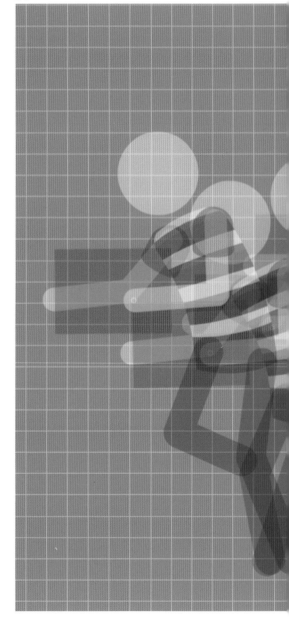

SAGAWA

Malika Henki and I work together on the TV commercials for Sagawa. We start with a group brainstorm, then divide up the drawing, and when it comes to animating we both direct. Working with the animators is very fulfilling; they're incredibly talented and each of them has their own speciality. We tell them what we want, but they often come up with their own ideas that are really surprising.

Paul McBride Airside seems to be producing more and more animation each year, and these are becoming ever more complex; for example, the series of Sagawa ads have become much more intricate. I think Airside's designers collaborate well with their pool of freelance animators; each of us understands the detail of how different animation techniques work so we're a powerful team. We always get to have some input, which as a freelancer is unusual!

Tim Bacon When you have worked with someone for a while you can to a certain extent intuit what they would like, which is very helpful when they are busy and you can't ask them, "Shall I make something blue or green?" Every now and then, however, you guess what you think they want and they surprise you by saying, "No, red please," which I like. Henki is a good one for that.

Atsushi Hamada (Hamada Planning, Sagawa CM Planner) Airside? Fast, Flexible, Fantastic! They churned out great ideas, one after another, like popcorn, as well as answering creatively to picky and persistent requests from us Japanese clients. We are working together again in the future, and are looking forward to more of their fabulous ideas.

佐川急便

マリカ ヘンキと私で、日本の運送会社、佐川急便のテレビCMを担当したの。まずはグループ・ブレインストーミングを行って、それから2人でドローイングを手分けして、アニメーションは一緒にディレクションを手がけたわ。アニメーターたちとの仕事には、とても満足している。皆とても才能があるし、それぞれが得意分野を持っているから、こちらの希望を伝えると、ほんとうに驚くようなアイデアを返してくることがよくあるのよ。

ポール・マクブライド 年を追うごとに、エアサイドはより多くのアニメーションを手がけるようになっていて、中身もさらに複雑になってきている。たとえば佐川急便のテレビCMシリーズなんか、相当込み入ったものになっているよ。エアサイドのデザイナーたちは、たくさんのフリーランス・アニメーターたちとうまくコラボレーションしていると思う。お互い が、異なるアニメーション技術の効果を細部まで理解しているから、チームとしても強力なんだ。僕らも絶えず意見を求められるけど、フリーランサーとしてはめずらしいことだよ！

ティム・ベーコン しばらく一緒に働いていると、相手の好みがある程度直感的にわかるようになってくるんだ。相手が忙しくて、いちいち「ここは青と緑、どちらがいい？」なんて聞けない時にはこれが役立つね。ただ、時々、予想を裏切って「赤がいいな」なんていうケースもあって、楽しいよ。ヘンキとか特にね。

濱田篤（濱田企画室：佐川急便CMプランナー） エアサイド、とにかく『早い。うまい。安い（？かどうかは、プロデューサーに聞いて）』面白いアイディアがポップコーンが出来るように次々と出てくる。しかもこちらからのしつこいリクエストにも素早く対応してくれる。今後もまたエアサイドとの仕事が待っている。みなさん、これからもよろしくね。

27

28

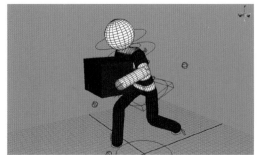

23 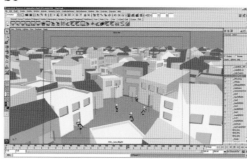 **24** **25**

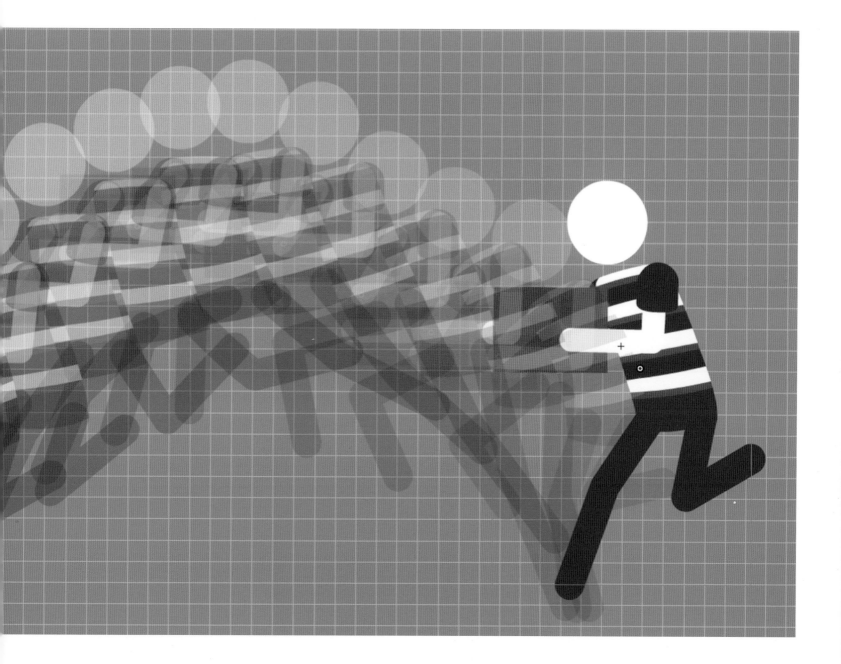

29

23– Sagawa – work in
30 progress, 2007–08

佐川急便 テレビCM
制作過程 2007–08

30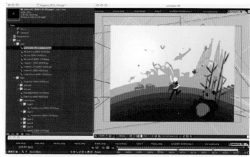

THE NO. 1 LADIES' DETECTIVE AGENCY

NO.1 レディーズ探偵社

Job name:	*The No.1 Ladies' Detective Agency* film titles
Client:	Anthony Minghella
Media:	Moving image
Summary:	Start and end film title sequences for BBC film.

The No. 1 Ladies' Detective Agency was Oscar-winning director Anthony Minghella's last work; a screen adaptation for the BBC of Alexander McCall Smith's popular novels, filmed on location in Botswana and featuring a precocious female lead amid a vibrant African backdrop. Airside was commissioned to create the titles and end credits for the film, and Anthony's brief was to capture the lushness of the film's colours, characters and the handmade signs that he saw everywhere during the shoot. Rather than trying to create this mimetically, the aesthetic was achieved by hand painting pieces of wood and using their texture as the basis for the character animations – which heavily referenced scenes in the film – alongside hand-drawn typography which plays out on top. These rougher treatments marked a new direction for Airside's illustration style. **FS**

Airside by Airside

エアサイド バイ エアサイド

The Way We Are Now

エアサイドの今

作品名:	「No.1 レディーズ探偵社」作品タイトル
クライアント:	アンソニー・ミンゲラ
メディア:	動画
内容:	BBC 映画のオープニングおよびエンディング・タイトル

――――――「No.1 レディーズ探偵社」は、アレクサンダー・マコール・スミスの人気小説を BBC が映画化した作品で、オスカー受賞監督アンソニー・ミンゲラの遺作となった。撮影はボツワナで行われ、活気あるアフリカの地を舞台に、進歩的な女性主人公を描きだしている。エアサイドが依頼されたのは、オープニング・タイトルとエンディング・クレジットで、アンソニーからの注文は、本編に登場する鮮やかな色彩やキャラクター、そして撮影中、随所で目にした手描きの看板を取り入れて欲しいということ。そこで、ただ模倣するのではなく、ペンキで色付けした木材を全体の質感に用い、本編の映像を参考にしたキャラクターをアニメ化、さらにその上に手描きのタイポグラフィーを施した。手描きの手法を用いた本作は、これまでのエアサイドのスタイルに一線を画す、新しい方向性を示す作品となった。(FS)

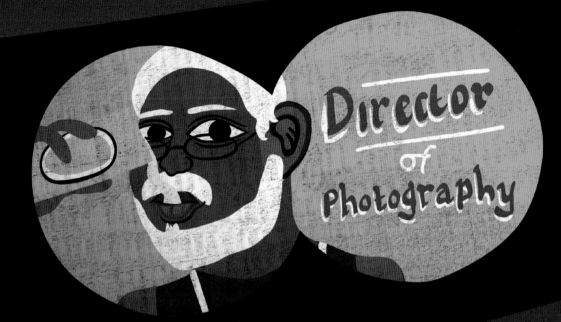

31

NO. 1 LADIES'

Alex We were asked to design the titles for Anthony Minghella's final film, *The No. 1 Ladies' Detective Agency,* which was the perfect project to explore some new styles. On location in Botswana, Anthony noticed a newspaper with satirical, salacious cartoons, and thought that was the right mixture of sexual intrigue and colourful character for the titles. We discussed the use of hand-painted signs, similar to those seen everywhere in Botswana and featured throughout the film, and responded to his ideas, scanning pieces of wood and painting on them, and creating some more hand-drawn treatments. Anthony loved all

NO.1 レディーズ探偵社

アレックス アンソニー・ミンゲラの最後の映像作品「No.1 レディーズ探偵社」のタイトル・デザインを手がけたんだけど、新しいスタイルを試みるにはうってつけのプロジェクトだったね。ボツワナでの撮影中、新聞に掲載された猥褻な風刺漫画を目にしたアンソニーは、そのスタイルが、サスペンスドラマとカラフルなキャラクターを盛り込んだオープニング映像にぴったりだと思った。さらに僕らは話し合いを重ね、ボツワナ各地で目にするような手書きの看板を、タイトルのあちらこちらに登場させることにした。アンソニーのアイデアを取り入れて、木材をスキャンして色づけし、さらに手書きの質感をつけ加えた。僕らが出した3つのアイデアをどれもアンソニーが気に入ってく

31– 32	Photos from *No1 Ladies'* launch party, 2008	**35– 37**	Development work for *No1 Ladies',* 2008
	「No.1 レディーズ探偵社」完成披露パーティー 2008		「No.1 レディーズ探偵社」制作過程 2008
33– 34	*No.1 Ladies'* end credit stills, 2008		
	「No.1 レディーズ探偵社」エンドクレジット 2008		

32

33

34

35

36

three directions we proposed, so we all jammed and cross-fertilised our ideas until we came up with something none of us had seen before.

——————— **Malika** This project is a really good example of collaboration. I like the fact that it has lots of different people's work in it: Chris created the type for the titles, while Jamie and I worked together on the illustration, and that was all inspired by the African signs.

——————— **Anthony Minghella** The titles and animation work from Airside on *The No. 1 Ladies' Detective Agency* was meticulous, perfectly judged, beautifully executed and achieved with minimal fuss and a real sense of enthusiastic collaboration. The whole process was impeccable.

れたから、すべてを掛け合わせた結果、今までに見たことがないような作品が出来上がったんだ。

——————— **マリカ** まさにコラボレーションの良いお手本ね。いろんな人たちが関わったという点が気に入っているの。タイトル文字を制作したのはクリス、イラストレーションはジェイミーと私、そしてすべての要素に影響を与えたのは、アフリカの看板、という風にね。

——————— **アンソニー・ミンゲラ** 「No.1レディーズ探偵社」のタイトルとアニメーションの制作に当たって、エアサイドは的確で完璧なスタイルを創造し、細やかな配慮とほんとうに熱心なコラボレーションによって、まったく美しい作品に仕上げてくれた。すべてのプロセスに、非の打ち所がなかったよ。

37

KONDITOR & COOK

コンディトワー & クック

Job name:	Konditor & Cook		**作品名：**	コンディトワー & クック	
Client:	Konditor & Cook		**クライアント：**	コンディトワー & クック	
Media:	Graphic design, packaging design		**メディア：**	グラフィックデザイン, パッケージデザイン	

Summary: A fresh identity for high-end food specialists including packaging design and in-store displays.

内容： 高級食品専門店のパッケージデザイン、店内ディスプレイを含めたブランドイメージの一新

Buying cakes from the Gherkin sounds like a confusing activity, but in rebranding the corporate identity for one of London's most sumptuous patisseries, this is what Airside has been helping Londoners to do. Prior to opening a new outlet at 30 St Mary Axe (London's infamously curvy skyscraper), Konditor and Cook approached Airside to help revisualise its presence on the high street. With eyes bigger than their bellies, Airside agreed, and thus began some crucial rounds of product familiarisation. The resulting branding is elegant and classic but with a colourful modern vibrancy that announces the special quality of the handmade goods transported inside. The branding was applied across cake boxes and bags, signage, window vinyls for the new shop during construction, and a wrapper for a giveaway chocolate bar for the shop's opening. **FS**

ガーキン（ピクルスビル）でケーキを購入するなんていうのは、なんだか紛らわしい行為だが、ロンドンで最も贅沢なパティスリーのひとつである企業の再ブランディングを通して、エアサイドはロンドンっ子たちにそれを薦めている。コンディトワー & クックは、セント・メリー・アクス30番地（ロンドンの悪名高いピクルス型ビル）に新店舗を開店するに先立ち、ショピングエリアでの彼らのブランドイメージを一新してほしいとエアサイドに依頼を持ちかけた。食意地の張ったエアサイドは、快く引き受け、まずは欠かせない作業として、商品に慣れ親しむことから始めた。結果として、彼らの扱う手作り商品の質の高さを思わせる、エレガントで古典的ながらも、カラフルでモダンな要素を取り入れたブランディング・デザインに仕上がった。ブランディングは、ケーキの箱から紙袋、看板、工事現場を覆うビニールシート、開店時に配ったチョコレートバーの包み紙にまで及んだ。（FS）

AIRSIDE BRANDING

エアサイド・ブランディング

Job name:	Airside Branding		**作品名:**	エアサイド・ブランディング
Client:	Airside		**クライアント:**	エアサイド
Media:	Print		**メディア:**	印刷物

Summary: An in-house identity refresh project.

内容: エアサイドのブランディング—新プロジェクト

It began with a new website, and unravelled into an entire rebrand of the organisation. Airside's desire to change its logo, corporate identity, and even its famous business cards, happily coincided with the decision to move its style forward from its famous vector illustration that characterised the existing branding. But how to achieve something new without throwing the baby out with the bathwater? The question plagued the team for six months. The breakthrough came when a new piece of type by Chris finally began to feel like a fully-fledged logo: Jamie adopted a favourite Airside technique of negative space, cutting off sections of the lettering and jerking their positioning to imply movement. Airside is renowned for its work in moving image, and the new branding reflects that. It works in different media: animating where it can on screen, and appearing fluid where it is printed. Being both the design consultant and the client created challenges, but the team eventually emerged victorious and on speaking terms. The business cards retained their popular portraits, but have been re-imagined as abstract profile silhouettes that at first glance appear to be a piece of non-Latin script. Only when the card is turned around does it reveal the person's profile, maintaining that all-important sense of interactivity. **FS**

まずはウェブサイトを一新することにはじまり、それから会社全体のブランディングの見直しへと発展した。ロゴ、CI、さらには評判のいいあの名刺を一新したいという想いは、エアサイドのスタイルとして広く世に知られ、現在のブランディングを特徴づけている、あのベクター・イラストレーションからさらに一歩前進しようという決意と、ぴったり合致していた。だが、どうすれば大切なものを失わずに、新たなものを手に入れることができるのか? この難題が、チームにのしかかって半年。遂にクリスが新しく作ったタイポグラフィーが、本命のロゴになりそうな気配と共に、ようやく事が動き出した。ジェイミーが、エアサイドお気に入りのネガティブ・スペースの手法を用いることを思いついて、文字の部分を切り取ってずらし、動きを演出。エアサイドの名は動画でも知られるようになってきたため、新ブランディングにもそれを反映させた。スクリーン上で見せる時は、アニメ化もでき、印刷でも、動きが感じられるという風に、様々なメディアに対応している。デザイン・コンサルタント兼クライアントであることは、これまでにないチャレンジではあったが、全員で話し合い、納得のいく結論に辿り着いた。名刺に関しても、お馴染みのポートレイトに代わって、一見、非ラテン語系の文字が書かれているように見える、抽象的な横顔のシルエットを描いた。名刺を縦にすると初めて、本人の横顔だとわかる仕組みで、重要なインタラクティブのセンスが保たれている。(FS)

The Way We Are Now

エアサイドの今

39

AIRSIDE BRANDING

Chris Working on the Airside rebrand was probably the most fraught experience the studio has ever had. Jamie and I felt we had something new, but it wasn't working properly and there was a majority feeling that we should ditch it. We had big arguments and discussions which ended in a very exciting meeting – Jamie and I were really pushing for it, and eventually our efforts paid off. To get consensus where 13 people, mostly designers, are approving every stage of the process – I think we've done well.

Jamie Wieck Chris had come up with a very bold piece of typography to use on our new website, and was pushing to adopt it as a new Airside logo. It caused arguments about whether a logo can just be a typeface or needs to be developed further; we felt we had the raw materials and just needed to develop it into a whole identity. I approached it with the rationale that Airside offers moving image as one of its core skills, so it was logical to create a sense of movement in the logotype,

and I ended up lopping off parts of the letters to give it a shifting quality. It was all about trying to turn something static into something fluid. I thought it was a great opportunity for Airside to shake off the idea that we only do cute characters that jump up and down when in fact we're very multidisciplinary.

Fred The biggest bone of contention was the illustrations on the back of our business cards. Everybody we gave the old cards to loved them; they encapsulated our style and reminded you of exactly who you had met the night before, but many of us felt that we had to move beyond that style and let them go. However, nobody could come up with anything that was as strong or worked nearly as well, so for ages we were going round in circles. The breakthrough came when I took one of Jamie's silhouettes and doubled it up, making it more abstract. Horizontally it just looks like random brush strokes, but turn the card ninety degrees and you see the face. It's a nice second beat realisation that fulfils the same function of the old illustrations in a more interactive way.

エアサイド・ブランディング

クリス エアサイドの再ブランディングは、スタジオが経験してきた中で、最も骨の折れる作業だったと思う。ジェイミーと僕が、やっと新しいものが出来たと思っても、なかなか馴染まなくて、大多数のネガティブな重圧を感じるんだ。みんなで激論を交わしては話し合い、とにかく活気あるミーティングをしたよ。ジェイミーと僕は、自分たちのアイデアを押しまくって、ようやく最後に報われたんだ。各プロセスで、スタジオの13人全員から毎回了承を得ないといけないんだから、よくやったと思うよ。

ジェイミー・ヴィエック クリスが、新しいウェブサイト用に太字のタイポグラフィーを思いついて、これをエアサイドの新しいロゴにしようと押していたんだ。そこで、ロゴを活字のままにするか、さらに発展させたデザインにするかで議論になった。僕らは、活字のままだとなんだか物足りなくて、ひと工夫加えてロゴマークにした方がいいと感じていた。エアサイドの得意分野のひとつがムービングイメージだから、ロゴ

にも動きを加えることは、理にかなっていると思ったんだ。そこで、動きのあるイメージを出すために、文字の一部を切り取ってみた。要は、静止していたロゴを、勢いのあるものに変えることが狙いだった。これまでの、キュートな文字が飛び跳ねているイメージを一掃する良い機会だと思った。実際、僕らは多様なスタイルに長けているからね。

フレッド 最大の論点は、名刺の裏のイラストレーションだった。今までの名刺は、僕らのスタイルが一目でわかるし、前夜に誰に会ったのか、はっきり思い出せるから好評だった。でもほとんど全員が、そろそろこのスタイルを離れて、新しい方向へ踏み出す時期だと感じていた。とはいえ、同じくらい説得力があって、かつうまく馴染むアイデアを誰も思いつかなかったから、長いこと堂々巡りだった。ところがジェイミーの作ったシルエットを、僕が二重にズラして抽象化したら、状況が一変したんだ。名刺を横にすると、無造作な筆さばきに見えるけど、90度回転させるとメンバーの横顔が浮かび上がる。かつての名刺のイラストレーションと同じ機能を、よりインタラクティブに表現した、僕らの第2章にふさわしい名刺だよ。

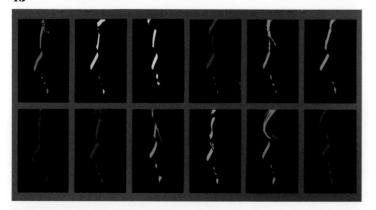

42

IT'S POP IT'S ART

イッツ・ポップ・イッツ・アート

Job name: *It's Pop It's Art*
Client: Airside / EMI Music Publishing
Media: Print, digital

Summary: A joint venture to produce limited edition screen-prints of well-known song lyrics.

What does a lyric look like? A piece of poetry is one answer, an art print is another. Airside and EMI Music Publishing have teamed up to generate a new tangent for music-related publishing – collectible music-related poster art, to rival the popularity enjoyed by film and exhibition posters, and Fred's beloved 1940's transport posters. Following the downturn in record-buying and the demise of creative record sleeves, the designers at Airside and executives at EMI settled on a shared passion: to create a new form of artwork merchandise that could play off the visual excitement of lyrics, as sleeves and posters once did. *It's Pop It's Art* is a series of posters designed by Airside, which take iconic lyrics from the EMI catalogue and turn them into illustrations. Simple, but effective, the idea is now being licensed out to widen the range beyond limited edition screen-prints to a covetable collection of objects and printed work, all bearing Airside's distinctive music-loving typographic illustrations. Little by little, Airside is finding creative ways to build up the feeling once more that music can be tangible and visually inspiring as well as sounding great. Each poster exudes the mood of the original song using hand-drawn typography, classic Airside illustration and – of course – the songwriting talents of masters like Marvin Gaye and The Rolling Stones. Like the Airside T-Shirt Club, the limited edition screen print versions are released in small quantities throughout the year. **FS**

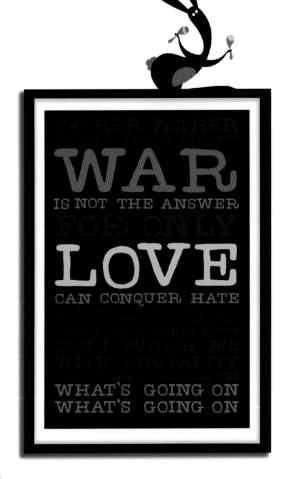

I'VE BEEN HOLDING OUT SO LONG
I'VE BEEN SLEEPING ALL ALONE

LORD I
MISS YOU

I'VE BEEN HANGING ON THE PHONE
I'VE BEEN SLEEPING ALL ALONE

I WANT TO
KISS YOU

Oooh Oooh Oooh
Oooh Oooh Oooh
Hoo Hoo Hoo
Hoo Hoo Hoo

LAST NIGHT A DJ
SAVED MY LIFE
LAST NIGHT A DJ SAVED MY LIFE FROM A BROKEN HEART
LAST NIGHT A DJ SAVED MY LIFE
LAST NIGHT A DJ SAVED MY LIFE
WITH A SONG

The Way We Are Now

エアサイドの今

作品名：	イッツ・ポップ・イッツ・アート
クライアント：	エアサイド／
	EMI ミュージック・パブリッシング
メディア：	ポスター、ウェブサイト

内容：	有名な歌詞を、枚数限定でスクリーン印刷の
	アートポスターにする共同事業

　　　　　　　　歌詞が目に見えたらどんな絵になるだろう？ 一篇の詩のようでもあり、アートポスターにもなり得る。エアサイドとEMIミュージック・パブリッシングは、音楽関連の新たな出版物を開発すべくタッグを組み、人気を集める映画や展示会のポスターや、フレッドが好む1940年代の交通局ポスターに匹敵するような、収集し甲斐のある音楽関連のポスターアートを創りだした。レコードの売上げ低迷の余波で、クリエイティブなレコードジャケットにお目にかかれなくなった今、エアサイドのデザイナーとEMIの経営陣は同じ想いを抱いていた。それは、かつてジャケットやポスターがそうであったように、歌詞を目で見る喜びが感じられる、何か新しい形のアートワークを創りたいということ。こうして始まったイッツ・ポップ・イッツ・アートは、EMIのリリースカタログから誰もが良く知る歌詞を選び出し、イラストレーション化した、エアサイドによるアートポスター・シリーズである。結果は、シンプルながらも効果絶大で、音楽をこよなく愛するエアサイドのタイポグラフィー・イラストレーションをより多くの人に楽しんでもらうべく、限定版スクリーン印刷に留まらず、誰もが購入可能な商品やポスターの制作も検討され始めている。エアサイドは、音楽が耳を喜ばせると同時に、手に取って視覚的にも人々に感動を与えることのできる創造的な方法を、徐々にではあるが、再び見出しつつある。手描きのタイポグラフィーとエアサイドらしいイラストレーション、そしてもちろんマーヴィン・ゲイやローリング・ストーンズら、ソングライティングの大家による素晴らしい歌詞が融合し、どのポスターもその歌のオリジナリティーを見事に表現している。エアサイド・Tシャツクラブと同様、限定版スクリーン印刷は、年間を通じてわずかな量のみ制作される。（FS）

THE ACE OF SPADES

YOU KNOW I'M BORN TO LOSE
AND GAMBLING'S FOR FOOLS
BUT THAT'S THE WAY
I LIKE IT BABY
I DON'T WANNA
LIVE FOR EVER
AND DON'T FORGET THE JOKER

ALWAYS LOOK ON
THE BRIGHT SIDE OF LIFE
FOR LIFE IS QUITE ABSURD, AND DEATH'S THE FINAL WORD
YOU MUST ALWAYS FACE THE CURTAIN WITH A BOW
FORGET ABOUT YOUR SIN, GIVE THE AUDIENCE A GRIN
ENJOY IT, IT'S YOUR LAST CHANCE ANYHOW
ALWAYS LOOK ON THE BRIGHT SIDE OF DEATH
JUST BEFORE YOU DRAW YOUR TERMINAL BREATH
LIFE'S A PIECE OF SHIT
WHEN YOU LOOK AT IT

I LOVE YOU
I GOTTA STAY TRUE
MY MORALS GOT ME ON MY KNEES
I'M BEGGING PLEASE
STOP PLAYING GAMES

I DON'T KNOW WHAT THIS IS BUT YOU GOT ME GOOD

(JUST LIKE YOU KNEW YOU WOULD)

YOU GOT ME BEGGIN' YOU FOR
"MERCY"

IT'S POP IT'S ART

Fred *It's Pop It's Art* is one of our collaborative projects: a separate business in itself, run jointly by EMI and Airside. We create poster art based on the EMI Music Publishing back catalogue which is packed full of iconic songs. Austin Wilde at EMI came up with the idea, and together we select appropriate songs and use them to inspire a piece of art. The idea of visualising music is right up our street; we get excited about interacting with a great song that we're really into. Yoko Ono totally got it – she was immediately up for letting us work with *Imagine*, and loved what we did.

Austin Wilde I'd worked with Airside before, and had some really positive experiences – the way they understand music is pretty unique. Initially we discussed the goals of *It's Pop It's Art* and where these posters fitted in. The iPod had transformed people's affection for music from being a real world package that you hold and cherish to this totally inanimate white object packed with virtual data. We realised we could do something visual that had a value to it, which would also give people a relationship with these records, and

particularly with the craft of songwriting. Seeing these amazing lyrics written down is so powerful – it really gives you an emotional connection to the songwriters. We began making limited edition prints to attract music-loving early adopters, the demographic which were probably first to have iPods but were most likely to be missing the physical connection to music. We're keen for younger music fans to have them on their walls as well as people who drink red wine in the evenings, so we're launching a more affordable range alongside the limited edition prints. It's all about having fun with the design and typography, and we want kids to get excited about it – I had posters on my wall when I was young and it was really important to me. From a music publisher's perspective, it's been really good to be able to show songwriters what we're able to do with their works. Lily Allen did a signing at the temporary Airside/IPIA shop last Christmas, and Duffy played a gig for us at Rough Trade to launch her poster. It offers artists another way to reach their audience. The way Airside understand the audience and the passion they put into their designs has really made the business a success.

46

44

45

イッツ・ポップ・イッツ・アート

フレッド 「イッツ・ポップ・イッツ・アート」は、コラボレーション企画のひとつで、それ自体ビジネスとして、EMIとエアサイドが共同で運営している。時代を象徴する名曲が詰まったEMIのリリース・アーカイブをベースに、ポスターアートを制作するんだ。EMIのオースティン・ワイルドが思いついた企画で、以来僕らは一緒に相応しい曲を選んでは、それにインスパイアされたアート作品を制作し続けている。音楽を視覚化することは、僕らの得意とするところだから、本当に好きな素晴らしい曲に関わることができて、最高の気分だよ。オノ・ヨーコは完璧に意図を汲んで、すぐに「イマジン」のアートワークを作らせてくれて、仕上がりも気に入ってくれた。

オースティン・ワイルド エアサイドとは以前仕事をしたことがあって、有意義な経験だった。彼らの音楽の解釈は相当ユニークだしね。まず最初に「イッツ・ポップ・イッツ・アート」の目的と、ポスターの需要がどこにあるかを話し合った。iPodの登場は、人々の音楽への愛着を、実際に手にとって大切にしていたパッケージから、バーチャルデータの入った無機質な白い物体へと、変えてしまった。そこで、何か価値のあるビジュアルを作成できるのではないか、それぞれのレコードにゆかりのある、特に歌詞にまつわる何かを作れないかと思いついた。素晴らしい歌詞が文字になって描かれているのは、とにかくパワフルなんだ。思わず歌詞に感情移入してしまうだろう。こうして、iPodをいち早く購入したものの、音楽との物理的接触を最も懐かし

がっている、新しもの好きな音楽ファンたちに向けて、限定版のポスターを制作し始めた。夜更けに赤ワインを楽しむような年齢層だけでなく、若い音楽ファンにもこのポスターを壁に貼って欲しいから、限定版ポスターだけでなく、より手ごろな価格で手に入るポスターも開発中なんだ。このプロジェクトは、デザインとタイポグラフィーを楽しむことが目的で、若者にも夢中になって欲しいんだ。僕自身、若い頃部屋にポスターを貼っていて、それが宝物だったからね。音楽を出版する立場の意見としては、ソングライターたちに、歌詞を使った作品を見せられるのは、本当に嬉しいね。去年のクリスマスには、期間限定エアサイド／IPIAショップで、リリー・アレンがサイン会を行ったし、ダフィーはポスター完成記念に、ラフトレードでギグを開いた。ポスターのおかげで、アーティストにもオーディエンスと触れ合う新たな機会が生まれている。エアサイドがオーディエンスをよく理解し、デザインに情熱を注いでくれることが、このビジネスの成功に繋がったんだ。

44 Screen for *Ace of Spades* print, 2006

「エース・オブ・スペイズ」
スクリーン印刷 2006

45 Print in situ, 2006

ポスター 展示風景 2006

THE TRIPTYCH

ザ・トリプティク

Job name: The Triptych
Client: Fred Deakin / Universal
Media: CD Packaging
Awards: Best CD Packaging,
2008 European Design Awards

Summary: Packaging for Fred's epic triple CD mix album

———— For his first official compilation, Fred was looking, as always, to push the boundaries and evolve Airside's graphic style into a new and appropriate area. The trademark abstract patterns that had characterised Lemon Jelly's releases were founded on key processes and by experimenting with these processes, introducing new variables and influences, came a system of more angular structures that mirrored the eclectic flow of the mix within. Dividing the pattern into three distinct elements was the final piece in the puzzle: the end result is an award-winning package that completes what the Guardian newspaper's front page described as "The best mix album ever". **FS**

作品名: ザ・トリプティク
クライアント: フレッド・ディーキン/ユニバーサル
メディア: CDパッケージ
受賞歴: 2008年ヨーロピアン・デザイン・アワード、 ベストCDパッケージ賞

内容: フレッドの傑作3部作、コンピレーションCD パッケージ

———— 初のオフィシャル・コンピレーション発売に際して、フレッドはいつもの如くパッケージにこだわり、エアサイドのグラフィックスタイルを然るべき新しい方向へ進化させようと模索していた。レモン・ジェリーのトレードマークの抽象模様をもとに、新たな変化や多様性を加えて試行を重ね、変化に富んだミックス版の内容を象徴する無数の鋭角を取り入れたパターンに辿り着いた。この模様を大きく3つに分けるというアイデアが、最後の決めてとなった。本品はベストパッケージ賞を獲得し、ガーディアン紙の一面で「史上最高のミックス・アルバム」と評された。(FS)

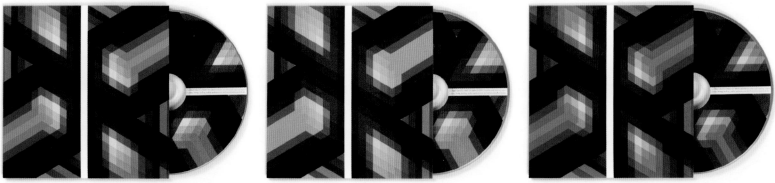

The Way We Are Now

エアサイドの今

NU BALEARICA

ヌー・バレアリカ

Job name: *Nu Balearica*
Client: Fred Deakin / Ministry of Sound
Media: CD Packaging

Summary: Packaging for Fred's Nu-Balearic double CD mix album

The second Fred Deakin mix album was a smoother affair than its predecessor, demanding a more playful and flowing aesthetic. Using colours from nature and gradients from sky and sea to evoke the elements of island life, Fred generated a signature tessellation, and applied it to a series of cardboard gatefold elements, celebrating the vinyl culture that spawned the music on the album. Uplifting and summery, abstract and meditative, these rhythmical images reflect the sights and sounds of the Nu-Balearic genre. **FS**

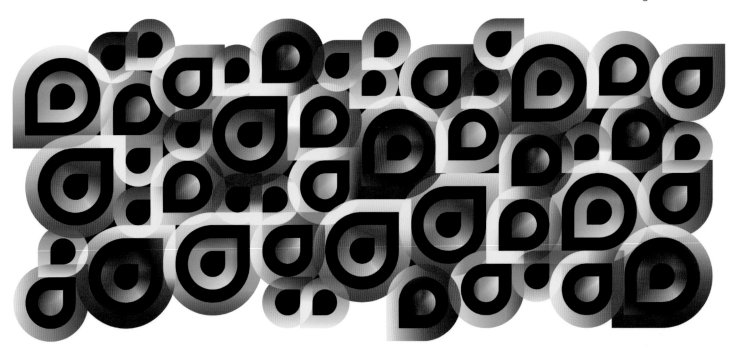

作品名:	ヌー・バレアリカ
クライアント:	フレッド・ディーキン／ ミニストリー・オブ・サウンド
メディア:	CDパッケージ

内容: フレッドのヌー・バレアリック2枚組コンピ
レーションアルバムのパッケージ

―――――― フレッド・ディーキン2作目のコンピレーショ
ンアルバムは、1作目よりもはるかにスムーズなテイストになった
ため、パッケージにもより遊び心のある、流れるようなデザイン
を追究した。島の生活を思い起こさせるような自然な色合いや、
空から海までのグラデーションなどを用いて、トレードマークの
モザイク模様を仕上げ、収録された音楽のルーツでもあるレコー
ド文化を思い出させる厚紙の見開きジャケットに印刷した。喜び
に満ちて、夏らしく、抽象的で瞑想的。これらのリズミカルなイ
メージは、ヌー・バレアリックというジャンルの音とビジョンを見
事に表現している。(FS)

ETHICS

——————— **Nat** We've always felt that we were ethical about the way we ran the company – treating our staff and our clients right and not taking the mickey. Over the last few years we've begun to consciously extend our ethics in order to respond to what's going on in the wider world, and to constantly strive for improvement in everything we do.

——————— Running the company with as light an environmental footprint as possible became a priority for us; we turned the studio round so that everything we do is considered in terms of its carbon footprint (and we got an outstanding achievement in Level 1 of the Green Mark awards). Then when it came to looking at what we were producing for ourselves and our clients in terms of paper, print, digital and packaging, we realised that we had a huge hole in our knowledge. I met two people, Sophie Thomas and Caroline Clark, who were fantastically helpful when we needed information about printing processes or finishing; so much so that we pooled our resources and have started a not-for-profit social enterprise called Three Trees Don't Make A Forest. We want to help other design agencies who want to become more sustainable but are finding it hard to know exactly what to do.

——————— **Fred** Of course, running the company in as democratic a way as possible also means not imposing our personal values on the people that work with us, which makes for some pretty lively debates! At the end of the day it's never black and white but we're always looking for the best way forward.

倫理観

——————— **ナット** 私たちは、スタッフやクライアントを、利益のために利用するのではなく、きちんと扱ってきたし、常に倫理的なやり方で、会社を運営してきたつもりなの。ここ数年は、より広く世界規模で起きていることに対応できるように、倫理意識を高めて、自分たちのやっていることを、いつも良い方向に改善していけるよう努めているわ。

——————— 今、私たちが何よりも優先しているのは、できるだけ環境を傷つけずに会社を経営すること。だから、スタジオで行うすべての活動において、二酸化炭素排出量削減を心がける方向に転換を図ったの。(その功績が認められて、グリーンマーク賞のレベル1を獲得した)それから今度は、紙、印刷、デジタル、パッケージの観点から、社内やクライアント用に自分たちが生産しているものを見直してみたら、自分たちがいかに無知かを気づかされたわ。印刷の工程や仕上げについて情報が必要だった時に、ソフィー・トーマスとキャロライン・クラークの2人に出会って、大いに助けてもらった。ものすごくためになったから、私たちは共同出資をして、非営利目的の社会事業として「Three Trees Don't Make A Forest (3本の木じゃ、森にはならない)」を立ち上げたの。もっと地球に優しい持続可能な会社になりたいけど、具体的にどうすればよいかわからないというデザイン会社の役に立ちたいと思っている。

——————— **フレッド** できる限り民主的に会社を経営していくということは、もちろん一緒に働く人たちに、僕らの価値観を押しつけないということ。これは、かなり活気に満ちた議論をもたらすけどね!結局のところ、物事は白黒割り切れるものじゃなく、常に最善の道を探し続けて行くしかないんだ。

49

49 Three Trees logo, 2008

スリー・トゥリーズ ロゴ
2008

50 A still from *A Beginner's Guide To Giving A Damn*, 2007

「ビギナーのための温暖化防止ガイド『小さいことは...気にしよう』」2007

Airside by Airside

エアサイド バイ エアサイド

The Way We Are Now

エアサイドの今

THE LAST WORD

——————— **Nat** Could we have predicted the way Airside has developed? Not at all – we had no idea we'd still be doing this ten years later. It hasn't been a conscious choice; we're just the kind of people who are greedy to experience the next thing. If Airside had evolved into the kind of company that only did one thing then none of us would still be here. We've chosen constant challenge and evolution over short term financial gain.

——————— **Alex** I remember at college thinking that there were all these talented people around me, and the best thing to do would be to work together with them rather than try to compete! If I could create a great working environment and be part of a team that would be ideal for me – and that's what Airside has been all about.

——————— **Fred** Ultimately, Airside is still just somewhere nice to hang out with our mates, only it's scaled up a bit since we started out. We're working with a much wider range of people and have got a bit more responsibility but it's still the same ideology. We're not going to compromise our creative ambitions or allow our working lives to be turned into drudgery. We try to make that core goal happen for ourselves, our staff, our clients and our audience, and we've stuck by that idea all along.

——————— **Alex** If you're not having fun and not enjoying your job, it's not worth it.

——————— **Fred** In retrospect, we worked very hard and had a lot of blind faith. It's been a team thing and we've been blessed with some very talented people to work with. There's a cliché that you start out loving what you do and end up running a business. That implies that it's a bad thing, but fortunately the three of us have discovered that we enjoy the challenge of running Airside. We've ended up being curators of the Airside resource: a big part of what we do as directors is about making sure the right work comes through the door, and that our staff are happy and have what they need to be as creative as they can be. Sometimes I think we've found a new kind of business model for the 21st century. We know that it could all end tomorrow, but if it does, we've been incredibly lucky to have had this experience and I don't know how we would top it. Having said that, bring it on – whatever it is!

結び

——————— **ナット**　エアサイドがどんなふうに成長するか予測していたかって？ 全然。この先10年後も、この仕事に就いているかなんて、わからないわ。意識してここを目指してきたわけではないの。ただみんな、貪欲に新しいことを経験したいタイプなのよ。もしエアサイドがひとつの専門業務しか行わない会社になってしまったら、その時は誰もここに残らないでしょうね。ひとつの成功をもとに大金を稼ぐより、常にチャレンジと進化を重ねることを選んできたから。

——————— **アレックス**　思い出すよ。大学時代、僕のまわりには優秀な奴らばかり揃っていたから、彼らと張り合うより、一緒にやっていくのが一番だって思ってた！ 素晴らしい仕事環境を作って、その一員として働けたら、どんなに理想的だろうって。エアサイドこそ、まさにそういう場所なんだ。

——————— **フレッド**　結局のところ、始めた頃に比べて少しは大きくなったものの、エアサイドは変わらず仲間とつるむのに最適の場所なんだ。いろんな人たちと仕事をするようになったし、責任も大きくなってきたけど、根本の哲学は変わらない。クリエイティブな野心は曲げないし、つまらない仕事に身を削ろうとも思わない。自分たちやスタッフのために、クライアントやオーディエンスのために、エアサイドを始めて以来ずっと、この確固たる信念を貫こうと努力しているよ。

——————— **アレックス**　仕事に面白みを感じられなくて、楽しくないと思うのなら、やる価値はないからね。

——————— **フレッド**　振り返ってみると、揺るぎない信念をもって、必死に働いてきた。僕らはチームだし、本当に才能のある人たちと組むことができてラッキーだと思う。好きなことを始めたのに、終いにはビジネスをやってるって話はよく聞くよね。それは本来、悲しい話なわけだけど、幸いなことに、実は僕ら3人とも、エアサイドの運営という挑戦をかなり楽しんでいるんだ。今では、僕らはエアサイドのキュレーターだからね。つまり、適切な仕事が来ているか、うちのスタッフが満足しているか、創造性を最大限発揮するのに必要な環境が整っているかを確かめることが、僕らディレクターの役割なんだ。時々、21世紀における、新たなビジネスモデルを発見したんじゃないかと思うよ。もしかしたら、明日にはすべて終わってしまうかもしれないけど、だとしても、この経験を味わえたことを誇りに思うし、これに勝るものなんてないと思っている。だからこれからも何が起ころうと全力で取り組んでいくよ！

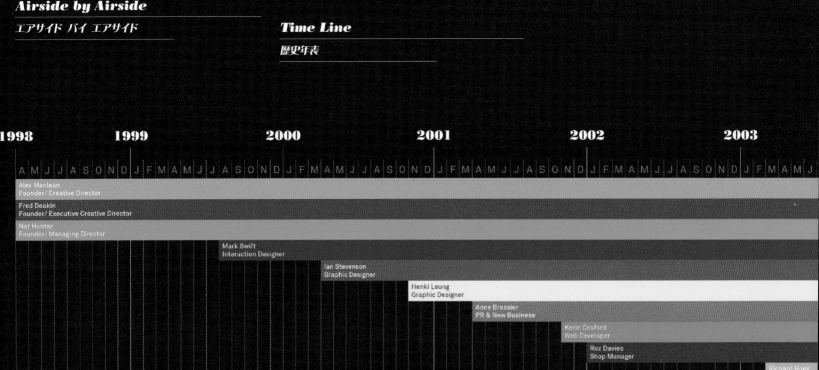

Airside by Airside

エアサイド バイ エアサイド

Time Line

歴史年表

| 1998 | 1999 | 2000 | 2001 | 2002 | 2003 |

A M J J A S O N D J F M A M J J A S O N D J F M A M J J A S O N D J F M A M J J A S O N D J F M A M J J A S O N D J F M A M J

Alex Maclean
Founder/ Creative Director

Fred Deakin
Founder/ Executive Creative Director

Nat Hunter
Founder/ Managing Director

Mark Swift
Interaction Designer

Ian Stevenson
Graphic Designer

Henki Leung
Graphic Designer

Anne Brassier
PR & New Business

Kerin Cosford
Web Developer

Roz Davies
Shop Manager

Richard Hogg

2004 2005 2006 2007 2008 2009

O N D J F M A M J J A S O N D J F M A M J J A S O N D J F M A M J J A S O N D J F M A M J J A S O N D J F M A M J J A S O N D

Pre-loaded / www.preloaded.co.uk
Artist / www.iilikedrawing.co.uk
Freelance
De-construct / www.de-construct.com
Artist / www.h099.com
Addiction
Freelance / www.sistastudios.com
Addiction / www.addiction.com

Colm Larkin
Accounts & Shop Manager

Sibylle Preuss
Project Manager

Chris Rain
Graphic Designer

Emma Hodson
Studio Manager

Guy Moorhouse
Interaction Designer

Jamie Wieck
Graphic Designer

Jessica Nash
Project Manager

Malika Favre
Graphic Designer

Natalie Wisdom
Studio Manager

Anthony Morgan / Placement
Chris Rain / Placement
Rob Gonzalez / Placement
Matt Bishop / Placement
Chloe Wolfe-Cowen / Placement
Malika Favre / Placement
Faiko Grentrup / Placement
Thale Vollaloken / Placement
Lucia Gaggiotti / Placement
Anna Fidalgo / Placement
Jamie Wieck / Placement
Joanne Murray / Placement
John White / Placement
Patrick Fry / Placement
Shahnaz Ahmed / Placement
Yostinobu Ku / Placement

Orange (p 128)
Coca-Cola (p 134)
Panasonic (p 124)
Meeghoteph (p 176)
MTV (p 240)
Mastercard (p 142)
Pet Shop Boys (p 224)
Mika (p 228)
Pop Art Gallery (p 238)
Sony Bravia (p 154)
Konditor & Cook (p 262)
IOTA (p 84)
The Triptych (p 276)
Sagawa (p 246)
Penguin in a Pickle (p 210)
A Beginner's Guide to Giving a Damn (p 204)
Storyman (p 216)
Airside Branding (p 266)
The No.1 Ladies' Detective Agency (p 254)
Nu Balearica (p 278)

AIRSIDERS

ALEX MACLEAN

FAVOURITE AIRSIDE PROJECT: FurWars
HAPPIEST WHEN: Constantly redesigning
my home
SPECIAL POWER: Uncanny baby impersonation
TOP HOBBY: History
DARK SECRET: D&D – For those who know what
that is, hang your head in shame
I'LL HAVE A: Private library and infinite
reading time
FINAL WORDS OF WISDOM: Geology is a study of
time and pressure

アレックス・マクレーン

お気に入りのプロジェクト: ファーウォーズ
至福のとき: 終わりのない我が家の改装
特技: 異様にうまい赤ちゃんの物まね
最高の趣味: 歴史
やましい秘密:
D&D…意味のわかったキミ、反省したほうがいいね
今欲しいのは: 専用図書館と無限の読書時間
座右の銘: 地質学は、時間と圧力の学問である

FRED DEAKIN

FAVOURITE AIRSIDE PROJECT: '64–'95
HAPPIEST WHEN: The group brain is really firing
SPECIAL POWER: Glow-in-the-dark hair
TOP HOBBY: Origami
DARK SECRET: I loved Spice The Movie
I'LL HAVE A: Black Russian
FINAL WORDS OF WISDOM: First thought
best thought

フレッド・ディーキン

お気に入りのプロジェクト: '64–'95
至福のとき:
グループ・ブレインストーミングが白熱しているとき
特技: 暗闇で髪を発光させる
最高の趣味: 折り紙
やましい秘密: スパイスガールズの映画に夢中だったこと
今飲むなら: ブラックルシアン
座右の銘: 最初のアイデアが最高のアイデア

NAT HUNTER

FAVOURITE AIRSIDE PROJECT: Calendar 2008
HAPPIEST WHEN: Making something better
SPECIAL POWER: Helicopter views
TOP HOBBY: Knitting
DARK SECRET: Take a torch
I'LL HAVE AN: Ume Shu
FINAL WORDS OF WISDOM: Be the change you
want to see in the world

ナット・ハンター

お気に入りのプロジェクト: 2008年度版カレンダー
至福のとき: 物事を改善するとき
特技: 物事を俯瞰してみること
最高の趣味: 編み物
やましい秘密: 探り当てて
今飲みたいのは: 梅酒
座右の銘: 何かを変えたければ、まずは自分が変わること

MARK SWIFT

FAVOURITE AIRSIDE PROJECT:
Nadav Kander & Pet Shop Boys
HAPPIEST WHEN: With my wife and children
SPECIAL POWER: Sleeping
TOP HOBBY: Anything outdoors
DARK SECRET: I like maths
I'LL HAVE A: Ice cream please
FINAL WORDS OF WISDOM: Take note of the small things in life they are just as important

マーク・スウィフト

お気に入りのプロジェクト：
ナダブ・カンダール＆ペット・ショップ・ボーイズ
至福のとき： 妻子と過ごす時間
特技： 寝ること
最高の趣味： アウトドア関連すべて
やましい秘密： 数学好き
今欲しいのは： アイスクリーム
座右の銘：
細部に配慮することが、人生の中で大きな意味を持つ

IAN STEVENSON

FAVOURITE AIRSIDE PROJECT:
Jam: Tokyo~London
HAPPIEST WHEN: Snoozing
SPECIAL POWER: Talking and walking
TOP HOBBY: Watching daytime TV
DARK SECRET: I know where she is
I'LL HAVE A: Fresh one please
FINAL WORDS OF WISDOM: You can see better through clean windows

イアン・スティーブンソン

お気に入りのプロジェクト： ジャム「東京―ロンドン」
至福のとき： 居眠り中
特技： しゃべり歩き
最高の趣味： 昼間のテレビ鑑賞
やましい秘密： 彼女の居場所はわかってる
今飲むなら： 新鮮なのをひとつ
座右の銘： キレイな窓越しには、モノが良く見える

HENKI LEUNG

FAVOURITE AIRSIDE PROJECT:
Greenpeace: Decentralised Energy
HAPPIEST WHEN: We have short briefs with tight deadlines
SPECIAL POWER: Make perfect cheese & ham toasties
TOP HOBBY: Nintendo and looking out of the window
DARK SECRET: 16th century civil war re-enactment of the 1st Battle of Newbury
I'LL HAVE A: Tonkatsu set meal
FINAL WORDS OF WISDOM: Apple S! Apple S! Apple S!

ヘンキ・レウン

お気に入りのプロジェクト：
グリーンピース「分散型エネルギー」
至福のとき：
タイトなスケジュールで、束縛の少ない仕事をするとき
特技： 完璧なチーズ＆ハムトースト作り
最高の趣味： 任天堂ゲーム、窓の外を眺めること
やましい秘密： 16世紀の内戦、ニューベリー第1戦のコスプレ
今欲しいのは： とんかつ定食
座右の銘： 保存！保存！保存！

ANNE BRASSIER

FAVOURITE AIRSIDE PROJECT: The Stitches
HAPPIEST WHEN: Lunchtimes
SPECIAL POWER: Blurry vision in right eye
TOP HOBBY: Wall of Death on rollerskates
DARK SECRET: My blood group is very rare and I am storing vials of my own blood
I'LL HAVE A: Martini with a twist
FINAL WORDS OF WISDOM: Leap. Then look. Then panic

アン・ブラーシエィ

お気に入りのプロジェクト： スティッチィズ
至福のとき： ランチタイム
特技： 右目でピンボケのビジョンを見ること
最高の趣味： ローラースケート場のウォール・オブ・デス
やましい秘密：
稀な血液型なので、小瓶に血液を保管していること
今飲むなら： マティーニをレモンピールつきで
座右の銘： 飛んで、見回して、それからパニック

Airsiders

エアサイダーズ

KERIN COSFORD

FAVOURITE AIRSIDE PROJECT:
Royal College of Arts
HAPPIEST WHEN: Creating something
genuinely novel
SPECIAL POWER: Can kill at 100 paces by
thought alone
TOP HOBBY: Collecting Diana memorial Franklin
Mint plates
DARK SECRET: Is buried under the patio
I'LL HAVE A: Fag and a mug of builders
FINAL WORDS OF WISDOM: Never trust a man
whose tie knot is bigger than his head

ケリン・コズフォード

お気に入りのプロジェクト： ロイヤル・カレッジ・オブ・アート
至福のとき： いまだかつてない、新たなものを創造するとき
特技： マインドパワーで100歩先の人を殺す
最高の趣味：
フランクリン・ミント製のダイアナ妃追悼プレート収集
やましい秘密： 中庭に葬ったよ
今欲しいのは： タバコとお茶を一杯
座右の銘： 頭よりデカいネクタイをつけた奴を信じるな

ROZ DAVIES

FAVOURITE AIRSIDE (SHOP) PROJECT:
Branding and product development – from
conception to completion
HAPPIEST WHEN: I am making decisions
SPECIAL POWER: Knowing everything
TOP HOBBY: Watching dark Dutch films with a bag
of pick 'n' mix
DARK SECRET: I have a crush on an Airsider
I'LL HAVE A: Bottle of Coke with a straw, please.
And a Chanel handbag
FINAL WORDS OF WISDOM: Gut instincts are good

ロズ・デイヴィス

お気に入りのプロジェクト：
エアサイドショップのブランディングと、企画から完成までの
製品開発プロセス
至福のとき： 決断するとき
特技： 全能
最高の趣味：
ジェリービーンズを片手に、ダークなオランダ映画の鑑賞
やましい秘密： エアサイドの一人にゾッこんなこと
今欲しいのは： ストローつきでコカコーラボトルをお願い
ついでにシャネルのバッグも
座右の銘： 本能に従うのが一番

RICHARD HOGG

FAVOURITE AIRSIDE PROJECT: Meeghoteph!
HAPPIEST WHEN: Asleep
SPECIAL POWER: I am quite good at drawing
TOP HOBBY: Go on then, twitching. Thats what
they wanted me to say
DARK SECRET: Everyone already knows
everything about my sexual perversions, Ha ha.
I can't think of anything worse
I'LL HAVE A: Pint of bitter!
FINAL WORDS OF WISDOM: Don't rush around
in the morning. It isn't healthy. Relax, have a
poached egg, two cups of tea, a bit of quality time
with the cat. That sort of thing

リチャード・ホッグ

お気に入りのプロジェクト： ミーゴテフ！
至福のとき： 睡眠中
特技： 絵を描くこと
最高の趣味： わかったよ、顔面痙攣。みんながそう言えって
やましい秘密： 僕の性倒錯はすべて知られてるし…ははは
それ以上の秘密はないよ
今飲むなら： ビールをジョッキで！
座右の銘： 朝からバタバタしない。健康的じゃないから。くつろ
いでポーチドエッグと紅茶を2杯飲みながら、猫と戯れるひと時
をもつ、といったようなこと

COLM LARKIN

FAVOURITE AIRSIDE PROJECT: The bank account
HAPPIEST WHEN: Surrounded by spreadsheets
SPECIAL POWER: Turning my pupils into pound signs
TOP HOBBY: Lighting cigars with bank notes
DARK SECRET: I'm not really an accountant
I'LL HAVE A: One way ticket to Rio please
FINAL WORDS OF WISDOM:
Watch The Princess Bride

コラム・ラーキン

お気に入りのプロジェクト： 銀行口座
至福のとき： 簿記用紙に囲まれているとき
特技： 瞳をポンドマークにすること
最高の趣味： 札束に火をつけて葉巻を一服
やましい秘密： ほんとは会計士じゃないこと
今欲しいのは： リオ行きの片道切符
座右の銘：「プリンセス・ブライド・ストーリー」は必見

SIBYLLE PREUSS

FAVOURITE AIRSIDE PROJECT: Sagawa
HAPPIEST WHEN: The Sun is shining
SPECIAL POWER: Make people do stuff
TOP HOBBY: Bikram Yoga to keep calm
DARK SECRET: David Hasselhoff – he has power over us Germans
I'LL HAVE A: Caipirinha and a residence on Ipanema beach
FINAL WORDS OF WISDOM: Be nice to people

シビラ・プルース

お気に入りのプロジェクト： 佐川急便
至福のとき： お天気のいい日
特技： みんなを働かせること
最高の趣味： ビクラム・ヨガで落ちつくこと
やましい秘密：
デビッド・ハッセルホフ…彼ってドイツ人好みなの
今飲むなら：
カイピリーニャを、イパネマビーチで暮らしながら
座右の銘： 人に優しく

CHRIS RAIN

FAVOURITE AIRSIDE PROJECT: Sony Bravia
HAPPIEST WHEN: Reading on the toilet
SPECIAL POWER: A backside 540 frontflip
TOP HOBBY: Collecting Atari 2600 games
DARK SECRET: I see dead people
I'LL HAVE A: Raise please
FINAL WORDS OF WISDOM: No Guts No Glory!

クリス・レイン

お気に入りのプロジェクト： ソニー・ブラビア
至福のとき： トイレでの読書
特技： スケボーでバックサイド540フロントフリップ
最高の趣味： アタリ2600のゲームソフト収集
やましい秘密： 死者が見えること
今欲しいのは： 昇給お願いします
座右の銘： 勇気なくして栄光なし！

Airsiders
エアサイダーズ

EMMA HODSON

FAVOURITE AIRSIDE PROJECT: Meeghoteph
HAPPIEST WHEN: It is sunny and I am outside and
there is a beach/picnic/ice cream van/pub nearby
and no work the next day
SPECIAL POWER: Weather control
(like Storm only less wintery)
TOP HOBBY: Coca-Cola bottle collecting,
glass and prefereably full
DARK SECRET: I recently ate 6 slices of cake for
a bet and I didn't even feel sick, in fact I quite
fancied another...
I'LL HAVE A: Bottle of Prosecco
FINAL WORDS OF WISDOM: In the words of
Anthony Burrill – "Work hard and
be nice to people"

エマ・ホドソン

お気に入りのプロジェクト： ミーゴテフ
至福のとき： 晴れた日に屋外で、ビーチピクニック
アイスクリーム屋さんやパブもあって、次の日もお休み
特技： 天候を操る（X-メンのストーム並みには無理だけど）
最高の趣味：
コカ・コーラボトルの収集。ガラス製で中身も入ってたら最高
やましい秘密：
近頃ケーキを6個食べる賭けをしたら、へっちゃらだった。
もう1つ食べたかったくらい…
今飲むなら： プロセッコ（イタリア産発泡ワイン）を1本
座右の銘： アントニー・ブリルの言葉、勤勉で人に優しく

GUY MOORHOUSE

FAVOURITE AIRSIDE PROJECT:
V&A China Design Now
HAPPIEST WHEN: Half drunk and out for a good
meal with friends
SPECIAL POWER: I can burn through steel with
my eyes
TOP HOBBY: I like taking photographs
DARK SECRET: I know the letter order of the keys
on a computer keyboard. This probably makes
me autistic
I'LL HAVE A: Tea, white no sugar. Thanks Chris
FINAL WORDS OF WISDOM: Try everything at
least once

ガイ・ムーアハウス

お気に入りのプロジェクト： V&A チャイナ・デザイン・ナウ
至福のとき：
ほろ酔い気分で友達と美味しい食事に出かけるとき
特技： 目力で鋼を溶かす
最高の趣味： 写真撮影
やましい秘密：
キーボードのキー配列を暗記していること。自閉症の原因かも
今飲むなら： クリス、ミルクティー砂糖抜きでよろしく
座右の銘： 何でも1度は挑戦してみよう

JAMIE WIECK

FAVOURITE AIRSIDE PROJECT: Airside's recent
re-branding and Storyman
HAPPIEST WHEN: Solving the problem
SPECIAL POWER: Action! Questions, cleaning up
and apologies later
TOP HOBBY: Being mistaken for Jack Black
DARK SECRET: I can't say the word 'innovative'
I'LL HAVE A: Piña colada please!
FINAL WORDS OF WISDOM: Go and read anything
by Bob Gill, the man's a genius

ジェイミー・ヴィエック

お気に入りのプロジェクト：
エアサイドの再ブランディングとストーリーマン
至福のとき： 問題を解決するとき
特技： まず行動、あれっと思って、片付けて、謝罪
最高の趣味： ジャック・ブラックに間違われること
隠したい秘密：「イノベイティブ（革新的）」と発音できないこと
今飲むなら： ピニャコラーダ！
座右の銘：
何でもいいからボブ・ギルの本を読むべし。彼は天才だ

JESSICA NASH

FAVOURITE AIRSIDE PROJECT: Visa for the team / FurWars for the fun
HAPPIEST WHEN: I am touched by compassion
SPECIAL POWER: my intuition
TOP HOBBY: Laughin', Dancin', Prancin'
DARK SECRET: I can't tell you
I'LL HAVE A: Havana Rum please
FINAL WORDS OF WISDOM: Be gentle on yourself

ジェシカ・ナッシュ

お気に入りのプロジェクト：
チームとしてはビザ、楽しさではファーウォーズ
至福のとき：思いやりに触れたとき
特技：直観力
最高の趣味：笑う、踊る、跳ねる
やましい秘密：それは秘密
今飲みたいのは：ハバナラムをお願い
座右の銘：自分を大切に

MALIKA FAVRE

FAVOURITE AIRSIDE PROJECT:
No.1 Ladies' Detective Agency
HAPPIEST WHEN: Yoshi makes me strong coffee in the morning
SPECIAL POWER: My bionic right hand
TOP HOBBY: Drawing naked girls doing naughty things
DARK SECRET: I watched almost every bad chick flick ever made
I'LL HAVE A: Glass of Muscat with my cheese, thanks
FINAL WORDS OF WISDOM: Work hard

マリカ・ファーヴ

お気に入りのプロジェクト：No.1 レディーズ探偵事務所
至福のとき：朝、ヨシが濃い目のコーヒーをいれてくれるとき
特技：右手の神業
最高の趣味：イケナイことをしている裸の女の子を描くこと
やましい秘密：悪趣味な女性映画を網羅している
今飲むなら：マスカットワインとチーズがいいわね
座右の銘：勤勉

NATALIE WISDOM

FAVOURITE AIRSIDE PROJECT: Nokia Vine/ Greenpeace Decentralised Energy
HAPPIEST WHEN: Wine is involved
SPECIAL POWER: I wish I had the power to find anything I look for but my only power seems to be to lose everything I touch
TOP HOBBY: Singing
DARK SECRET: I'm in love with Henki because when he can be bothered he makes a nice cup of tea
I'LL HAVE: Another glass of wine… make it fizzy this time!
FINAL WORDS OF WISDOM: Any words spoken by someone with the surname Wisdom are technically words of Wisdom

ナタリー・ウィズダム

お気に入りのプロジェクト：
ノキア「ヴァイン」＆グリーンピース「分散型エネルギー」
至福のとき：ワインがあればいつでも
特技：探し物を見つける能力が欲しいのに、触るものすべて無くなっちゃうの
最高の趣味：歌うこと
やましい秘密：美味しいお茶をいれてくれるヘンキに惚れてること
今飲むなら：ワインをもう一杯、今度はソーダ割で！
座右の銘：
「賢人」という名の人が発した言葉は、すべて「賢人の言葉」

ACKNOWLEDGMENTS

謝辞

Airside Shop Customers	Paul Bradshaw	Andy Creed	Deborah Ford	Andy Haslim	Joe Jones
Charles Aboah	Denis Briant	Paul Curtis	Pete Fowler	Kit Hawkins	John Paul Jones
Kid Acne	Tim Bricknell	Camilla Deakin	Sarah Frain	John Hegarty	Anna Jones
Mark Adams	Nilly Brook	Ellen Deakin	Nick Franglen	James Hilton	Jay Jopling
Matt Adams	Danielle Brooks	Nicholas Deakin	Jane Fraser Hay	Simon Hilton	James Joyce
Sodge Adams	Nick Brooks	Rose Deakin	Mike Frogley	Johnny Hines	Nadav Kander
Ibrahim Ahmed	Matt Brown	Alex Dean	Patrick Fry	Tom Hingston	Kirsten Kates
Shahnaz Ahmed	Steve Brown	Lars Denicke	Kwok Fung Lam	Bill Hobbins	Boris Kaz
Sonita Alleyne	Peter Browne	Katy Dent	Lucia Gaggiotti	Rebecca Hodgson	Johnny Kelly
Rosie Allimonos	Calum Buchanan	Rory Dodd	Ofir Gal	Richard Hogg	Roger Kelly
Nick Appleton	Ann Bukantas	Richard Doust	Terry Gallagher	Henry Holland	Mick Kent
Manish Arora	Nick Bullock	Ruth Ducker	Tony Garment	Erika Horiguchi	Nazenin Khajenouri
Noriko Ashino	Sam Burford	Olivier Dumont	Lucy Gaster	Nick Hornby	Hera King
Neil Aspinall	Jon Burgerman	Neil Durber	Lorraine Geoghegan	Ed Horrox	Howard Kingston
Sean Atherton	Patrick Burgoyne	Paul Earnshaw	Michael Gillette	Julian House	Dave Knox
Tim Bacon	Anthony Burrill	Astrid Edwards	Rob Gonzalez	Michael Howe	Jason Kotey
Mick Bailey	Johnny Bute	Paul Edwards	Jasper Goodall	Mike Howell	Kozyndan
Justine Bannister	Mitchy Bwoy	Roly Edwards	Alison Graham	Peter Howell	Yoshinobu Ku
Lucy Barber	Juan Cabral	Eh?	Gill Graham Maw	Rhian Hughes	Toshiya Kubo
Stuart Barter	James Chads	Angela Eleini	Nigel Graham Maw	Alistair Hunter	Phil Kwan
John Barton	Simona Ciraolo	Sally Ann Elliot	Falko Grentrup	Harriet Hunter	Donna Lambert
John Bates	Caroline Clark	Yanny Elliot	Mike Griffin	Helge Hunter	Karen Lamond
Robbie Bear	Eoin Clarke	Alex Ely	Steph Gruar	Mat Hunter	Adam Larkum
Mike Bell	Jesse Cleverly	Miwa Enomoto	Mark Haley	Sophie Hunter	David Law
Paul Bennun	Andrew Clover	Stuart Evans	Eben Halford	Simone Ireland	Stewart Lawman
Rupert Bentley	Phil Cockrell	Matt Ewbank	Catherine Hall	David Jaquin	Rachel Leach
Miranda Benzies	Stephen Coedel	Marcus Fairs	Dee Halligan	Christian Jelen	Phil Lee
Kam Bhogal	Miko Coffey	Daniel Farmer	Atsushi Hamada	Mark Jenkins	Laura Lees
Matthew Bishop	Dylan Connerton	Joe Ferry	Elliot Hammer	Gerhard Jenne	Barrie Legg
Andy Blundell	Chris Cooke	Laurent Fetis	Jane Harrison	Max Jerschke	Katharina Leuzinger
Neil Boorman	Nathan Cooper	Anna Fidalgo	Kate Harrison	Murray John	Cam Levin
Paul Bowman	John Cossey	Tosh Fieldsend	Ben Hartman	Lucy Johnson	Paul Logan
Chris Bradbury	Simon Costin	Sally Findlay	Takahiro Hashimoto	Kirstie Johnstone	Kieran Long

Giles Lovell Wilson
Honey Luard
Gavin Lucas
Al MacCuish
Andrew MacDonald
Clare Maclean
Gordon Maclean
Ian Maclean
Ewan Macleod
Alex MacNutt
Kate Mahon
Natalie Malla
Rika Manabe
Rob Manley
Andre Marot
Justina Marot
Marc Marot
Matt Marsh
Kiyokazu Matsumoto
Dylan Matthew
Paul McBride
Wayne McCann
Murray McKean
Lucy McLauchlan
Craig McLean
Camille McMillan
Pete Menich
Tom Middleton
Youki Mikami
Mina Mileva
Sam Miller
Robert Milne
Gillian Milner

Anthony Minghella
Neil Minty
Donald Mitchell
Hitoshi Miyata
Mode 2
Sue Modral
Bill Moggridge
Sam Monck
Montse
Anthony Morgan
Kate Moross
Helen Morrell
Lou Mumford
Torri Mundell
Jason Munn
Akiko Murakami
Kazumi Murano
Al Murphy
Joanne Murray
Ravi Nadoo
Jeremy Neech
Damian Nelson
Jez Nelson
Louis Neubert
Jimi Newport
Lucinda Newton-Dunn
Joelle Newton-Mold
Kerry Nichols
Katy Niker
Misha Nikolic
Alex Nisbet
Ros Noctor
Marion Nove-Josserand

Martin Oliver
Owen Oppenheimer
Greg Orme
Pam Oskam
Anna Pank
Evan Parker
Kip Parker
Mark Pawson
Nigel Pay
Caroline Pay
Clare Pegrum
Yasmine Penniman
Simone Pereira-Hind
Julia Peyton-Jones
Nat Phelan
Michael Pinsky
Phillip Pinsky
Neilon Pitamber
Amanda Posey
Manuel Puro
Jack Rain
Damon Rainer
Alex Reddicliffe
Mark Reddy
Tom Redfern
Gary Reich
Lynda Relph-Knight
Julian Richardson
Francesco Riginelli
Rob Riley
Rinsen
Piers Roberts
Marc Robinson

Tom Roope
Dean Rose
Graham Rounthwaite
Ju Row-Farr
Richard Russell
Kashmir Salhan
Michael Salkeld
Danielle Sandler
John Sauven
Lisa Sawada
Derrin Schlesinger
Roger Scott
Mr Scruff
Olga Sonia
    Sepulveda Miranda
Rebecca Shallcross
Adrian Shaugnessy
June Shinozaki
Shoboshobo
Fiona Sibley
Leo Silverman
Stephen Simmonds
Neil Simpson
Dennis Sisterston
Flick Skinner
Cynthia Smith
Milly Snell
Tom Spiers
Erin Staniland
John Stewart
Graham Storey
Daniel Strachan
Graeme Stuart

Matt Stuart
Simon Summerscales
Nadia Swarovski
Sweden Graphics
Ian Swift
Melody Sylvester
Hanako Tabata
Jarin Tabata
Rumi Takahashi
Hideaki Takemura
Anna Takimoto
Stephanie Tayler
John Taylor
Neil Tennant
Nobuhiko Terasawa
Peter Thaler
Andrew Thomas
Sophie Thomas
Matt Thornhill
Elin Tiberg
Tony Tonge
John Tosh
Charlotte Troy
Hiromi Tsuchiya
Paul Tully
Kuei-Ju Tung
Alex Turner
Marc Valli
Anne Van Haeverbecke
Thale Vollalokken
Andy Votel
Rosie Walford
Chris Walker

Shane Walter
Simon Waterfall
Iain Watt
Sophie Webb
Stokely Webster
Richenda Wheeler
Jon White
Rachel Wickham
Austin Wilde
Ian Willingham
Mathew Wilson
Bob Wilson
Chloe Wolfe-Cowen
Sam Wooldridge
Deborah Woolfe
Edgar Wright
Ian Wright
Maki Yoshikura
Carey Young
Rob Zajac
Jeremy Zimmermann

THANK YOU!